# University Success

## ORAL COMMUNICATION

### ADVANCED

Christina Cavage

Series Editor: Robyn Brinks Lockwood

Authentic Content Contributor: Ronnie Hess II

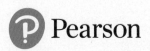

*University Success Oral Communication, Advanced Level*

Copyright © 2018 by Pearson Education, Inc.

All rights reserved.

Pearson Education, 221 River Street, Hoboken, NJ 07030

**Staff credits:** The people who made up the *University Success* team, representing content development, design, manufacturing, marketing, multimedia, project management, publishing, rights management, and testing, are Pietro Alongi, Stephanie Callahan, Kimberly Casey, Tracey Cataldo, Sara Davila, Dave Dickey, Gina DiLillo, Warren Fischbach, Nancy Flaggman, Lucy Hart, Sarah Henrich, Gosia Jaros-White, Niki Lee, Amy McCormick, Jennifer Raspiller, Robert Ruvo, Katarzyna Skiba, Kristina Skof, Katarzyna Starzynska-Kosciuszko, Joanna Szyszynska, John Thompson, Paula Van Ells, Joseph Vella, Rebecca Wicker, and Natalia Zaremba.

**Project coordination:** Robyn Brinks Lockwood

**Project supervision:** Debbie Sistino

**Contributing editors:** Lida Baker, Eleanor Barnes, Andrea Bryant, Barbara Lyons, Leigh Stolle, and Sarah Wales-McGrath

**Cover image:** Oleksandr Prykhodko / Alamy Stock Photo

**Video research:** Constance Rylance

**Video production:** Kristine Stolakis, assisted by Melissa Langer

**Text composition:** EMC Design Ltd

**Library of Congress Cataloging-in-Publication Data**

A catalog record for the print edition is available from the Library of Congress.

Printed in the United States of America

ISBN-10: 0-13-465268-1

ISBN-13: 978-0-13-465268-9

1  18

# Contents

## PART 1: FUNDAMENTAL ORAL COMMUNICATION SKILLS

## PART 2: CRITICAL THINKING SKILLS

## PART 3: EXTENDED LECTURES

# Welcome to *University Success*

## INTRODUCTION

*University Success* is a new academic skills series designed to equip intermediate- to transition-level English learners with the reading, writing, and oral communication skills necessary to succeed in courses in an English-speaking university setting. The blended instructional model provides students with an inspiring collection of extensive authentic content, expertly developed in cooperation with five subject matter experts, all "thought leaders" in their fields. By utilizing both online and in-class instructional materials, *University Success* models the type of "real life" learning expected of students studying for a degree. *University Success* recognizes the unique linguistic needs of English language learners and carefully scaffolds skill development to help students successfully work with challenging and engaging authentic content.

## SERIES ORGANIZATION: *THREE STRANDS*

This three-strand series, **Reading**, **Writing**, and **Oral Communication**, includes five distinct content areas: the Human Experience, Money and Commerce, the Science of Nature, Arts and Letters, and Structural Science, all popular fields of study among English language learners. The three strands are fully aligned across content areas and skills, allowing teachers to utilize material from different strands to support learning. Teachers can delve deeply into skill development in a single area, or provide additional support materials from other areas for richer development across the four skills.

## THE *UNIVERSITY SUCCESS* APPROACH: *AN AUTHENTIC EXPERIENCE*

This blended program combines the utility of an interactive student book, online learner lab, and print course to create a flexible approach that adjusts to the needs of teachers and learners. Its skill-based and step-by-step instruction enables students to master essential skills and become confident in their ability to perform successfully in academic degree courses taught in English. Students at this level need to engage with content that provides them with the same challenges native speakers face in a university setting. Many English language learners are not prepared for the quantity of reading and writing required in college-level courses, nor are they properly prepared to listen to full-length lectures that have not been scaffolded for them. These learners, away from the safety of an ESL classroom, must keep up with the rigors of a class led by a professor who may be unaware of the challenges a second-language learner faces. Strategies for academic success, delivered via online videos, help increase students' confidence and ability to cope with the challenges of academic student and college culture. *University Success* steps up to the podium to represent academic content realistically with the appropriate skill development and scaffolding essential for English language learners to be successful.

# PUTTING STUDENTS ON THE PATH TO *UNIVERSITY SUCCESS*

Intensive skill development and extended application—tied to specific learning outcomes—provide the scaffolding English language learners need to become confident and successful in a university setting.

| Global Scale of English | 10 | 20 | 30 | 40 | 50 | 60 | 70 | 80 | 90 |
|---|---|---|---|---|---|---|---|---|---|
| CEFR | | <A1 | A1 | A2 + | B1 + | B2 + | C1 | C2 | |

| INTERMEDIATE TO HIGH-INTERMEDIATE LEVEL<br>B1–B1+ \| 43–58 | ADVANCED LEVEL<br>B2–B2+ \| 59–75 | TRANSITION LEVEL<br>B2+–C1 \| 68–80 |
|---|---|---|
| Authentic content with careful integration of essential skills, the Intermediate to High-Intermediate level familiarizes students with real-world academic contexts. | Challenging, authentic content with level-appropriate skills, the Advanced level prepares students to exit the ESL safety net. | A deep dive for transition-level students, the Transition level mirrors the academic rigor of college courses. |
| **INTENSIVE SKILL PRACTICE** | **INTENSIVE SKILL PRACTICE** | **INTENSIVE SKILL PRACTICE** |
| Intensive skill practice tied to learning objectives informed by the Global Scale of English | Intensive skill practice tied to learning objectives informed by the Global Scale of English | Intensive skill practice tied to learning objectives informed by the Global Scale of English |
| **AUTHENTIC CONTENT** | **AUTHENTIC CONTENT** | **AUTHENTIC CONTENT** |
| ■ Readings: 200–2,000 words<br>■ Lectures: 15–20 minutes<br>■ Multiple exposures and chunking | ■ Readings: 200–3,000 words<br>■ Lectures: 20 minutes | Readings and lectures of significant length:<br>■ 200–3,500-word readings<br>■ 25-minute lectures |
| **EXPLICIT VOCABULARY INSTRUCTION** | **EXPLICIT VOCABULARY INSTRUCTION** | **CONTENT AND FLUENCY VOCABULARY APPROACH** |
| ■ Pre- and post-reading and listening vocabulary tasks<br>■ Glossing of receptive vocabulary<br>■ Recycling throughout each part and online | ■ Pre- and post-reading and listening vocabulary tasks<br>■ Glossing of receptive vocabulary<br>■ Recycling throughout each part and online | ■ No direct vocabulary instruction<br>■ Online vocabulary practice for remediation |
| **SCAFFOLDED APPROACH** | **MODERATELY SCAFFOLDED** | |
| Multiple guided exercises focus on comprehension, application, and clarification of productive skills. | Guided exercises focus on comprehension, application, and clarification of productive skills. | |
| **VOCABULARY STRATEGIES** | **VOCABULARY STRATEGIES** | |
| Vocabulary strategy sections focus on form, use, and meaning. | Vocabulary strategy sections focus on form, use, and meaning to help students process complex content. | |
| **GRAPHIC ORGANIZERS** | | |
| Extensive integration of graphic organizers throughout to support note-taking and help students process complex content. | | |

# Key Features

## UNIQUE PART STRUCTURE

*University Success* employs a unique three-part structure, providing maximum flexibility and multiple opportunities to customize the content. The series is "horizontally" aligned to teach across a specific content area and "vertically" aligned allowing a teacher to gradually build skills.

Each part is a self-contained module allowing teachers to customize a non-linear program that will best address the needs of students. Parts are aligned around science, technology, engineering, arts, and mathematics (STEAM) content relevant to mainstream academic areas of study.

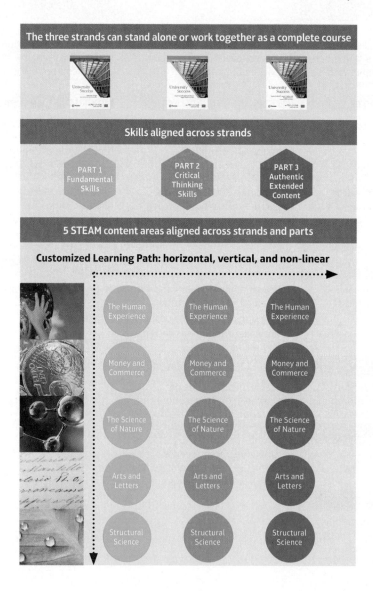

The three strands can stand alone or work together as a complete course

Skills aligned across strands

PART 1
Fundamental
Skills

PART 2
Critical
Thinking
Skills

PART 3
Authentic
Extended
Content

5 STEAM content areas aligned across strands and parts

Customized Learning Path: horizontal, vertical, and non-linear

The Human Experience
The Human Experience
The Human Experience

Money and Commerce
Money and Commerce
Money and Commerce

The Science of Nature
The Science of Nature
The Science of Nature

Arts and Letters
Arts and Letters
Arts and Letters

Structural Science
Structural Science
Structural Science

# THE THREE PARTS AT A GLANCE

**Parts 1 and 2** focus on the fundamental and critical thinking skills most relevant for students preparing for university degrees. In Part 1 and Part 2, students work with comprehensive skills that include:

• Preparing an argument
• Identifying and understanding audience
• Understanding rhetorical styles
• Utilizing persuasive techniques
• Participating in academic discussions

**Part 3** introduces students to extended practice with skills. Content created by top university professors provides students with a challenging experience that replicates the authentic experience of studying in a mainstream university class.

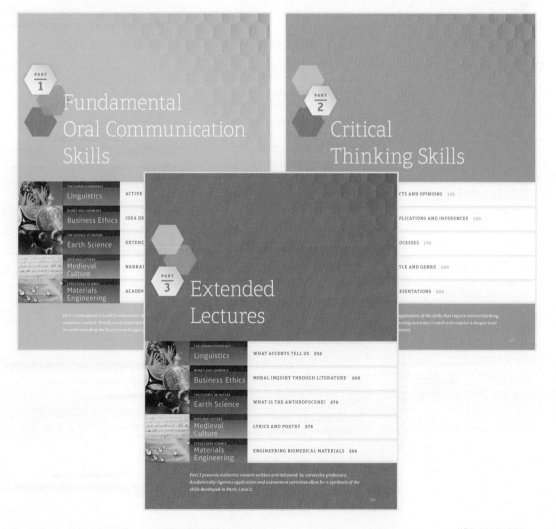

**Student Book**

**MyEnglishLab**

A **unit profile** outlines the content.

**Outcomes** aligned with the Global Scale of English (GSE) are clearly stated to ensure student awareness of skills.

**Self-assessments** provide opportunities for students to identify skill areas for improvement and provide teachers with information that can inform lesson planning.

Professors provide a **preview** and a **summary** of the content.

**Why It's Useful** sections highlight the need for developing skills and support transfer of skills to mainstream class content.

A **detailed presentation** demonstrates the skills' value in academic study.

A **variety of listening types**, including lectures, academic discussions, and expert panel discussions, represent "real life" university experiences.

Additional **listenings online** encourage the application of skills.

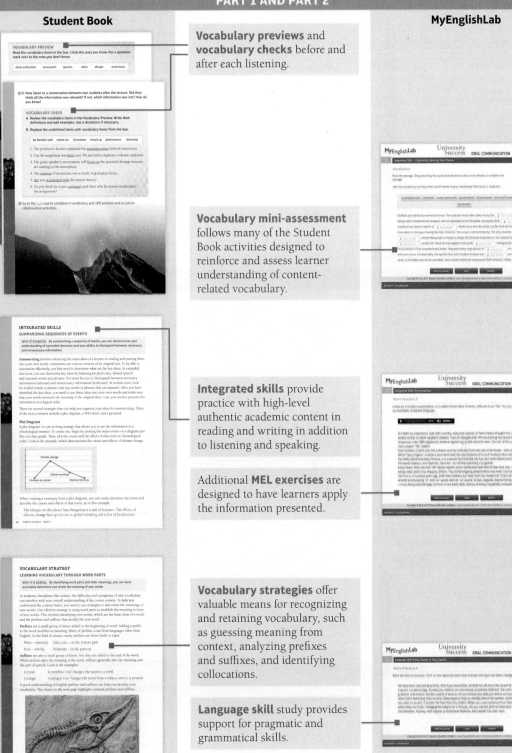

# PART 1 AND PART 2

**Student Book**

**MyEnglishLab**

**Vocabulary previews** and **vocabulary checks** before and after each listening.

**Vocabulary mini-assessment** follows many of the Student Book activities designed to reinforce and assess learner understanding of content-related vocabulary.

**Integrated skills** provide practice with high-level authentic academic content in reading and writing in addition to listening and speaking.

Additional **MEL exercises** are designed to have learners apply the information presented.

**Vocabulary strategies** offer valuable means for recognizing and retaining vocabulary, such as guessing meaning from context, analyzing prefixes and suffixes, and identifying collocations.

**Language skill** study provides support for pragmatic and grammatical skills.

KEY FEATURES    ix

## Student Book

### APPLY YOUR SKILLS

**WHY IT'S USEFUL** By applying the skills you have learned in this unit, you will be able to make accurate inferences when listening to discussions and presentations, as well as successfully prepare for and give presentations in a college-level course.

### ASSIGNMENT

Prepare a persuasive presentation with a partner on how a global corporation of your choice is acting socially responsible. You will select appropriate evidence, identify your audience and utilize connotative meanings, words, and phrases to make your claim that this corporation acts in a socially responsible manner.

### BEFORE YOU LISTEN

A. Before you listen, discuss the questions with one or more students.

1. People today are increasingly concerned with the environment. However, at the same time, consumers are demanding more products that make their lives easier. These products often are produced in factories that add to environmental problems. How can these two work together? What can be done to ensure we are not harming our environment, and still have access to new products?

2. In recent years more companies are claiming to be "green" to help protect our environment. Are you familiar with any companies? What do they produce? Do you feel they are actually helping the environment?

3. Historically, producing and driving automobiles has been especially harmful to the environment. What can the automobile industry do to be more socially responsible? How can they become more "green"?

Parts 1 and 2 end with an extended **Apply Your Skills** section that functions as a diagnostic or formative assessment.

## PART 3

## Student Book

## MyEnglishLab

### THINKING CRITICALLY

Discuss the questions with another student.

1. What are the arguments for and against a new epoch? How does the professor support each argument?

2. Based on the lecture, how would you describe the speaker's opinion? In your discussion, provide examples that illustrate your understanding.

3. The professor questions when exactly the epoch would begin. What significant events does he use as potential boundaries? How certain is he that one of these events would mark a new epoch?

### THINKING VISUALLY

A. Look at the graphic from the bottom to top. Discuss the questions with a partner.

**MESOZOIC ERA**

Cretaceous Period
• Extinction of dinosaurs
• First birds
• First flowering plants

Jurassic Period
• Dinosaurs diversify

Triassic Period
• First dinosaurs

1. How would you summarize plant and animal life during the Mesozoic era?

2. Based on the animals in each period, what can you infer about the climate during each period?

3. How did plant and animal life change between each period? What do you think can be said about the relationship between climate and animal and plant life?

B. Go online and investigate another geological era. Create a visual like the one above, highlighting the periods and the plant and animal life of each era. Share it with your classmates. Summarize the information in the visual for your classmates.

Go to MyEnglishLab to record your results.

**Critical thinking** activities ask learners to engage at a deep level with the content, using information from the lecture to address specific real-world applications.

**Thinking Visually** sections provide an opportunity for students to create and analyze charts, graphs, and other visuals.

Decisions we make today will shape our future

### EXTENDED LECTURE
### BEFORE YOU VIEW

Think about these questions before you view the lecture "An Introduction to Materials Science and Engineering and Their Application to Biomedical Materials." Discuss them with another student.

1. Look around and consider some of the objects near you. What materials are they made of?

2. What determines which material is used in the production of an object?

3. How many objects near you appear to be made from plants?

4. What are some everyday objects made from plants? How do you objects used in the healthcare industry?

### LECTURE

Go to MyEnglishLab to view Professor Heilshorn's lecture. Take notes while you listen. Then answer the questions in Check What You Learned.

**TIP**

When listening to a lecture, it is important to listen for cues that signal the organizational pattern of the lecture. Signal words can help you better follow and take notes on these lectures. To learn more on signal words, refer to MATERIALS ENGINEERING, Part 1.

### Glossary

**Microstructure:** the arrangement of molecules that can be seen under a microscope
**Bulk metals properties:** obvious, practical characteristics rather than theoretical ones
**Metallic bonds:** chemical bonds that hold metal together through the attraction of fixed and mobile, positive electrons
**Ductile:** able to be deformed or distorted, not brittle (easily broken)
**Conductors:** materials that allow heat and electricity to move freely
**Ionic bonds:** chemical bonds in which an atom loans one or more electrons to another atom
**Insulators:** a material that allows little or no heat to go into or out of something
**Polymers:** long molecules made up of repeating units
**Covalent bonds:** a chemical bond which is formed by a shared electron
**Elasticity:** the ability to return to an original shape
**Crystalline:** a three-dimensional arrangement of atoms

**Closer listening** and **collaborative activities.**

Students view an **authentic lecture** presented by a professor working in a specific STEAM field.

## STRATEGIES FOR ACADEMIC SUCCESS AND SOFT SKILLS

Strategies for academic success and soft skills, delivered via online videos, help increase students' confidence and ability to cope with the challenges of academic study and college culture. Study skills include how to talk to professors during office hours and time management techniques.

## TEACHER SUPPORT

Each of the three strands is supported with:

- Comprehensive **downloadable teaching notes** in MyEnglishLab that detail key points for all of the specialized, academic content in addition to tips and suggestions for how to teach skills and strategies.
- **An easy-to-use online learning management system** offering a flexible gradebook and tools for monitoring student progress
- Essential tools, such as **audio** and **video scripts** and **word lists**, to help in lesson planning and follow-up.

## ASSESSMENT

*University Success* provides a package of assessments that can be used as precourse diagnostics, midcourse assessments, and final summative assessments. The flexible nature of these assessments allows teachers to choose which assessments will be most appropriate at various stages of the program. These assessments are embedded in the student book and are available online in MyEnglishLab.

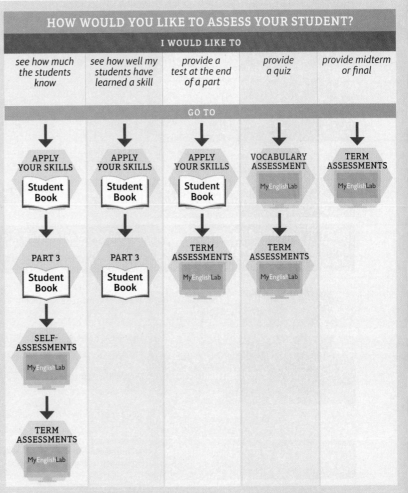

# Scope and Sequence

| Integrated Skills | Language Skills | Vocabulary Strategy | Apply Your Skills |
|---|---|---|---|
| Annotate texts | Use interjections | Learn new words through context | Prepare and deliver a group presentation on an accent that is disappearing or has disappeared |
| Prepare an argument | Use adverb clauses to describe relationships | Utilize stance adverbials to determine affective meaning | Participate in a class debate regarding corporate ethics and social responsibility |
| Summarize sequences of events | Use modals to describe possibilities and probabilities | Learn vocabulary through word parts | Prepare a presentation on a geologic time period and the changes that occurred. |
| Identify narrative elements | Recognize time frames and aspect | Identify collocations | Prepare a presentation of a culturally-important narrative, and employ prosodic features. |
| Compare and contrast textbooks and lectures | Use language of comparison and contrast | Learn vocabulary through graphic organizers | Prepare and deliver a pair presentation comparing the suitability of two different materials for a product. |

| Integrated Skills | Language Skills | Vocabulary Strategy | Apply Your Skills |
|---|---|---|---|
| Detect bias | Use change of topic signals | Create an idiom journal | Participate in a class debate on the need for having and using an official national dialect. |
| Select appropriate evidence | Use noun clauses to clarify | Determine connotative meaning | Prepare a pair presentation on a socially responsible global corporation and how it can serve as a model of good business practice. |
| Recognize definitions | Notice boosting language | Recognizing collocations | Participate in a roundtable discussion on greenhouse gases and examine possible solutions to the problem. |
| Utilize descriptive imagery | Use similes and metaphors | Recognize idioms based on medieval culture | Prepare a presentation on how a song or film is representative of today's cultural values. |
| Synthesize resources | Use language for linking ideas | Learn vocabulary through categorization | Prepare a formal presentation examining how synthetic polymers are aiding product development in a field of your interest. |

### Research / Assignment

Research, prepare, and deliver an individual presentation on the regional and educational background of a well-known American, and use that information to analyze that person's accent and dialect.

Research, prepare, and deliver a pair presentation on a prominent business leader, and how that person's behavior reflects the company's ethics and impacts their brand.

Research, prepare, and hold a class debate on the role that humanity has played in the current climate change.

Research, prepare, and participate in a panel discussion of a historical period and the ways in which the culture of that period still influences contemporary music, art, and literature.

Research, prepare, and deliver an individual presentation on the reasons that a change was made from a product's original manufacturing material to the material currently being used

# A Note from Robyn Brinks Lockwood

Series Editor for *University Success Oral Communication*

Many second-language students study English for years in order to be admitted into an English-speaking university. Despite their efforts, many are still not ready for the rigors of study that include academic lectures and discussions. Academic lectures are far longer than the excerpted or scripted lectures that they encountered in language classes. Additionally, these lectures are given by speakers who do not always use the language with the perfect grammar, clear pronunciation, and easily identifiable main ideas that learners experienced in language class. Rather, these lecturers interweave their content with stories, digressions, and slang.

Often, these learners are not prepared for this type of authentic language. Also, they can be ill-equipped to participate in academic discussions. At times, lacking confidence and experience, they are silent during class discussions even when they understand the content.

For these reasons, *University Success* has developed its Advanced Level to take students beyond their current level to a higher mastery which is necessary for success at a university. The Advanced Level, which is designed for students in the B2 range, contains challenging and authentic language with a focus on skills that will propel language students from the cocoon of the ESL classroom, out into an L1 world.

That does not mean learners are thrown into the deep end of the pool. Rather, this course provides systematic skills practice. The skills and their practice are carefully tied to specific learning objectives informed by the Global Scale of English, so students will see their progress as they learn. The course's authentic content is provided by prominent educators. Each of their five lectures is roughly 20 minutes long, exposing students to longer lectures and providing sufficient context for comprehension. Interestingly, students actually understand more than they would with short, scripted lecture excerpts that are too short to provide adequate information.

In contrast to the Transition Level, the Advanced Level offers both pre- and post- listening vocabulary tasks. Multiple exposures to vocabulary help it become ingrained so that students are more apt to retain it.

Additionally, this level of the series offers moderate scaffolding. Guided exercises focus on comprehension, application, and clarification that lead students smoothly into the Transition Level, and from there, onto a valid learning experience at the university they choose to attend.

## PART 1 – FUNDAMENTAL SKILLS

The first five units cover the five main schools of university study: Business, Engineering, Humanities, Science, and Social Sciences. Regardless of their major, students will encounter these five subjects as they progress through the general education requirements of undergraduate programs—or prerequisite courses necessary for graduate programs. This part offers listening passages ranging from two to five minutes to review what students know and build confidence. Although students may have encountered some of the featured skills before, it is unlikely that they will have applied them to authentic content.

## PART 2—CRITICAL THINKING SKILLS

In the next five units, the same five areas of study are explored; however, listening passages range from five to eight minutes to allow more practice. A wide range of genres common in university settings is included: lectures, presentations, panel discussions, and study groups. Critical thinking skills, such as detecting inferences and assessing an audience, are explicitly elicited to better prepare them for the lectures they will hear in Part 3.

## PART 3—EXTENDED LECTURES

The last five units in the book feature lectures given by instructors and professors at Stanford University. Each lecture is approximately 20 minutes and contains authentic content, vocabulary, and syntax. The lecturers were not given guidelines, so the material and its delivery is the same as they would use in their mainstream classes, where no concessions are made for L1 or L2 learners. The lectures contain humor, imperfect pronunciation and grammar, fast rate of speech, hesitations, and digressions, without the bells and whistles of a TED Talk or the easy content of a scripted lecture—in other words, all the variables that native speakers encounter regularly. This series offers something unlike any other: it presents content from professors at a world-renowned university while allowing students the targeted practice that will help them continue across the bridge from EAP to mainstream academic studies.

# SUBJECT MATTER EXPERTS

 **Marisa Galvez** specializes in the literature of the Middle Ages in France and Western Europe, especially literature written in Occitan and Old French. Her courses at Stanford focus on medieval and Renaissance French literature and the medieval imaginary in modern literature, film, and art. Her recent book, *Songbook: How Lyrics Became Poetry in Medieval Europe* is the first comparative study of songbooks, and was awarded the John Nicholas Brown Prize from the Medieval Academy of America.

 **Sarah Heilshorn** is an Associate Professor in the Department of Materials Science and Engineering and, by courtesy, of Bioengineering and Chemical Engineering at Stanford University. She completed her Ph.D. and M.S. degrees in Chemical Engineering at California Institute of Technology. She earned a B.S. in Chemical Engineering at Georgia Institute of Technology. She is an expert in the design of new materials that mimic those found in our own bodies.

 **Scotty McLennan** is a Lecturer in Political Economy at the Stanford Graduate School of Business (GSB), where he teaches in the areas of business ethics and business and spirituality. He taught business ethics at the Harvard Business School between 1988-2000, and from 2000-2014 he was the Stanford University Dean for Religious Life as well as Lecturer at the GSB. He is the author of four books and a number of book chapters and articles.

 **Michael Osborne** is a climate scientist turned multimedia producer for Worldview Stanford who teaches science communication classes at Stanford. He co-founded and produces the award-winning *Generation Anthropocene* podcast, a partnership between Stanford and Smithsonian.com featuring stories and conversations about planetary change. "Through the podcasts, we want to capture stories about the changing environmental and cultural landscapes from diverse perspectives. . . to help guide strategic, editorial, and partnership decisions that bolster Worldview's mission of creating unique learning experiences."

 **Robert Podesva** is an Assistant Professor of Linguistics at Stanford University. He holds degrees from Stanford University (PhD, MA) and Cornell University (BA) and has been an Assistant Professor at Georgetown University. His research examines the social significance of phonetic variation and its role in the construction of identity, most notably gender, sexuality, and race. His most recent projects focus on the interrelation between linguistic variation and embodiment in the expression of affect. He has co-edited *Research Methods in Linguistics, Language and Sexuality*, and the forthcoming *Social Meaning and Linguistic Variation*.

# SERIES EDITORS

 **Robyn Brinks Lockwood** teaches courses in spoken and written English at Stanford University in the English for Foreign Students graduate program and is the program education coordinator of the American Language and Culture undergraduate summer program. She is an active member of the international TESOL organization, serves as Chairperson of the Publishing Professional Council, and is a past chair of the Materials Writers Interest Section. She is a frequent presenter at TESOL regional and international conferences. Robyn has edited and written numerous textbooks, online courses, and ancillary components for ESL courses and TOEFL preparation.

 **Maggie Sokolik** holds a BA in Anthropology from Reed College, and an MA in Romance Linguistics and Ph.D. in Applied Linguistics from UCLA. She is the author of over 20 ESL and composition textbooks. She has taught at MIT, Harvard, Texas A&M, and currently UC Berkeley, where she is Director of College Writing Programs. She has developed and taught several popular MOOC courses in English language writing and literature. She is the founding editor of *TESL-EJ*, a peer-reviewed journal for ESL / EFL professionals, one of the first online journals. Maggie travels frequently to speak about grammar, writing, and instructor education. She lives in the San Francisco Bay area, where she and her husband play bluegrass music.

 **Lawrence J. Zwier** is an Associate Director of the English Language Center, Michigan State University. He holds a bachelor's degree in English Literature from Aquinas College, Grand Rapids, MI, and an MA in TESL from the University of Minnesota. He has taught ESL / EFL at universities in Saudi Arabia, Malaysia, Japan, Singapore, and the US. He is the author of numerous ELT textbooks, mostly about reading and vocabulary, and also writes nonfiction books about history and geography for middle school and high school students. He is married with two children and lives in Okemos, Michigan.

# Acknowledgments

Working on *University Success* has been a wonderful, collaborative experience. My deepest gratitude to the staff at Pearson not only for giving me this opportunity, but also for their vision and professionalism. Special thanks to Amy McCormick for her undying support and cheerleading along the way, and to Niki Cunnion for helping keep me organized and providing me with the resources I needed. My deep gratitude as well to all those at Pearson working behind the scenes to create a wonderful tool for teachers and students. A continuing thanks to Debbie Sistino whose leadership, guidance, and desire to truly provide students with what they need, are unparalleled. And to Ronnie Hess, thank you for your contributions; your ability to simplify difficult content has once again proven to be excellent. Great books are not the work of great authors, but of great editors. Eleanor Barnes, what can I say—you helped me muddle through materials science, medieval literature, and geology. Through the way, you helped me break down challenging content in a way to make it approachable for our ESL students. You always made me laugh and served as a great sounding board. Thank you.

And above all, thank you to all the students of SCAD (Savannah College of Arts and Design) who have walked through my classroom doors. You make me want to do my best. I am forever grateful to you for challenging me to create innovative, dynamic lessons which meet your needs and help you seamlessly transition into mainstream university classes. Lastly, thank you, Bill, Emma, Berkley, and Glory. You gave me time when I needed it, helped me with science and encouraged me along the way. —*Christina Cavage*

# Reviewers

We would like to thank the following reviewers for their many helpful comments and suggestions:

**Jamila Barton**, North Seattle Community College, Seattle, WA; **Joan Chamberlin**, Iowa State University, Ames IA; **Lyam Christopher**, Palm Beach State College, Boynton Beach, FL; **Robin Corcos**, University of California, Santa Barbara, Goleta, CA; **Tanya Davis**, University of California, San Diego, CA; **Brendan DeCoster**, University of Oregon, Eugene, OR; **Thomas Dougherty**, University of St. Mary of the Lake, Mundelein, IL; **Bina Dugan**, Bergen County Community College, Hackensack, NJ; **Priscilla Faucette**, University of Hawaii at Manoa, Honolulu, HI; **Lisa Fischer**, St. Louis University, St. Louis, MO; **Kathleen Flynn**, Glendale Community College, Glendale, CA; **Mary Gawienowski**, William Rainey Harper College, Palatine, IL; **Sally Gearhart**, Santa Rosa Junior College, Santa Rosa, CA; **Carl Guerriere**, Capital Community College, Hartford, CT; **Vera Guillen**, Eastfield College, Mesquite, TX; **Angela Hakim**, St. Louis University, St. Louis, MO; **Pamela Hartmann**, Evans Community Adult School, Los Angeles Unified School District, Los Angeles, CA; **Shelly Hedstrom**, Palm Beach State University, Lake Worth, FL; **Sherie Henderson**, University of Oregon, Eugene, OR; **Lisse Hildebrandt**, English Language Program, Virginia Commonwealth University, Richmond, VA; **Barbara Inerfeld**, Rutgers University, Piscataway, NJ; **Zaimah Khan**, Northern Virginia Community College, Loudon Campus, Sterling, VA; **Tricia Kinman**, St. Louis University, St. Louis, MO; **Kathleen Klaiber**, Genesee Community College, Batavia, NY; **Kevin Lamkins**, Capital Community College, Hartford, CT; **Mayetta Lee**, Palm Beach State College, Lake Worth, FL; **Kirsten Lillegard**, English Language Institute, Divine Word College, Epworth, IA; **Craig Machado**, Norwalk Community College, Norwalk, CT; **Cheryl Madrid**, Spring International Language Center, Denver, CO; **Ann Meechai**, St. Louis University, St. Louis, MO; **Melissa Mendelson**, Department of Linguistics, University of Utah, Salt Lake City, UT; **Tamara Milbourn**, University of Colorado, Boulder, CO; **Debbie Ockey**, Fresno City College, Fresno, CA; **Diana Pascoe-Chavez**, St. Louis University, St. Louis, MO; **Kathleen Reynolds**, William Rainey Harper College, Palatine, IL; **Linda Roth**, Vanderbilt University ELC, Greensboro, NC; **Minati Roychoudhuri**, Capital Community College, Hartford, CT; **Bruce Rubin**, California State University, Fullerton, CA; **Margo Sampson**, Syracuse University, Syracuse, NY; **Sarah Saxer**, Howard Community College, Ellicott City, MD; **Anne-Marie Schlender**, Austin Community College, Austin, TX; **Susan Shields**, Santa Barbara Community College, Santa Barbara, CA; **Barbara Smith-Palinkas**, Hillsborough Community College, Dale Mabry Campus, Tampa, FL; **Sara Stapleton**, North Seattle Community College, Seattle, WA; **Lisa Stelle**, Northern Virginia Community College Loudon, Sterling, VA; **Jamie Tanzman**, Northern Kentucky University, Highland Heights, KY; **Jeffrey Welliver**, Soka University of America, Aliso Viejo, CA; **Mark Wolfersberger**, Brigham Young University, Hawaii, Laie, HI; **May Youn**, California State University, Fullerton, CA

# Fundamental Oral Communication Skills

*Part 1 is designed to build fundamental skills step by step through exploration of rigorous, academic content. Practice activities tied to specific learning outcomes in each unit focus on understanding the function and application of the skills.*

*Language communicates who we are*

# Active Participation

## UNIT PROFILE

In this unit, you will learn about how factors like age, gender, social class, and race influence people's manner of speaking or accent. You will also learn how the differences between Standard and Non-standard American English accents have changed throughout the years.

**You will prepare a group presentation on a lost or disappearing accent.**

## OUTCOMES

- Demonstrate interest and engage in lectures and discussions
- Utilize appropriate examples to clarify discussion points
- Annotate texts to identify key points and support your point of view
- Use interjections to actively participate in lectures and discussions
- Acquire new vocabulary using context clues and identifying synonyms

For more about **LINGUISTICS**, see ❷ ❸. See also ⬛R and ⬛W **LINGUISTICS** ❶ ❷ ❸.

## GETTING STARTED

Go to MyEnglishLab to watch Professor Podesva's introductory video and to complete a self-assessment.

**Discuss these questions with a partner or group.**

1. Do languages change? If so, in what ways?

2. How does the language of your generation differ from that of your grandparents' generation?

3. In Professor Podesva's introduction, he mentions that social factors can affect accents. How might factors, such as age, gender, and economic status affect one's accent?

## FUNDAMENTAL SKILL

### BEING AN ACTIVE PARTICIPANT

> **WHY IT'S USEFUL** By being an active participant, you can increase your learning by actively collaborating with your professors and peers.

To be successful in a North American college classroom, you need to be an **active participant**. Active participation often means collaborating with your professors and peers. Collaboration can help you better understand complex topics because you are able to share and exchange ideas and information. Universities and colleges value active participation, and often make it a large part of the classroom experience. There are several things you can do to become a more active participant.

First, it is important that you **express interest** in the subject, speaker, and the speaker's ideas. Showing interest indicates your level of **engagement** with the subject matter. Being engaged with the subject matter not only helps you to retain the information, but also demonstrates your desire to learn.

A second important strategy is being able to **incorporate appropriate examples** to illustrate your ideas. Selecting examples that are relevant to the context of the lesson demonstrates your understanding of a topic and improves your ability to contribute to a discussion.

### VOCABULARY PREVIEW

**Read the vocabulary items in the box. Circle the ones you know. Put a question mark next to the ones you don't know.**

| flabbergasted | arduous | replicate | hurdle | dialect | sway |
|---|---|---|---|---|---|

## EXERCISE 1

🔊 A. Listen to a lecture about age and accents. How does the student show interest in the topic?

.................................................................................................................................................

🔊 B. Listen again. What examples does the professor use to illustrate how age influences accent? List any additional details the professor provides.

.................................................................................................................................................

.................................................................................................................................................

C. What questions might you ask to show interest in the topic? Compare your questions with a partner.

🔊 D. Now listen to a conversation between two students after the lecture. Were they engaged? What does each one do to actively participate in the conversation?

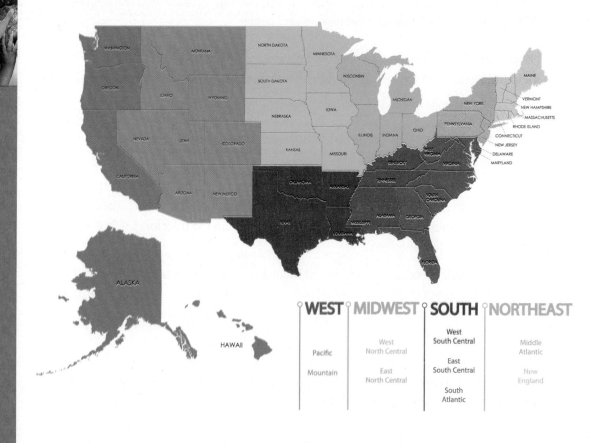

**CULTURE NOTE**

North American accents vary by region. There are variations in the pronunciation of various sounds, words, and even some grammatical features. Although the map on page 4 indicates the main accents spoken by each area, there are variations within each region.

## VOCABULARY CHECK

**A.** Review the vocabulary items in the Vocabulary Preview. Write their definitions and add examples. Use a dictionary if necessary.

**B.** Choose the sentence that correctly describes the underlined vocabulary items.

1. a. Trying to change your accent can be <u>arduous</u> work; it is as difficult as running a marathon.

   b. Trying to change your accent can be <u>arduous</u>—as fun as visiting with a friend.

2. a. How many <u>dialects</u> can you speak? I can speak Spanish and English.

   b. How many <u>dialects</u> can you recognize? I can recognize a southern dialect and the northeastern dialect.

3. a. Mary was <u>flabbergasted</u>. She was astonished.

   b. Mary was <u>flabbergasted</u>. She was heartbroken.

4. a. Juan overcame many <u>hurdles</u> when he began learning English. There were successes, and he was glad to experience them.

   b. Juan overcame many <u>hurdles</u> when he began learning English. There were barriers, but he found a way around them.

5. a. Many people try to <u>replicate</u> great speakers, copying their vocal patterns.

   b. Many people try to <u>replicate</u> great speakers, making fun of their word choices and voice.

6. a. Did she <u>sway</u> you? She can be so funny.

   b. Did she <u>sway</u> you? She can be so persuasive.

🔵 Go to MyEnglishLab to complete a listening and vocabulary practice and to join in collaborative activities.

# SUPPORTING SKILL 1

## DEMONSTRATING INTEREST AND ENGAGEMENT

**WHY IT'S USEFUL** By demonstrating your interest and engagement in a lecture, class discussion, or other academic activity, you can show your professors you are ready to learn, activate your critical thinking skills, and get the most out of the course.

College professors expect **active participation** from their students, and this participation can take either a verbal or nonverbal form. Using the strategies below can help you demonstrate your interest and engagement as well as further your understanding of a topic.

While in class, listen carefully to your professor and classmates. Participating in class can sometimes be intimidating; however, if you follow these steps, you can ease your anxiety.

One way to **demonstrate your interest** in a topic is to come to class prepared with questions on the readings and course material from the previous class. Reviewing the material critically requires added thought, which deepens your understanding of the content. In order to ask questions either before or during the class, it is important to signal the professor that you would like to speak. You can do this either verbally or nonverbally.

| Verbal Signals | Non-verbal Signals |
| --- | --- |
| Excuse me, ... | Raise your hand |
| May I ask a question? | Make eye contact with your professor |
| Could I interrupt you for a minute? | Sit up straighter in your chair |
| Would you mind if I interrupted you? | |

### TIP

North American classrooms are often relatively friendly and informal. It is common to ask the professor questions in class, and many students raise their hand at the same time they begin to speak. This is not considered rude. If someone is talking, however, wait until they are finished before speaking up. Remember, too that not all professors like to be interrupted. Sometimes it is best to wait for a pause in the lecture before asking a question.

Second, the signal you use will depend on the situation you are in. Verbal signals are typically used when you are involved in a class discussion, or working with a small group or partner. However, they are not common during a lecture, or a presentation. Using verbal signals at these times may be considered disruptive. In these situations, non-verbal signals are useful. They not only show the speaker you are engaged, but they also can help the speaker "see" what may and may not be challenging to understand. Thus, it is important to listen carefully to your professor and your classmates and use these signals to show interest in and understanding of what they are saying.

| Verbal Signals | Non-verbal Signals |
|---|---|
| Uh-huh. | Make eye contact with the speaker |
| Hmm. | Nod |
| That's interesting/great/fascinating/terrific. | Lean forward |
| | Take notes |
| Wow! | |
| (Oh) Really? | |
| Sure. | |

These verbal signals are referred to as *interjections*. You will have more practice with interjections in the Language Skill section in MyEnglishLab. Refer to page 18.

## VOCABULARY PREVIEW

Read the vocabulary items in the box. Circle the ones you know. Put a question mark next to the ones you don't know.

| pitch | intonation | precise | hit the nail on the head | impact | ethnicity |
|---|---|---|---|---|---|

## EXERCISE 2

A. Brainstorm with a partner. What factors influence our accents?

.................................................................................................................................

.................................................................................................................................

.................................................................................................................................

**B.** Listen to a class discussion on factors influencing accents. As you listen, complete the sentences.

1. I thought speaking .............................. between men and women were just a matter of women's voices being higher .............................. and men's voices being lower pitched, right?

2. Oh? How does where you live on a map .............................. your accent?

3. Uh-huh. You hit the nail on the head. Regional .............................. .

4. Could I .............................. you for a minute? Is that why some accents seem related to .............................. ?

5. But over a .............................. ago, people tended to stay in one place and not move around as much. With no television, radio, or .............................. , people mostly spoke like their neighbors.

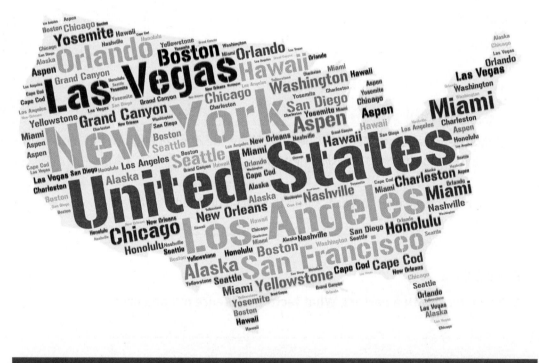

| TIP |
| --- |
| When students participate in academic discussions they are often "thinking on their feet." That means what they are saying has not been prepared. Speakers usually pause before their main point. Listen for a pause, and the main point is likely to follow. |

**C. Listen again. Which ways did the students use to show their interest and engagement?**

Asked a question by...

- ☐ Excuse me, ...
- ☐ May I ask a question?
- ☐ Could I interrupt you for a minute?
- ☐ Would you mind if I interrupted you?

Used a verbal signal to show interest by...

- ☐ Uh-huh.
- ☐ Hmm.
- ☐ That's interesting.
- ☐ Wow!
- ☐ Really?
- ☐ Sure.
- ☐ Oh.

**D. Read each statement. After each, show your interest by either asking a question or by using a verbal signal.**

1. Our accents are definitely influenced by our friends.

   ........................................................................................................................

2. I believe family and geography are the greatest factors influencing our accents.

   ........................................................................................................................

3. Social class can also influence our accents.

   ........................................................................................................................

4. Our professions influence our accents. If we need to communicate with a wide variety of speakers, this definitely impacts how we say things.

   ........................................................................................................................

**E. Work in a small group. Discuss which factor from Part D has the greatest influence over your accent. As you listen to your classmates, be sure to give both verbal and non-verbal signals that you are interested and engaged.**

## VOCABULARY CHECK

A. Review the vocabulary items in the Vocabulary Preview. Write their definitions and add examples. Use a dictionary if necessary.

B. Write synonyms for each vocabulary item. Use a thesaurus to help you.

1. ethnicity ............................

2. hit the nail on the head ............................

3. impact ............................

4. intonation ............................

5. pitch ............................

6. precise ............................

⬤ Go to MyEnglishLab to complete vocabulary and skill practices and to join in collaborative activities.

# SUPPORTING SKILL 2

## IDENTIFYING AND INCORPORATING APPROPRIATE EXAMPLES

**WHY IT'S USEFUL** By identifying and incorporating appropriate examples, you can reveal your understanding of a topic, clarify your points of view, and gain support for your ideas.

When participating in an academic discussion, it is important to **identify and incorporate appropriate examples** not only to demonstrate your understanding of the topic, but also to clarify your main ideas for your listeners and to gain support for your ideas. There are several types of examples you can incorporate when speaking. Choosing the best one depends on the topic, the situation, and your audience.

### Using a Model

While listening to, and participating in academic discussions, you will hear a good number of examples that provide a very specific illustration of an idea. The use of a model is effective in presentations, debates, and group discussions.

"Uptalk" is using rising intonation at the end of a statement.

For example: "My name is Meghan."

> **CULTURE NOTE**
>
> *Uptalk* is common among many young people. Because it resembles question intonation, young people using uptalk can often seem timid, or less confident. In situations such as talking with authority figures, their listeners may misinterpret uptalk as an indication of self-doubt.

## Using an Anecdote

*Anecdotes* are short stories that help to illustrate a point or idea. Anecdotes can be a very helpful way to clarify something because they are memorable. They are most effective when giving a presentation. They leave your listeners with a clear, memorable picture.

> I was walking down the street the other day, and a woman was talking quite excitedly. At the end of every sentence, her pitch rose sharply, and she sounded child-like. I thought something was wrong. My friend assured me nothing was wrong, she was just "uptalking."

## Using a Scenario

*Scenarios* are similar to anecdotes, but they often indicate what might happen in a hypothetical situation rather than what has already happened. Scenarios are especially effective to use when you want to gain support for your idea. You are essentially persuading your listeners by establishing a context for your point. The use of a scenario is quite effective in argumentative presentations, debates, and group discussions.

> Imagine walking down the street one day in a place where people speak your first language, and you hear sounds you have never heard before. You cannot understand what is being said. You look around, and everyone is much younger than you, they are all young children …

| Type of Example | Ways to Introduce |
|---|---|
| Model | For example … <br> For instance … <br> Such as … <br> Let me give you an example … |
| Anecdote | To illustrate … <br> Let me tell you a story … <br> Consider this story … |
| Scenario | Imagine … <br> Suppose … |

## VOCABULARY PREVIEW

Read the vocabulary items in the box. Circle the ones you know.
Put a question mark next to the ones you don't know.

| | | | |
|---|---|---|---|
| non-standard | identifiable | determine | exceptionally |
| entirely | notably | mimic | strict |

## EXERCISE 3

### A. Work with a partner. Answer the questions.

1. Can you think of anyone who has a Standard American accent? How does it sound?

2. What part of the country do you think this accent might be spoken?

**TIP**

You can extract key information by listening carefully to how a professor speaks during a lecture or a class discussion. Main ideas are generally spoken more slowly and clearly. In other words, professors often lengthen the syllables of important information. Pay close attention when speakers slow their speech. This often indicates a main idea.

### B. Listen to a discussion on Standard and Non-standard American English accents. Choose the ideas that you hear.

☐ 1. Everyone in Kansas speaks Standard American English.

☐ 2. Newscasters try to sound the same.

☐ 3. In the 1930's and 1940's, newscasters spoke with their unique regional accents.

☐ 4. What we call Standard American English is what we agree to call it.

☐ 5. Speaking with a New York accent is considered desirable.

☐ 6. Defining Standard American English is very difficult.

### C. Listen again for the types of examples that are used. Make notes of details.

MODEL: ................................................................................................................

ANECDOTE: ..........................................................................................................

SCENARIO: ...........................................................................................................

**CULTURE NOTE**

As you have learned, American accents vary greatly from region to region. Two very distinct regional accents are the Southern accent and the New York City accent. The Southern accent has long, drawn-out vowels that can sound like two syllables and which have a continuous pitch. Whereas the New York City accent of many native New Yorkers drops the "r" in the middle and at the end of words. It also replaces the "th" sounds in words with "d" or "t".

D. Work with a partner. Consider your native language. Are there regional differences? Share some regional differences with a partner by using a model, an anecdote, or a scenario.

E. Work in a small group. Discuss how your native languages differ from English. Be sure to give examples that illustrate the difference.

## VOCABULARY CHECK

A. Review the vocabulary items in the Vocabulary Preview. Write their definitions and add examples. Use a dictionary if necessary.

B. Complete the sentences with the correct vocabulary items.

1. Young children often stand behind adults and _____ their actions.

2. Some vowels sounds are _____ different in their pronunciation from one part of the country to another.

3. Accents are not determined _____ by where we are born, but other factors as well.

4. Many people feel that a southern accent is a _____ accent, except, of course, those who live in the South.

5. In order to _____ where someone is from, pay close attention to the way they pronounce certain words.

6. Languages have _____ rules regarding grammar and word choice.

7. Each regional accent has _____ features that help us distinguish it from other accents.

8. People have to work _____ hard to reduce their regional accent.

Go to MyEnglishLab to complete vocabulary and listening practices and to join in collaborative activities.

# INTEGRATED SKILLS

## ANNOTATING TEXTS

**WHY IT'S USEFUL**  By developing a system for annotating texts, you can easily identify key points of a reading, and make connections between a reading and a lecture. In addition, identifying those connections can aid you in developing talking points for a classroom discussion.

In your classes, you will most likely participate in many different learning activities, and be exposed to a wide variety of learning materials. In a typical college classroom, professors will lecture; you will be required to read course texts, asked to participate in classroom discussions, and perhaps even attend out of class excursions, like field trips. It can be challenging to synthesize all this material. One effective way to make connections between learning experiences is through annotating.

**Annotating** a text involves marking it up. It is an active strategy that permits you to engage deeper with the material. Annotating allows you to have an active "dialogue" with the text, and make connections to lectures, classroom discussions, and assignments. This often leads to better understanding of the course material.

What exactly is annotating? Annotating can take two forms: in-text markings and out-of-text markings. **In-text markings** involve highlighting and circling key points in the text. Highlighting and circling can help you quickly identify these key points and become familiar with new vocabulary when you review the material. It also allows you to easily see the organization of the text. Look at this excerpt:

> ## Introduction: Rhoticity, Radio, and a Rapid Shift
>
> Just a few decades ago, "well-spoken" English was associated with a radically different accent. Speech instructors, teachers, and broadcasters all agreed that a British-influenced, North-east Coast accent was the voice of prestige. After the Second World War, however, the ideal "American" voice quickly changed to an accent associated with the American Midwest. The rise of broadcast television, and the concomitant rise of the TV news anchor, propelled this style of speaking to prominence around the world. Today it is this "Midland," accent, with its distinctive rhoticity that is most commonly associated with American speech.

A second type of text annotation, **out-of-text markings**, involves writing in the margins. Good annotators pull out information that helps to explain why in-text notations are important, or that make connections to other learning materials. Out-of-text annotations may include definitions, examples, paraphrases, numbering of key ideas, connections to lectures or class discussions, and questions. Annotations can also be used to create an outline of the key information in the reading. When annotating, it is important to develop your own system, with your own set of symbols. Some common symbols appear below.

| Symbol | Meaning |
|--------|---------|
| $*$ | This is important |
| ✓ | I agree/I understand |
| ? | I don't understand/I have a question about this |
| ! | I really agree/that's surprising |
| ∞ | There's a connection to lecture/class discussion/between points |
| ↓ | More detail to above |
| *Ex* | example |

Look at this excerpt:

## Introduction: Rhoticity, Radio, and a Rapid Shift

Just a few decades ago, "well-spoken" English was associated with a radically different accent. Speech instructors, teachers, and broadcasters all agreed that a British-influenced, North-east Coast accent was the voice of prestige. After the Second World War, however, the ideal "American" voice quickly changed to an accent associated with the American Midwest. The rise of broadcast television, and the concomitant rise of the TV news anchor, propelled this style of speaking to prominence around the world. Today it is this "Midland," accent, with its distinctive rhoticity that is most commonly associated with American speech.

*? What was that accent?*

*∞ Lecture midwest*

*Ex → Midland*

## EXERCISE 4

**A.** With a partner, discuss in-text and out-of-text annotations. What are the advantages of each type? Develop a symbol chart for out-of-text annotations.

**B.** Listen again to the class discussion on Standard American accents. As you listen, take notes and add annotations to mark key ideas.

**C.** Now read the textbook excerpt on Standard American accents. Annotate the text. Be sure to include connections to the classroom discussion.

---

# Introduction: Rhoticity, Radio, and a Rapid Shift

Just a few decades ago, well-spoken English was associated with a radically different accent. Speech instructors, teachers, and broadcasters all agreed that a British-influenced, Northeast Coast accent was the voice of prestige. After the second World War, however, the ideal "American" voice quickly changed to an accent associated with the American Midwest. The rise of broadcast television, and the concomitant rise of the TV news anchor, propelled this style of speaking to prominence around the world. Today, it is this Midland accent, with its distinctive rhoticity, that is most commonly associated with American speech.

## A Change of Scenery

What caused the sudden change in speaking style? Theories abound, with some bordering on the outlandish. Did the mixing of accents, which occurred when thousands of US citizens entered the military in wartime, give the coastal elite a new appreciation for Midwestern honesty and its associated voice? It's possible that technological advancement played a role; the older, coastal accents were easy to pick up clearly on less sensitive audio equipment. As the sound quality of broadcast radio and television improved, however, voices could be reproduced with greater clarity. Now speakers could be understood clearly without having to dramatically alter their speaking style. On a more practical level, however, the fact that early Hollywood drew most of its talent from Westerners and Midwesterners who moved to California was probably the biggest single cause of the accent's rise to prominence.

## Rhoticity—The Sound of America

Among non-English speakers, and even non-American speakers of English, the most distinctive quality of American English is almost certainly its *rhoticity*—or use of the sound associated with the letter "R." Many varieties of English—including many in the United States and most varieties in countries historically associated with the British Commonwealth—are *non-rhotic*. In these forms of English, the "R" sound is only fully vocalized at certain times. A *rhotic* accent, like that associated with Standard American English, fully pronounces the "R" sound at all times. While mastering the intricacies of rhoticity can prove especially difficult for those learning English, it remains the most important sound to practice for those wishing to "sound American."

## The American Accent Today

While language instructors and news anchors may seem to have an agreed-upon standard, it is worth remembering that the fundamental characteristics of language change continue to apply—even in places associated with "standard" speech! The northern cities vowel shift, for example, continues to influence many areas that were historically associated with Standard American English. While this change was well underway at the time, a blend of Midwestern accents became seen as the standard, regional changes continue; this gradually pushes regional accents to diverge further along their own path.

Even if the "standard" is destined to change, that doesn't mean you should prepare yourself by learning an entirely new way to speak English. Languages always change, but the change is gradual; the sound of Standard American English will continue to be influenced by regional dialects and social trends. We may notice changes over the course of our lifetime, but generally they will be easy to adapt to. What is seen as standard will certainly change—but only when large portions of society gradually change of their own volition. Even with large-scale changes like those seen in the twentieth century, the sounds of a language don't change without user input!

D. With your partner, compare your annotations. What is similar? What is different? What connections did you make to the classroom discussion?

E. Work in small groups. Discuss the questions.

1. How would you define Standard American English? How has the definition changed over the last century?

2. What factors are responsible for that shift?

3. How do you think Standard American English might change in the future?

○ Go to MyEnglishLab to complete a skill practice.

## LANGUAGE SKILL

### USING INTERJECTIONS

**WHY IT'S USEFUL** By identifying and utilizing interjections, you can easily show your interest and engagement with the topic.

○ Go to MyEnglishLab for the Language Skill presentation and practice.

# VOCABULARY STRATEGY

## LEARNING NEW WORDS THROUGH CONTEXT

**WHY IT'S USEFUL**  By using context clues to identify synonyms for unknown words, you can learn new vocabulary in a meaningful way, and connect it to the content.

One obstacle when listening to a lecture, a class discussion, or reading course materials is understanding new vocabulary. **Learning new words in context**, using the surrounding words and phrases, is a very effective and meaningful way to learn vocabulary.

How can you learn vocabulary in context? There are several strategies you can use, and speakers and writers often give **context clues** to the meaning of new words. One very common context cue is a **synonym**. Synonyms are words that have the same or similar meaning. Speakers and writers vary their vocabulary, and will frequently incorporate synonyms to avoid too much repetition.

> Some accents and dialects are considered to be **prestigious**. These **high-status** accents are associated with wealthy and successful social groups.

Although you may not know the word *prestigious*, there is a synonym that explains it in the very next sentence. The same is true with the unknown word *rhoticity*; there is a synonym/definition later in the same sentence.

> The most distinctive quality of American English is almost certainly its **rhoticity—or use of the sound associated with the letter R.**

Synonyms can occur in either the previous or following sentence, as they do in the first example with *prestigious* and *high-status*. In addition, they can occur in the same sentence with a punctuation marker with or without the word *or*, as in the sentence with *rhoticity*. Punctuation and the word *or* are context clues that alert you that a definition or a synonym is coming. Other common punctuation markers for synonyms are two commas, a hyphen, or even parentheses. By learning vocabulary in this way, you will see how the word is actually used to help you better understand the content. You can associate the word with context, and that association helps you to retain that new vocabulary word.

## EXERCISE 5

### A. Read the sentences. Choose the context clue that helps you learn the meaning of the underlined word.

1. The most widespread American accent is the Midwestern accent. Early Hollywood drew most of its talent from Westerners and Midwesterners who moved to California, which was probably the biggest single cause of the accent's <u>ubiquitous</u> use.

   a. Synonym in previous or following sentence

   b. Definition/synonym with punctuation

2. Changing your accent is an <u>arduous</u>, or difficult, task even for trained individuals who grew up as native speakers of the language.

   a. Synonym in previous or following sentence

   b. Definition/synonym with punctuation

3. In North American English, the differences usually involve something called <u>*prosodic variation*</u>—this includes things such as the emphasis placed on individual syllables, how pauses are used, and things like that.

   a. Synonym in previous or following sentence

   b. Definition/synonym with punctuation

4. Accents that are not widely accepted by all occur in various places in the US. Accents which are commonly heard in movies and on television programs like colloquial accents from New York City, are often perceived as <u>Non-standard</u> accents.

   a. Synonym in previous or following sentence

   b. Definition/synonym with punctuation

### B. Read the sentences. Use context clues to identify the meaning of the underlined word. Write in a synonym.

1. Some North American accents are very noticeable. These <u>distinct</u> accents have been influenced by the region, and its early immigrants. ........................

2. It is very important to be very <u>precise</u>, or exact, when explaining how to do something in a second language. ........................

3. Regional accents can vary slightly by tiny details. The <u>intricacies</u> of where exactly a sound is made in the mouth is one thing linguists consider when studying regional accents. ........................

4. Many actors set a goal of adopting Standard American English. This <u>target</u> is obtainable for some, and difficult for others. ........................

C. Work with a partner. Make sentences using the words and their synonyms below. Be sure to use context clues with the synonyms.

1. mimic / copy

2. elite / privileged

3. trends / current happenings

4. impact / influence

5. strict / firm

## APPLY YOUR SKILLS

**WHY IT'S USEFUL**  By applying the skills you have learned in this unit, you will be able to more actively participate and engage in a college-level course.

### ASSIGNMENT

Prepare a group presentation on a disappearing or lost accent. You and your group members will present key elements of the accent, such as who spoke it, where it was spoken, elements of the accent that may still exist today, and the factors that led to its disappearance.

### BEFORE YOU LISTEN

A. Before you listen, discuss the questions with one or more students.

1. Do you think an accent can be changed? If so, how?

2. Why would someone want to change their accent?

3. What are some factors that may be responsible for variations in accents?

B. You will listen to a lecture on Standard and Non-standard American English. As you listen, think about these questions:

1. What is the goal of an accent-reduction course?

2. What are some factors that influence someone's accent?

3. How has Standard American English changed over the last 70 years?

4. Why do some people attempt to change their accent?

C. Review the Unit Skills Summary on page 22. As you listen to the lecture and prepare for your group presentation, apply the skills you learned in this unit.

# UNIT SKILLS SUMMARY

## BECOME AN ACTIVE PARTICIPANT BY USING THESE SKILLS:

### Utilize strategies to express interest and engagement

- Ask questions and use non-verbal cues to show your interest.
- Use verbal and non-verbal signals to engage in a lecture or class discussion.
- Identify and utilize a wide variety of examples to support your ideas.

### Annotate texts

- Utilize in-text and out-of-text annotations to identify key information.
- Use annotations to make connections to other course content.

### Utilize interjections

- Participate in lectures and class discussions by using interjections to show your agreement, disbelief, or surprise.

### Identify synonyms in context to learn new words

- Utilize context clues to recognize synonyms of unknown words.

## LISTEN

A. Listen to a lecture about Standard and Non-standard American English. Take notes on key ideas.

B. Compare your notes with a partner. Do you both have the same key ideas? What skills from this unit helped you identify key ideas?

C. Review the questions from Before You Listen, Part B. Listen to the lecture again. Work with a partner and use your notes on the lecture to answer the questions.

Go to MyEnglishLab to listen more closely and answer the critical thinking questions.

## THINKING CRITICALLY

**Discuss the questions with another student.**

1. What connection does the speaker suggest exists between where you grow up and your accent? How about your ethnic group and your accent? How do these two work together to influence your accent?

2. How would you summarize the main point of the lecture?

3. Based on the lecture, how would you describe the speaker's point of view? Be sure to provide appropriate examples that demonstrate your understanding.

4. The professor makes the point that accents change. How do you think accents will change in the future? What other influences might affect your accent?

## THINKING VISUALLY

**A. Look at the graph. Discuss the questions with a partner.**

1. What can you say about the trend of the Mid-Atlantic accent?

2. What can you say about the trend of the Midland accent?

3. Can you determine when a change in each occurred?

4. What other accents from the lecture could you plot on the line graph?

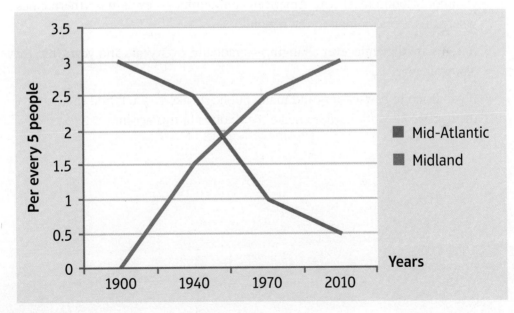

B. Go online and investigate the trends regarding another common accent in the United States. Add your findings to the graph on page 23.

C. Share your findings with your classmates. Discuss the trend. Is there a change in the trend? What could be responsible for the change?

---

**TIP**

When describing trends, such as the one in the line graph, the focus is on whether something is going up (increasing), going down (decreasing), or remaining about the same (holding steady). Verbs and nouns are used for this purpose. Common words for going up include these verbs and nouns: to increase/see an increase, rising/see a rise. Common words for going down include to decrease/see a decrease, to fall/ see a fall/to drop/see a drop. Some adjectives and adverbs used with these words include: sharp/sharply, steady/steadily, slight/slightly. For example, "Use of the Midland accent began rising sharply after 1900."

---

Go to MyEnglishLab to record your results.

## THINKING ABOUT LANGUAGE

Read these excerpts from the lecture. After the end of each excerpt, add an interjection. Circle any synonyms you find in the excerpt.

1. Some accents and dialects are considered to be elite or prestigious and are associated with wealthy and successful social groups. .........................

2. R-dropping, for example, is still common in many Southern accents and is commonly found in African-American communities—even in northern cities where this is uncommon in the region! .........................

3. Accents are dynamic, ever changing—gradually, over years and years, but they *always* change. .........................

4. If you listen to newscasters and many public speakers, you'll find that most of them strive, or work hard, to make their voices fit this accent. .........................

## GROUP PRESENTATION

**A. Discuss the questions with one or more students.**

1. Accents change, and some accents even disappear. Do you know of any accents that have disappeared?

2. What might cause an accent to no longer be used?

**B. You will work with a small group to prepare a presentation on a lost accent. Brainstorm disappearing or lost accents. Think about North American accents and other English accents across the globe. Then select an accent, and think about these questions as you research and prepare. Consider using a wide variety of examples to illustrate your ideas.**

1. What is the accent?

2. Where was it spoken?

3. Are there remnants of it today? Where?

4. Why is the accent now considered extinct?

**C. Listen to each presentation.**

Listen carefully and take notes on each presentation. As you listen, remember to actively participate by asking questions, and using interjections to show your feelings. Discuss the similarities and differences between all the accents presented.

⬆ Go to MyEnglishLab to watch Professor Podesva's concluding video and to complete a self-assessment.

# BUSINESS ETHICS

# Idea Development

## UNIT PROFILE

In this unit, you will learn about commerce and about the fiduciary system of the United States. You will also learn about three ethical frameworks for making business decisions and how these frameworks influence company culture. In addition, you will see the role that ethics play in the success or failure of a business.

**You will prepare a debate on the social responsibilities of a business in your community.**

## OUTCOMES

- Identify main ideas
- Distinguish supporting details
- Prepare a formal argument
- Use adverbial clauses to describe relationships
- Determine affective meaning through stance adverbials

For more about **BUSINESS ETHICS**, see ② ③.
See also Ⓡ and Ⓦ **BUSINESS ETHICS** ① ② ③.

## GETTING STARTED

⏺ Go to MyEnglishLab to watch Dr. McLennan's introductory video and to complete a self-assessment.

**Discuss these questions with a partner or group.**

1. In what ways might ethics guide a business or organization?

2. Do you think there is the relationship between a company's ethics and their success? If so, what is it?

3. In Dr. McLennan's introduction, he introduces you to fiduciary responsibility. How does he define a fiduciary?

## FUNDAMENTAL SKILL

### DEVELOPING AN IDEA

> **WHY IT'S USEFUL** By focusing and developing your ideas, you can present them in a clearer, more organized, and more effective manner.

When preparing for college presentations, panel discussions, and other speaking assignments, you will need to develop your ideas so they have a clear focus and good support. This will allow you to present your ideas clearly and coherently. The process of **idea development** involves using techniques like brainstorming, adding, deleting, organizing, and prioritizing ideas. There are several strategies that can help you develop your ideas. All of these strategies can help you **identify a main idea**, or focus. They can also help you determine how to break down your focus or main idea into **supporting ideas**. The first strategy is brainstorming. Brainstorming involves writing down everything that comes to mind on a topic.

| A successful business |
| --- |
| • makes money |
| • has good benefits |
| • treats employees well |
| • (acts ethically) |
| • has innovative products/ideas |

Once you find a topic, you can brainstorm supporting ideas.

One method to help guide you in finding supporting ideas is by asking WH-questions.

_What_ does it mean to act ethically?

_Who_ is responsible for ethical behavior?

_Why_ do companies benefit when they behave ethically?

_Where_ do employees learn the company's ethical policies?

_How_ is ethical behavior enforced?

A second effective strategy to developing ideas is using a visual map, sometimes called a "cluster-map" or a "mind-map." A visual map allows you to see potential connections between main ideas and supporting topics.

Once you have a visual map, you can add or delete ideas. Visual maps are especially helpful to see the relationships between main and supporting ideas. The further you branch out, the more specific your ideas are.

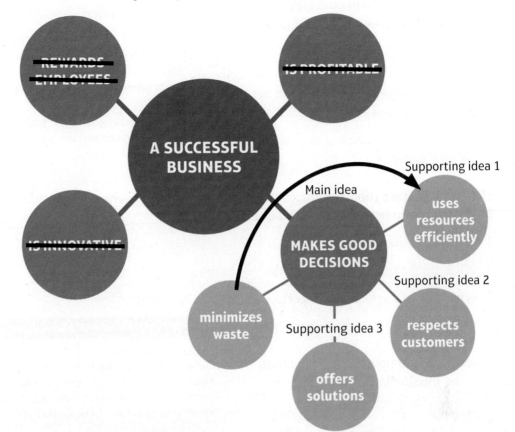

Idea development helps you prepare for all types of oral assignments, and it is especially helpful when preparing an argument. Preparing an argument involves making a claim, stating your reasons for that claim, and providing appropriate evidence to support your claim. Utilizing a visual map can help you clearly identify the supporting reasons for your claim, and their relationship to one another. By utilizing this strategy, you can deliver your position more clearly and coherently.

## VOCABULARY PREVIEW

Read the vocabulary items. Circle the ones you know. Put a question mark next to the ones you don't know.

| | | |
|---|---|---|
| frameworks | at the heart | core concept |
| a great deal of consideration | ambiguous | driving force |

## EXERCISE 1

### A. Work with a partner. Discuss the questions.

1. What does it mean to be ethical? What do you think it means for businesses or corporations to be ethical?

2. What are some business practices that you feel are unethical? What are some business practices that you feel are ethical?

3. How do you think businesses establish their policies about ethics?

> **Glossary**
>
> **Mission:** the main goal or purpose of a person, business, or organization
>
> **Scenarios:** describing things that might happen in different possible situations
>
> **Virtue:** morally good, right, and honest character and behavior

### B. Listen to a lecture that introduces three common ethical frameworks used in business. As you listen, answer the questions.

1. What is business ethics?

2. What are the three common ethical frameworks?

3. Where can the ethical frameworks of a business be found?

4. Who does each framework benefit?

### C. Listen again. Complete the visual map with the missing information.

> **TIP**
>
> Lectures that introduce new ideas and concepts generally move from general to specific. Major ideas are generally introduced first and then explained in greater depth with supporting ideas. Finally, the speaker will supply details or examples.

example: ........................................

mission statement outline

highly ...............................................

**Consequentialist**

**BUSINESS ETHICS FRAMEWORKS**
– how a business will act
– in mission statements

...........................................

works to become virtuous

full set of rules

example: consumer research agency

example: ...........................................

........................................... and actively working towards being ethical

D. Use your visual map to identify ideas and details. Write *M* (main idea), *S* (supporting idea), and *D* (detail or example).

1. .............. Ethical codes serve as a framework for decision making in business.

2. .............. According to the consequentialist framework, the best decision is the best outcome for all involved.

3. .............. A pharmaceutical company uses childproof bottles to avoid harming customers.

4. .............. The duty-based framework of ethics follows a complete set of rules.

5. .............. Consumer research agencies have strict guidelines regarding customer data.

6. .............. The virtue framework of ethics is about constant self-examination and working towards being ethical.

E. Now listen to a conversation between two students who attended the lecture. What do they think the main ideas of the lecture were?

# BUSINESS ETHICS

**SOCIAL RESPONSIBILITY**     **TRUST**     **CONNECTION**

**HONESTY**     **INTEGRITY**     **COMMITMENT**

**TRANSPARENCY**     **CORE VALUES**     **RELIABILITY**

## VOCABULARY CHECK

A. Review the vocabulary items in the Vocabulary Preview. Write their definitions and add examples. Use a dictionary if necessary.

B. Match the vocabulary items with their synonyms.

............ 1. a great deal of consideration     a. beliefs

............ 2. ambiguous     b. organizational method

............ 3. at the heart     c. unclear

............ 4. core concept     d. push

............ 5. driving force     e. basis

............ 6. framework     f. much attention

> Go to MyEnglishLab to complete a listening and vocabulary skill practice and to join in collaborative activities.

# SUPPORTING SKILL 1
## IDENTIFYING MAIN IDEAS

**WHY IT'S USEFUL** By identifying main ideas in a lecture, discussion, or presentation, you can better understand the overall content and the relationship between ideas.

Each lecture, discussion, or presentation has a main idea. The **main idea** refers to the key point being made or examined. Without understanding the main idea, nothing else will seem to make sense, and once you have a clear picture of the main idea, all the supporting ideas and details will fall into place. Understanding every single word is not necessary for determining the main idea. However, there are several strategies that can help you determine the main idea.

The first strategy is listening for word chains. A word chain refers to when words that are the same, or have the same meaning, are strung together, repeated, and linked. Look at the example.

What makes a business **ethical**? Businesses are all built on their mission statements. These mission statements reflect a company's **values**, or their **beliefs** of how to behave in the market. These **beliefs** are their **ethics**. Can they offer the customers a lower price because the economy is not doing well, or should they charge more because the product is in demand? The **values** the company holds often dictates their **ethics**.

In this example, you see the words *ethical, values, beliefs, ethics, values,* and *ethics* in a word chain. The ideas in these sentences are linked by these words. Therefore, these words make up the key idea. Listening for word chains can help you identify the main topic of a lecture, presentation, or discussion.

A second method involves listening for signals. In academic settings, the speaker often signals listeners to the structure of the lecture, that a main idea is coming, and reviews main ideas.

| Signals to the structure | Signals that introduce a main idea | Signals that review main ideas |
|---|---|---|
| Today we are going to… <br> Our focus today is… <br> First I am going to X, then I will… | Our first point is… <br> Now that we've looked at X, let's take a look at Y. <br> The key concept is… | Let me recap what we discussed… <br> We've looked at… <br> Here's a quick review of X… |

Professors are often passionate about the subjects they teach, so listening carefully to voice and speaking rate can also help you distinguish main ideas from other ideas. The voices of American English speakers naturally rise and get slightly louder when mentioning key points. This means that their pitch goes up, has increased volume, and the syllables are generally lengthened. When syllables are lengthened, the vowels are pronounced carefully and more clearly; there are few reduced words, or syllables. Main ideas are often spoken more slowly than less important ideas. For example, if our main topic is business ethics, it may sound like this when professor introduces the topic:

Today, we are going to examine what ex-A C T-ly a fi-D U-ciary relationship is.

## VOCABULARY PREVIEW
**Read the vocabulary items. Circle the ones you know. Put a question mark next to the ones you don't know.**

| | | |
|---|---|---|
| empower | liable | act in your best interest |
| turmoil | thorough | best of their ability |

## EXERCISE 2

### A. Work with a partner. Discuss the questions.

1. What is the relationship between a doctor and a patient? How about a lawyer and a client? What responsibilities do doctors have to their patients? How about lawyers to their clients?

2. Do you think a bank has the same responsibility to its clients? Why or why not?

3. Who should be responsible if someone invests and then loses a large sum of money—the client or the person who helped them invest? Why?

### B. Listen to a class discussion on fiduciary relationships. Choose the ideas you hear.

1. Investment advisors are responsible for someone's financial loss.

2. A fiduciary is responsible for the financial well-being of a person.

3. Many fiduciary relationships are established by contracts.

4. A fiduciary relationship is preferable to clients.

5. Fiduciary relationships do not function well in our modern commerce system.

---

**CULTURE NOTE**

The United States, and much of the world, experienced an economic decline in the first decade of the 2000's, primarily because of a housing and real estate bubble which affected over 50 percent of the US population. During the bubble, many home buyers obtained loans without proper security. The surge in home buying caused housing and property prices to rise higher than their real value. However, in 2008, these high prices could no longer be sustained, and prices fell quickly and drastically to more realistic levels. Consequently, a large number of homeowners owed more money on their homes than their homes were worth. Numerous homeowners could not repay the money they owed, and therefore, many families lost their homes. Many large US and European banks that had loaned money were forced to close, and a large number of companies in the financial industry reported record losses.

C. **Listen again. As you listen, circle the words in each excerpt that make up a word chain. Use the circled words to determine the main idea.**

**TIP**

One way to improve note-taking is to use word chains. Word chains will help you determine key ideas and help you organize your notes. After the lecture, review your notes for word chains, and place the key ideas in the margin. Then determine the relationship of these ideas to one another. By identifying and organizing key words after a lecture, you will become a better listener and a better notetaker.

### Excerpt One

Good afternoon. Let's begin today by examining what exactly a fiduciary relationship is. In my experience, it's easiest to explain what a fiduciary is in terms of other legally defined relationships. When we speak of a "legal guardian," or discuss the special relationship between a doctor and a patient, we know that we're referring to a relationship between a person and someone who is legally empowered to assist that person. A fiduciary is similar—but rather than being a full caretaker or a health professional, a fiduciary is responsible for the financial well-being of a person.

Main Idea: .............................................................................................................................

### Excerpt Two

If someone has a fiduciary relationship with you, he or she is responsible for all or part of your finances; it is that person's job and responsibility to protect your money, and, if appropriate, to work to increase your finances to the best of his or her abilities. Investment managers and accountants often have liable relationships with clients— meaning that person is legally responsible for any errors.

Main Idea: .............................................................................................................................

### Excerpt Three

It's true that many clients would prefer a fiduciary relationship especially after the financial turmoil of the last ten years! Keep in mind that fiduciaries have two main responsibilities to their clients: first, a duty of loyalty. They must act solely in the interest of their client. If not, it becomes a conflict of interest. Secondly, fiduciaries have a duty to care. The duty of care requires fiduciaries to be thorough and competent, and follow industry standards. Businesses are more successful when they establish loyalty, and demonstrate care for their clients.

Main Idea: .............................................................................................................................

🎧 D. Listen again and write the signal words and phrases that you hear.

1. Signal about the lecture structure: ......................................................................

2. Signal that introduces a main idea: ....................................................................

3. Signal that highlights or reviews a main idea: ...................................................

E. Work with a partner. Take turns restating the main ideas of the lecture. Use signals and your voice to highlight the main ideas.

## VOCABULARY CHECK

A. Review the vocabulary items in the Vocabulary Preview. Write their definitions and add examples. Use a dictionary if necessary.

B. Match the underlined vocabulary items with their definitions.

............... 1. You need to do the task to the best of your ability.

............... 2. Her work is very complete; she's a thorough person.

............... 3. Giving him access to my finances has empowered him.

............... 4. By law, your fiduciary must act in your best interest.

............... 5. The turmoil from the real estate crash affected many industries.

............... 6. If I lose all my money in the stock market, who is liable?

a. responsible

b. benefits you

c. instability

d. inspired; given authority to

e. detailed; in depth

f. as completely as you can

🔵 Go to MyEnglishLab to complete vocabulary and skill practices and to join in collaborative activities.

# SUPPORTING SKILL 2
## IDENTIFYING SUPPORTING IDEAS

**WHY IT'S USEFUL** By identifying supporting ideas, you can gain a better understanding of the main idea, see the relationships between ideas, and distinguish factual details that support a claim.

Throughout your college career, you need to take accurate notes to successfully understand the content being presented in your classes. A fundamental part of note-taking is distinguishing between the key points, or main ideas, and the supporting ideas and details. **Supporting ideas** help to explain, clarify, and illuminate the main idea. They often answer WH-questions about the main idea. Supporting ideas generally fall under two categories: major supporting ideas and minor supporting ideas.

**Major supporting ideas** develop or illustrate the main idea. Speakers may use a comparison, contrast, statistic, or graph to help develop the main idea.

> Unlike the consequentialist framework, the duty-based framework is not situational, but built around one's obligation to do the right thing according to certain rules.

**Minor supporting ideas**, such as examples, testimonials, or illustrations, add interest to and help clarify the main idea.

> A car manufacturer, for example, would draw on industry standards and government safety regulations.

An effective method for distinguishing between main ideas and supporting ideas is using a graphic organizer to take notes. Graphic organizers organize information in a way that makes it easy to distinguish between main ideas and details. A hierarchy map is a very effective graphic organizer when distinguishing between main ideas and major and minor supporting ideas.

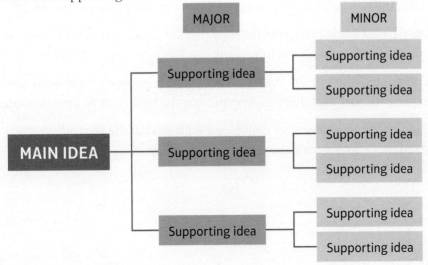

**VOCABULARY PREVIEW**

Read the vocabulary items. Circle the ones you know. Put a question mark next to the ones you don't know.

| | | | |
|---|---|---|---|
| adhered to | hazardous | rigidity | novel |
| consequences | catastrophe | straw man argument | anticipate |

## EXERCISE 3

**A.** Look at the list of businesses. Choose those that you think need a strict code of conduct (exact rules for behavior).

............ Airlines          ............ Educational institutions

............ Car dealerships          ............ Energy companies

............ Computer manufacturers          ............ Food manufacturers

............ Construction companies          ............ Real estate companies

**B.** Compare your list with your partner. Are they similar? Discuss why you feel the businesses you checked need a strict code of conduct. What might their mission statements look like?

**C.** Listen to a class discussion on duty-based ethics. As you listen, identify main ideas and supporting ideas. Write *M* (main idea) or *S* (supporting ideas).

............ 1. A duty-based framework is built around the company's obligation to do the right thing.

............ 2. Adhering to a strict code of conduct is part of a duty-based framework.

............ 3. Duty-based work environments may include construction businesses and other hazardous work environments.

............ 4. Companies who operate under a duty-based framework have many years of experience that aids them in determining the best rules to operate under.

............ 5. Duty-based companies are concerned with examining the industry standards and government regulations when developing new products.

🎧 **D. Listen again and complete the graphic organizer to help you distinguish between major and minor supporting ideas.**

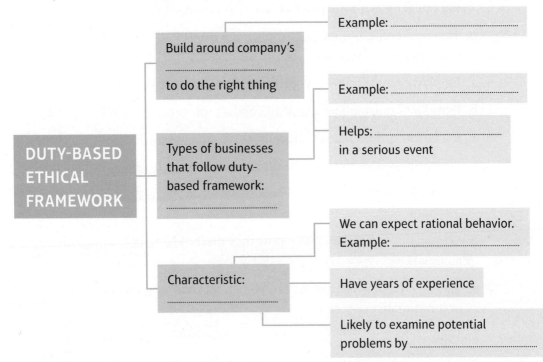

**DUTY-BASED ETHICAL FRAMEWORK**

Build around company's
..............................
to do the right thing

Example: ...................................................

Types of businesses that follow duty-based framework:
..............................

Example: ...................................................

Helps: ...................................................
in a serious event

Characteristic:
..............................

We can expect rational behavior.
Example: ...............................................

Have years of experience

Likely to examine potential problems by .......................................

**E. Work with a partner. Choose a business from Part A and explain why you think it is duty-based. Begin by giving your main idea, add two to three major supporting ideas, and two to three minor supporting ideas.**

## VOCABULARY CHECK

**A. Review the vocabulary items in the Vocabulary Preview. Write their definitions and add examples. Use a dictionary if necessary.**

**B. Choose the sentence that correctly paraphrases the meaning of each underlined vocabulary item.**

1. a. It's important that corporations <u>adhere to</u>, or follow, governmental policies and regulations.

   b. It's important that corporations <u>adhere to</u>, or develop, governmental policies and regulations.

2. a. We do not <u>anticipate</u>, or expect, any issues with the new flexible work schedule.

   b. We do not <u>anticipate</u>, or demand, any issues with the new flexible work schedule.

*(Continued)*

3. a. This could have been a <u>catastrophe</u>, or a real success, if we hadn't seen the problems with the product before we released it.

   b. This could have been a <u>catastrophe</u>, or a disaster, if we hadn't seen the problems with the product before we released it.

4. a. Employees must follow a <u>code of conduct</u>, or set rules, at their workplace.

   b. Employees must follow a <u>code of conduct</u>, or steps, at their workplace.

5. a. If a business does not act ethically, there are <u>consequences</u>, or concerns.

   b. If a business does not act ethically, there are <u>consequences</u>, or penalties.

6. a. Corporations must be careful how they discard <u>hazardous</u>, or dangerous, materials.

   b. Corporations must be careful how they discard <u>hazardous</u>, or costly, materials.

7. a. Many technology companies are known for their <u>novel</u> ideas, or innovations.

   b. Many technology companies are known for their <u>novel</u> ideas, or interesting stories.

8. a. He is making a <u>straw man argument</u>; it is accurate and based on truths.

   b. He is making a <u>straw man argument</u>; it is weak and based on untruths.

▶ Go to MyEnglishLab to complete vocabulary and skill practices and to join in collaborative activities.

## INTEGRATED SKILLS

### PREPARING AN ARGUMENT

**WHY IT'S USEFUL** By utilizing strategies to prepare an effective argument, you can better establish your claim and supporting evidence and demonstrate your critical thinking ability.

Throughout college you will be asked to present your side of an issue and expected to support your position with appropriate evidence. This is referred to as *argumentation*. Argumentation is different from persuasion. Where persuasion generally focuses on personal beliefs and experiences, argumentation focuses on logic, which is supported by facts and examples. Preparing for an argument involves outlining your claim, the reasons of your claim, and providing evidence.

To begin **preparing an academic argument**, you first need to have a good understanding of the topic. Begin by thinking about what you already know on the topic. You can do this by reviewing class notes, reading textbook articles, or speaking to your professors and classmates. After you have a good understanding of the topic, you are ready to begin preparing your argument. There are five main steps to preparing an argument:

> **TIP**
>
> *Argument*, like many words in English, has different meanings and applications. In academic usage, making an *argument* refers to presenting a claim about an often-controversial issue, and supporting that claim with reasons backed by evidence. In everyday usage, *argument* usually refers to a quarrel or disagreement. Common collocations for this use include: *have an argument, get into an argument, develop into an argument,* and *erupt into an argument.*

1. Establish your claim.

2. Outline the reasons why you made the claim.

3. Identify evidence to support your reasons.

4. Connect the evidence to your claim.

5. Acknowledge the opposition's position (the counterargument), and show the problems with (refute) the counterargument.

To establish your claim, you simply need to prepare a position statement or assertion. Do this by creating a sentence that states your viewpoint and uses clear, concise language. Do not use opinion phrases like *I think, I believe,* or *In my opinion* and avoid using modals. These weaken your position.

Determining the supporting reasons for your argument means thinking about why you are taking that position. Why do you feel the way you do? Your reasons answer that question. These reasons are your supporting ideas. Once again, use clear, concise, direct language to support your claim.

Identify evidence to support your claim. There are several different types of evidence, for example, print and electronic sources, such as your textbook, digital databases, and other course materials. Other good sources of information are interviews and surveys.

The last two steps involve explaining how the evidence supports your claim and acknowledging and refuting the opposition's counterarguments. To do this successfully, you need to combine your ideas with your evidence. It is very important that your listeners understand how the supporting reasons and their evidence connect to the claim. Make sure that you do not end your argument with your evidence. That is known as *dumping*. Dumping means waste. By throwing your evidence out there, without making connections for your listeners, you are wasting your evidence.

Acknowledging the opposing argument is critical in a coherent argument. It shows a deeper understanding of the topic, as well as your ability to think critically and evaluate an issue. Showing why the opposition argument is weak strengthens your own argument. Look at the examples:

## 1. MAKE YOUR CLAIM

"Corporations need to be environmentally responsible if they are going to be successful in the 21st century."

## 2. OUTLINE YOUR REASONS

"Good practice can draw new customers, improve sustainability, and demonstrate commitment to our planet."

## 4. CONNECT EVIDENCE WITH YOUR CLAIM

[evidence from recent report] "So, as the research dictates, you can increase your customer base, which in turn, leads to a more successful company by utilizing green practices."

## 3. IDENTIFY EVIDENCE TO SUPPORT REASONS

[reason: drawing customers] "According to a recent report published in a quarterly business journal, your business can be set apart from your competitors if you promote environmentally friendly practices."

## 5. ACKNOWLEDGE AND REFUTE THE COUNTERARGUMENT

"While opponents may argue that the primary function of a business is to generate profits for its shareholders, they fail to see the cost of not going green. Depleting our natural resources will not only close their doors faster, and cause greater harm to our planet, but also increase their production costs, and reduce their overall profits."

## EXERCISE 4

**A. Work with a partner. Discuss the questions.**

1. What does it mean for a business to be socially responsible?

2. What are the advantages of a business being socially responsible?

3. What are the disadvantages of a business being socially responsible?

**B. Using the information from your discussion, establish a claim about businesses and social responsibility. Write your claim below.**

.............................................................................................................................................................

.............................................................................................................................................................

**C. Write three reasons to support your claim.**

.............................................................................................................................................................

.............................................................................................................................................................

.............................................................................................................................................................

D. Read the article below and the article on page 44.

# For the Future of Business Success

We live in a connected, globalized world where the actions of one company can have a proportionately enormous impact on society at large. In recent decades, we've seen both the economy and the environment harmed through the irresponsible actions of a small handful of businesses. These businesses must adopt an ethical framework of corporate social responsibility for the greater good of the world.

According to the modern ethical framework of corporate social responsibility, a business is not merely obligated to produce profit for its shareholders, but also to actively avoid harming society and the environment. Corporate social responsibility has arisen in response to social and environmental issues of the last century. Anyone willing to examine the issues will realize that business decisions often have a significant impact on the larger world, beyond the simple concerns of buyers and sellers. If a company's business practices can harm the environment, the company is responsible to all people harmed as a result; there are more people with something at stake in these scenarios than the small number of parties directly involved in a company's business.

While some businesses may initially be reluctant to cut into profit for the sake of the social good, businesses need to realize that not only is corporate social responsibility the appropriate ethical decision, but it is also quite profitable if undertaken with intelligence and sensitivity. Most businesses, large and small, employ experts that would be well-suited to doing charitable work in a variety of areas. By applying their charitable efforts to an issue they are already well-equipped to tackle, businesses cannot only help others, but also raise brand awareness and get a great deal of positive publicity.

Finally, at least some form of corporate social responsibility will be necessary for long-term profit. In the most pessimistic and extreme scenarios, a lack of social responsibility from influential businesses can result in environmental and societal destabilization that drives down profits. Even from a perspective of self-interest, it is best for a business to operate under an ethical framework of corporate social responsibility. In doing so, businesses can help create a stable, healthy world that will be more willing and able to buy their services.

Contributing Author: Dr. Jami Scales, professor of Business Ethics

# It's Business!

"Corporate social responsibility," has become a popular catchphrase recently, both for businesses that seek to improve media presence and for advocates who think that the role of a company should extend beyond the generation of profit. Now, if a business wishes to improve their image through carefully managed charity and public donations, that is a sensible practice. Some now advocate for a broader form of corporate social responsibility, in which a company is obligated to engage in social, charitable, and environmental practices beyond the scope of the law and the company's pursuit of profit; these people sorely misunderstand the purpose and nature of a business.

The primary purpose of any business is to generate profit for shareholders. An ethical code of conduct serves as a valuable and important way to achieve this—after all, how could a business hope to survive if none of its employees could be trusted to act appropriately? A well-formulated code of conduct and an ethical code clearly defined in the company's mission statement, if followed and enforced, should be more than sufficient to ensure profitability and create a safe environment for employees.

Part of ethical business practice involves following laws and governmental regulations. Because every government will regulate industry according to that government's needs and expectations, there is absolutely no need for a business to formally institute corporate social responsibility as a practice. If a social or environmental issue is truly important, either the government or the influence of the free market will compel businesses to follow rules related to it. If a new, previously unknown environmental problem becomes known, governments will take steps to regulate it and ethical businesses will subsequently adapt to new regulations.

Contributing Author: Rebecca Brown, CEO and Vice-Chairman

---

E. Complete the T-chart with the main ideas from each article.

## SOCIAL RESPONSIBILITY AND BUSINESS

| Article One: For the Future of Business Success | Article Two: It's Business! |
|---|---|
| Claims: | Claims: |
| Reasons: | Reasons: |

**F.** Use evidence from the articles to support your claim. Complete the outline.

Claim: .............................................................................................................................................................

Reason #1: ......................................................................................................................................................

Support/Evidence: .......................................................................................................................................

Reason #2: ......................................................................................................................................................

Support/Evidence: .......................................................................................................................................

Reason #3: ......................................................................................................................................................

Support/Evidence: .......................................................................................................................................

Counterargument: ......................................................................................................................................

Flaw with counterargument: ...................................................................................................................

🔊 Go to MyEnglishLab to complete skill practices.

## LANGUAGE SKILL

### ADVERBIAL CLAUSES TO DESCRIBE RELATIONSHIPS

**WHY IT'S USEFUL** By identifying and utilizing adverbial clauses to describe relationships, you can add meaning and clarify when, where, how, why, and to what extent something happens.

🔊 Go to MyEnglishLab for the Language Skill presentation and practice.

# VOCABULARY STRATEGY

## DETERMINING AFFECTIVE MEANINGS THROUGH ADVERBIALS

**WHY IT'S USEFUL** By recognizing adverbials in a sentence, you can better determine the speaker's position and feelings about their statement.

Adverbs, single words, adverbials, and groups of words add meaning by providing further description. They can also tell us how the speaker feels about something. Adverbs and adverbials that describe how a speaker feels are often referred to as **stance adverbials** because they tell us where the speakers "stand." In other words, they inform us of the speakers' attitude toward, feeling about, or commitment to what they are saying. These words carry an affective meaning. An affective meaning refers to speakers' personal feelings, attitudes, or values. Look at these examples:

> **Thankfully**, the company decided to review their policies.

> **Actually**, the company decided to review their policies.

> **No doubt** that Joe's company is concerned with its image.

> **Frankly speaking**, Joe's company is concerned with its image.

The first example indicates that the speaker is grateful, or happy, that the company is reviewing their policies. This person clearly feels the company needed to do so. The second sentence indicates that the speaker may be correcting someone or giving someone new information.

The third example is conceding or even agreeing that Joe's company is concerned with its image. However, the last sentence adds a bit more affective meaning. It gives the listener the feeling that Joe's company might be *too* concerned with its image and not concerned enough about other issues. In these examples, adverbials alter the meaning of the sentence by adding an affective meaning. These affective meanings can range from expressing surprise to conceding or reluctantly accepting someone else's idea. Look at the chart.

| Meaning | Adverbials | Example |
|---|---|---|
| Conceding | Admittedly<br>No doubt | **Admittedly**, we are in the business of making money.<br>There's **no doubt** that we are here to make money. |
| Correcting | Actually<br>As a matter of fact | **Actually**, the company decided to review their policies.<br>**As a matter of fact**, the company posted record profits this year. |

| Meaning | Adverbials | Example |
|---|---|---|
| Expressing preference | Ideally | **Ideally**, if we could reduce waste, our costs would go down. |
| Expressing certainty | Certainly<br>Clearly<br>Obviously | **Certainly**, the company has a return policy.<br>**Clearly**, the code of conduct must be followed.<br>**Obviously**, our employees are evaluated annually. |
| Introducing a fact | Frankly<br>In fact<br>To be honest | **Frankly**, we were in the red last year.<br>**In fact**, we were in the red last year.<br>**To be honest**, they're understaffed. |
| Giving an opinion | If you ask me<br>I'm afraid | **If you ask me**, they should close their doors.<br>**I'm afraid** they are only concerned with making money. |
| Exemplifying and explaining | Basically<br>Essentially | **Basically**, our policies have been established and are enforced.<br>**Essentially**, we want our employees to volunteer when they can. |

## EXERCISE 5

**A. Read each sentence. Use the stance adverbials to determine how the speaker feels about the topic. Choose the correct answer.**

1. You make a good point. Admittedly, we should probably review those policies.

    a. Reluctantly agrees     b. Giving a fact     c. Correcting

2. We obviously need to establish a new dress policy.

    a. Reluctantly agrees     b. Is certain     c. Correcting

3. The new business down the street actually opened up about six months ago.

    a. Is certain     b. Giving a fact     c. Correcting

4. If you ask me, our main goal is to make a profit.

    a. Reluctantly agrees     b. Giving an opinion     c. Correcting

5. Ideally, we need to establish greener policies.

    a. Express preference     b. Giving an opinion     c. Is certain

6. As a matter of fact, that's not at all what the policy states.

    a. Express preference     b. Introducing a fact     c. Correcting

**B. Use the cues to complete each statement with a stance adverbial.**

1. .............................., (exemplify) more companies need to be concerned with the environment.

2. .............................., (opinion) it is wonderful when a company encourages its' employees to volunteer.

3. .............................., (fact) a company must act ethical if they want to retain customers.

4. .............................., (concede) there is a lot more to do to ensure companies act in the best interest of their customers.

5. .............................., (preference) I would like to work for a company that values the environment.

6. .............................., (certainty) they have made a large profit this year, did you see the car the CEO was driving?

**C. Work with a partner. Exchange ideas on what companies can do to be more ethical. Include stance adverbials in your statements to add an affective meaning.**

◑ Go to MyEnglishLab to complete a skill practice.

## APPLY YOUR SKILLS

**WHY IT'S USEFUL** By applying the skills you have learned in this unit, you will be able to distinguish between main ideas and supporting ideas in academic lectures and discussions in a college-level course.

### ASSIGNMENT
Prepare an argument and participate in a debate on the responsibilities of a business within your community.

### BEFORE YOU LISTEN

**A. Before you listen, discuss the questions with one or more students.**

1. Who was Henry Ford, and what is he best known for?

2. Do you think business practices have changed since the early 20th century? If so, how have they changed?

3. What did it mean to be innovative in the early 20th century? How has that concept changed today?

B. You will listen to a lecture on Henry Ford and his business practices. As you listen, think about these questions.

1. What was Ford's reputation?

2. What was his relationship with the assembly line?

3. What was Ford's perspective of his employees?

4. Why is he described as innovative?

5. What are some examples of Ford's business practices that highlight his personality?

C. Review the Unit Skills Summary. As you listen to the lecture and prepare for your presentation, apply the skills you learned in this unit.

## UNIT SKILLS SUMMARY

### DEVELOP IDEAS FOR ACADEMIC PRESENTATIONS AND DISCUSSIONS USING THESE SKILLS:

**Identify main ideas in a lecture or discussion**

- Recognize word chains.
- Identify signals for main ideas.
- Differentiate between stressed and non-stressed ideas.

**Distinguish supporting ideas from main ideas**

- Recognize major and minor supporting ideas.
- Utilize a graphic organizer to differentiate between main ideas and supporting ideas.

**Prepare a formal argument**

- Determine your claim.
- Identify reasons and support for your claim.
- Connect evidence to your claim.
- Acknowledge the opposition and refute their claim.

**Utilize adverbial clauses to describe relationships**

- Clarify your meaning by using an adverbial clause.
- Distinguish between different types of adverbial clauses.

**Recognize adverbials that clarify speaker's point of view**

- Determine their affective meaning.

## LISTEN

A. Listen to a lecture on Henry Ford and his business practices. Take notes.

B. Compare your notes with a partner. Do you have the same key ideas? What skills from this unit can help you identify key ideas?

C. Review the questions from Before You Listen, Part B. Listen to the lecture again. Work with a partner and use your notes on the lecture to answer the questions.

Go to MyEnglishLab to listen more closely, and answer the critical thinking questions.

## THINKING CRITICALLY

Discuss the questions with another student.

1. Based on the lecture, what lessons can be learned from Ford's business practices?

2. A monopoly is when one company controls the market. Are there monopolies around today? If so, can you name some? What disadvantages exist for consumers when there is a monopoly?

3. The lecturer mentions that Ford attempted to stop his competition by putting all profits back into the company. It didn't go into research and development, or production methods. Where do you think the money went?

## THINKING VISUALLY

A. Look at the graphic. Discuss the questions with a partner.

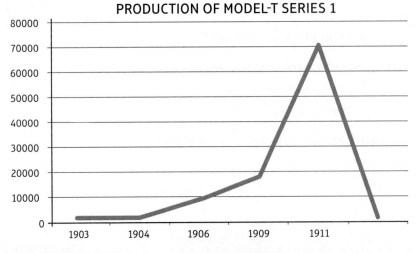

PRODUCTION OF MODEL-T SERIES 1

1. How can you describe the growth of Model-T production and ownership?

2. Why do you think it grew so quickly?

3. In your opinion, are there any problems when a product's production grows so rapidly and how could that affect the market?

**B.** Go online and investigate another automobile. Create a graph like the one in Part A. Indicate how many were produced each year. Evaluate the pattern and share it with your classmates.

⬆ Go to MyEnglishLab to record your results.

> **TIP**
>
> There are several common expressions you can use to describe graphs:
>
> If the line rises or falls quickly, we might say: *There was a rapid/steep/sharp increase or decrease.*
>
> If the line rises or falls slowly, we might say: *There was a slow/gradual growth or decrease.*
>
> If there is little change, we might say: *It has remained steady.*

## THINKING ABOUT LANGUAGE

Complete each adverbial clause in the sentences with an adverb.

1. ............................................. Henry Ford was innovative, he was criticized for his business practices.

2. The Model T was the first affordable automobile of its time ............................................. of Ford's cost reducing measures on the assembly line.

3. Automobile workers formed unions ............................................. having been mistreated at the workplace.

4. ............................................. Henry Ford had listened to his customers, he might have had more success.

5. Henry Ford tried to stop the Dodges' plan to open their own automobile production company ............................................. they had worked with Ford.

6. ............................................. Henry Ford's shortcomings, he still is viewed as a successful businessman.

## GROUP DEBATE

A. Think about the lecture, and the other information presented in the unit. There are definite benefits to listening to your customers, following an ethical framework, and being a socially responsible company. Are there drawbacks? What are they? Complete the chart with your ideas.

|  | Benefits | Drawbacks |
| --- | --- | --- |
| Listening to customers |  |  |
| Following an ethical framework |  |  |
| Being socially responsible |  |  |

**B. Share your chart with your classmates. What should be a corporation's primary focus? Divide into two teams: in favor of corporations focusing more on social responsibility and opposed to corporations focusing more on social responsibility. Follow these steps:**

1. Prepare an argument for your position. Research business practices.

2. Develop your argument by incorporating evidence.

3. Prepare for the debate against the other team.

**C. Debate**

Establish the rules of your debate. Each team takes a turn presenting its claim and argument. As the opposing team speaks, take notes. After the opposition has presented their argument, ask questions to make sure you understand any implications made by the other team. After the debate, take a class vote to determine which team supported their claim best.

⊙ Go to MyEnglishLab to watch Dr. McLennan's concluding video and to complete a self-assessment.

# EARTH SCIENCE

# Extended Discourse

## UNIT PROFILE

In this unit, you will learn about the differences between several geological eras. You will also investigate how the events in each era have impacted biodiversity on our planet.

**You will prepare an individual presentation on a geologic time period, outlining the changes that occurred during that period.**

## OUTCOMES

- Examine time frames in discourse
- Organize events in time frames
- Summarize sequences of events
- Identify and utilize modals to discuss possibilities and probabilities
- Utilize word parts to comprehend new vocabulary

For more about **EARTH SCIENCE**, see ②③. See also R and W **EARTH SCIENCE** ①②③.

# GETTING STARTED

⏵ Go to MyEnglishLab to watch Dr. Osborne's introductory video and to complete a self-assessment.

**Discuss these questions with a partner or group.**

1. Biology is the study of life in all its forms from microscopic to very large. What is geology?

2. Have you heard of the geologic time scale? If so, what do you know about it? If not, based on the name, what do you think it is?

3. In Dr. Osborne's introduction, he refers to Earth's history of mass extinctions. Can you think of one mass extinction he might be referring to?

# FUNDAMENTAL SKILL

## ENGAGING WITH EXTENDED DISCOURSE

**WHY IT'S USEFUL**  By utilizing listening strategies during extended discourse, you can better identify the speaker's main ideas. You can also distinguish supporting ideas, details, and examples.

Academic listening involves listening to **extended discourse**. Class lectures are a type of extended discourse; the lecturer speaks for an extended time. Therefore, professors will give a sizeable amount of critical information without taking a break. In turn, while listening, you must be able to extract main ideas, distinguish them from supporting ideas, and identify details and examples.

There are several things you can do to better identify the main ideas, supporting topics, details and examples. First, listen carefully for stressed words. Speakers will stress key terms and ideas. These are often said at a higher pitch, and with longer syllables. The speaker might also repeat key words. Stressed and repeated words often indicate main ideas. When listening for supporting ideas, details, and examples, pay close attention to cues the speaker gives. Supporting ideas may be numbered: first, second, next. Examples may be introduced using *for example*, *for instance*, and *such as*. It is also important to distinguish information that is not directly related to the content. Information not directly related to the content of the lecture is considered irrelevant. Determining which information is **relevant** and which is **irrelevant** can help you better understand the overall organization of the lecture.

When listening to a lecture, it is also very important to pay close attention to the **time frame** the speaker is using. Interestingly, time frames can indicate more than when an action occurred. They also indicate if the speaker believes something is true or not.

*(Continued)*

For example, if a speaker uses the past to describe a particular theory or belief, they are telling you that it is no longer believed to be true, or, in other words, is no longer the accepted theory. Speakers generally organize lectures and narratives into time frames, moving from past beliefs to current, and even beliefs about what might take place in the future. Identifying these time frames can help you determine the overall organizational pattern of the lecture, which can help you better understand the overall content.

## VOCABULARY PREVIEW

Read the vocabulary items in the box. Circle the ones you know. Put a question mark next to the ones you don't know.

| | | |
|---|---|---|
| phenomena | to center on | formation |
| be familiar with | mixed up | relatively |

## EXERCISE 1

### A. Look at the diagram. Answer the questions.

## Geologic Time Scale

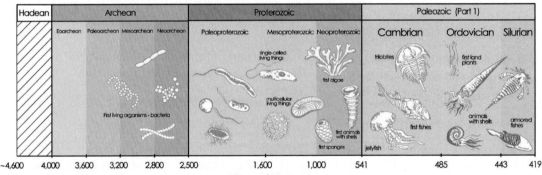

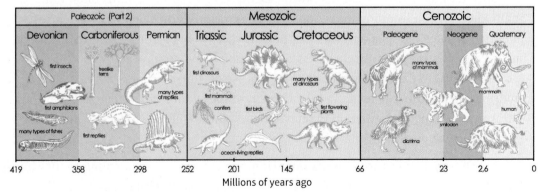

1. According to the diagram, how old is the Earth?

2. About how long ago did plant life first appear? Dinosaurs?

**B. Listen to a lecture about the geologic time scale. Write *M* next to a main idea, and *S* next to a supporting idea. Then compare your notes with a partner.**

> ## Glossary
>
> Eon: a unit of time equal to about a billion years
>
> Era: a division of geologic time usually shorter than an eon
>
> Period: a division of geologic time usually shorter than an era
>
> Epoch: a division of an era; the smallest division of geologic time

........ 1. A geological time scale is a way in which geologists keep track of events and changes on Earth.

........ 2. The geological time scale uses 4 units of measure.

........ 3. Eons are broken into eras, eras are broken into periods, and periods are broken into epochs.

........ 4. We are currently in the Phanerozoic Eon.

........ 5. Dinosaurs lived during the Triassic, Jurassic, and Cretaceous Periods of the Mesozoic Era.

> ### TIP
>
> In conversational English, native speakers often either drop the past tense *-ed* ending, or link it to the word that follows. For example, *talked to me* sounds like *talkta me*, and *lived alone* sounds like *liv dlone*. When listening for the past, pay close attention to any time markers the speaker may use. Listening for time markers like *before*, *previously*, and *ago* can help you determine the time frame when something occurred.

**C. Listen again. Listen carefully for the verbs the speaker uses. Write them under the correct heading.**

| Past | Present | Future |
|------|---------|--------|
| ........................................ | ........................................ | ........................................ |
| ........................................ | ........................................ | ........................................ |
| ........................................ | ........................................ | ........................................ |

### CULTURE NOTE

The geologic time scale, or GTS, was created to simplify and record a large number of events that have shaped our planet. Geologists and other Earth scientists have discovered these events by investigating layers of the Earth, and the study of fossil records.

🔊 D. Now listen to a conversation between two students after the lecture. Did they think all the information was relevant? If not, which information was not? How do you know?

## VOCABULARY CHECK

A. Review the vocabulary items in the Vocabulary Preview. Write their definitions and add examples. Use a dictionary if necessary.

B. Replace the underlined items with vocabulary items from the box.

| be familiar with | center on | formation | mixed up | phenomena | relatively |
|---|---|---|---|---|---|

1. The professor's lecture explained the <u>amazing events</u> behind extinctions.

2. Our lab assignment was <u>fairly</u> easy. We just had to duplicate a volcanic explosion.

3. The guest speaker's presentation will <u>focus on</u> the potential damage humans are making to the atmosphere.

4. The <u>creation</u> of mountains was a result of geological forces.

5. <u>Are</u> you <u>acquainted with</u> the meteor theory?

6. Do you think he is just <u>confused</u>, and that's why he doesn't understand the assignment?

🔗 Go to MyEnglishLab to complete a vocabulary and skill practice and to join in collaborative activities.

# SUPPORTING SKILL 1
## EXAMINING TIME FRAMES IN TEXTS

**WHY IT'S USEFUL**  By examining time frames in listening and reading texts, you can better determine when something occurred, the order of occurrence, and if the information is a fact.

Lecturers often speak in chronological order. Chronological order refers to organizing events in sequence by time. Paying attention to the **time frames** the speaker uses can help you determine when something has occurred. There are three time frames in English: past, present, and future. In addition to the verb form, there are key words that you can listen for to help you determine the time frame, and the order in which something has occurred.

| Words to indicate *before* | Words to indicate *during* | Words to indicate *next* | Words to indicate *now* |
|---|---|---|---|
| at that time | at the same time | after that | at the moment |
| earlier | meanwhile | afterward | currently |
| long ago | simultaneously | following | presently |
| previously | when | later | today |
| prior to | while | not long after | |
| up until that time | | soon after | |

Time frames not only indicate approximately when something happened, but the choice of a time frame also tells you *how the speakers may feel* about the topic. For example, if something is a fact, and therefore believed to be always true, speakers use the present time frame, and the present tense. If speakers feel that something is no longer generally believed to be true, they may use the past time frame to indicate the information is no longer thought to be a fact. Each time frame has a function and can tell us more about the topic.

| Present is used for... | Past is used for... | Future is used for... |
|---|---|---|
| • timeless truths (this includes scientific laws)<br>• habitual actions<br>• conversations of historical narration (to retell something)<br>• planned or scheduled future events<br>• actions in progress | • a single completed action<br>• an event that occurred in the past for a period of time, but is no longer true in the present<br>• an imagined event (if these formations had taken a different process, our world would look different today.) | • an action that will take place at a definite time in the future<br>• a prediction<br>• an action that will be completed by a specific time in the future |

## VOCABULARY PREVIEW

Read the vocabulary items in the box. Circle the ones you know. Put a question mark next to the ones you don't know.

| | | | | | |
|---|---|---|---|---|---|
| mass extinction | ecosystem | species | alien | abrupt | enormous |

## EXERCISE 2

A. Brainstorm with a partner. What changes have occurred on Earth over the last two hundred and fifty million years? Consider things such as climate and temperature, plant life, and animal life. Use the visual on page 56 to help you.

### Glossary

Biodiversity:  the existence of many different kinds of plants and animals

Ecological niche:  the role an animal or plant plays in the environment

(Geologic) event:  a large, natural disaster that greatly changes the environment

B. Listen to a lecture on the Mesozoic Era. Choose the nine different time markers you hear mentioned.

| | | | |
|---|---|---|---|
| after/after that | at that time | currently | next |
| at the same time | meanwhile | prior to | later |
| in the meantime | not long after | during | soon |
| up until that time | simultaneously | before | when |
| by the end of | previously | earlier | while |

### TIP

Listening to lectures involving time can be challenging if speakers are not using time markers. However, they often give clues with their body language. For instance, they may use their hands to point to a direction of time. Moving their hand to the right or backwards over their shoulder away from students can indicate an event that happened before another event. Moving their hand to the left or toward students could indicate an event that happened next. Therefore, it's important to pay close attention to body language as well as the words the speaker uses.

C. Listen again. Add events to the timeline. Use key words and verb time frames to help you determine the order of events.

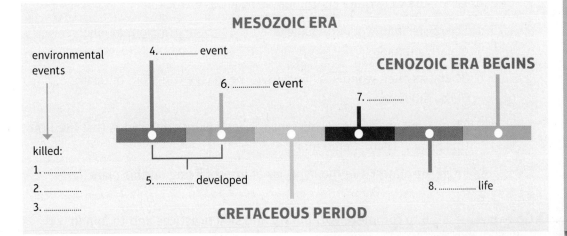

**MESOZOIC ERA**

environmental events

4. ................. event

**CENOZOIC ERA BEGINS**

6. ................. event

7. .................

killed:

1. .................

2. .................

3. .................

5. ................. developed

8. ................. life

**CRETACEOUS PERIOD**

D. Work with a partner. Take turns restating events from the lecture. Be sure to use key words to indicate when an event happened.

Partner A: There was an extinction event in the Permian-Triassic Period.

Partner B: Prior to that, there were several environmental events.

**CULTURE NOTE**

According to geologists and other scientists, the Earth moved from the Mesozoic Era into the Cenozoic Era due to a geologic event: an enormous meteorite struck the Earth. Scientists believe that this meteorite destroyed over ¾ of all species of life on the planet. Animals that survived destruction include the leatherback sea turtle and crocodiles.

## VOCABULARY CHECK

A. Review the vocabulary items in the Vocabulary Preview. Write their definitions and add examples. Use a dictionary if necessary.

B. Choose the sentence that correctly describes the underlined vocabulary item.

1. a. An <u>alien</u> is someone who is from another country.

   b. An <u>alien</u> is a being from another planet.

2. a. There have been <u>abrupt</u> changes on our planet, happening faster than ever thought.

   b. The planet is <u>abrupt</u>; it changes frequently and expectedly.

3. a. An <u>ecosystem</u> includes all living things—people, plants, and animals.

   b. An <u>ecosystem</u> includes natural disasters like earthquakes and hurricanes.

*(Continued)*

4. a. Dinosaurs were quite <u>enormous</u>; as large as today's skyscrapers!

   b. Dinosaurs were quite <u>enormous</u>; as heavy as a truck.

5. a. Scientists often wonder what caused the <u>mass extinction</u>, or emergence, of early humans.

   b. Scientists often wonder what caused the <u>mass extinction</u>, or death, of the dinosaurs.

6. a. There were once several different <u>species</u>, such as dinosaurs, that lived on this planet. There are no more.

   b. There are almost a million <u>species</u> of insects living on this planet.

⚫ Go to MyEnglishLab to complete vocabulary and skill practices and to join in collaborative activities.

## SUPPORTING SKILL 2

### ORGANIZE EVENTS BY TIME FRAMES

**WHY IT'S USEFUL**   By understanding how time frames are used to organize a lecture, you can better understand its overall content. You can also clearly communicate your ideas in a way that makes it easier for listeners to follow your ideas.

Throughout your college career you will be asked to recount events, summarize findings, and describe developments. Choosing an appropriate pattern of organization is a critical first step.

A common organizational pattern in the field of science is the **chronological** pattern. A chronological pattern of organization structures narratives, or stories, by the order in which they occurred. Generally, this pattern begins at the oldest event and moves forward to the most current. Therefore, the speaker will most likely begin in the past time frame and move into the present time frame.

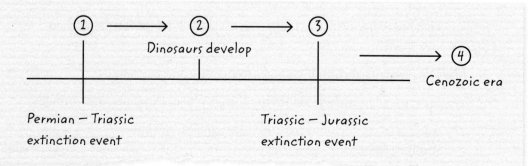

Another common pattern is the **significant event** pattern or causal pattern. In this pattern, a speaker will mention an important event and describe what happened before or after it. Usually, the speaker will identify the causes (past time frame) first and then move to the effects (present time frame). However, occasionally, the speaker might begin by looking at the effects of the event first and then look back to discuss its causes.

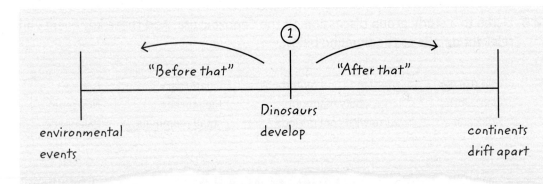

The key to understanding a lecture is to identify its organizational pattern. Listening closely for key words, verb tense, and time markers can help you better understand the events, and the order in which they happened.

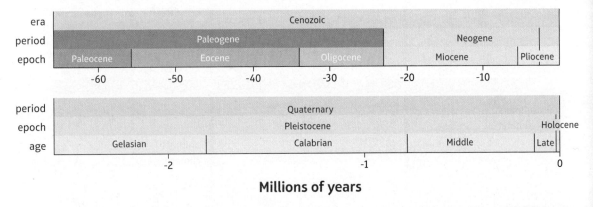

**Millions of years**

## VOCABULARY PREVIEW

Read the vocabulary items in the box. Circle the ones you know.
Put a question mark next to the ones you don't know.

| | | | |
|---|---|---|---|
| mammals | grasslands | ancestral humans | ground sloths |
| herd animals | ice age | wooly mammoths | domesticated |

## EXERCISE 3

**A. Work with a partner. Answer the questions.**

1. How has the climate changed over time?

2. How have climate changes impacted animals and plant life?

**B. Listen to a study group discussion on the Cenozoic era. Add these key events and relevant details to the timeline below.**

| | | | |
|---|---|---|---|
| cold (ice age) | grasslands and mountains | Quaternary | hot |
| giant sloths | large wooly mammoths | Pleistocene | Neogene |
| Holocene | warm with cool periods | small mammals | Paleogene |

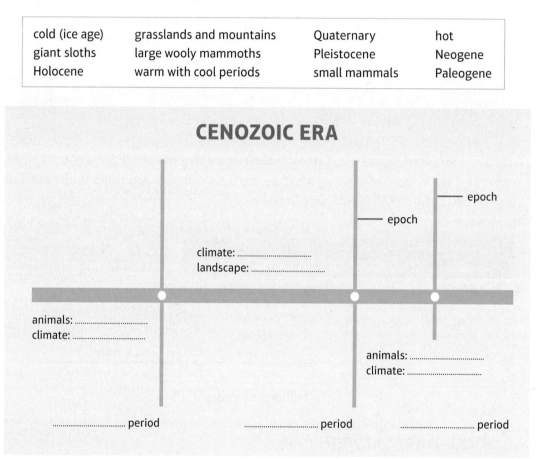

**C. Listen again and decide which organizational pattern is being used. How did you know?**

**D. Work with a partner. Take turns describing a historical event using chronological or significant event order.**

## VOCABULARY CHECK

A. Review the vocabulary items in the Vocabulary Preview. Write their definitions and add examples. Use a dictionary if necessary.

B. Match the vocabulary items with their definitions.

......... 1. ancestral humans

......... 2. domesticated

......... 3. grasslands

......... 4. ground sloths

......... 5. herd animals

......... 6. ice age

......... 7. mammals

......... 8. wooly mammoths

a. bred or trained to live and work with humans

b. a warm-blooded animal born live, with hair or fur covering its body

c. the first humans which developed into modern man

d. giant, slow-moving, hairy, ground-dwelling animal now extinct

e. land with trees and covered with grass

f. animals that live in large groups

g. a giant, hairy elephant, now extinct

h. a past period when much of the world was covered with ice and snow

◎ Go to MyEnglishLab to complete vocabulary and skill practices and to join in collaborative activities.

# INTEGRATED SKILLS

## SUMMARIZING SEQUENCES OF EVENTS

**WHY IT'S USEFUL** By summarizing a sequence of events, you can demonstrate your understanding of extended discourse and your ability to distinguish between necessary and unnecessary information.

**Summarizing** involves extracting the main ideas of a lecture or reading and putting them into your own words. Summaries are concise versions of an original text. To be able to summarize effectively, you first need to determine what are the key ideas. In extended discourse, you can determine key ideas by listening for pitch rises, slowed speech, and repeated words and phrases. You must be sure to distinguish between necessary information (relevant) and unnecessary information (irrelevant). In written texts, look for bolded words or phrases and any words or phrases that are repeated. After you have identified the key ideas, you need to put these ideas into your own words and make sure that your words maintain the meaning of the original ideas. Last, you need to present this information in a logical order.

There are several strategies that can help you organize your ideas for summarizing. Three of the most common include a plot diagram, a WH-chart, and a pyramid.

### Plot Diagram

A plot diagram is a pre-writing strategy that allows you to see the information in a chronological manner. To create one, begin by plotting the major events on a diagram just like on a line graph. Then, plot the causes and the effects of that event in chronological order. Look at the example, which demonstrates the causes and effects of climate change.

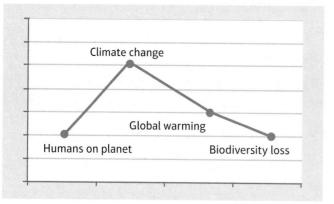

When creating a summary from a plot diagram, you can easily introduce the event and describe the causes and effects of that event, as in this example:

> The climate on this planet has changed as a result of humans. The effects of climate change have given rise to global warming and a loss of biodiversity.

## WH-Chart

Like the plot diagram, a WH-Chart is a pre-writing strategy. It organizes information based on answers to the five critical WH- questions. Look at the example:

| Who or what? | When? | Where? | Why? | How or in what way? |
|---|---|---|---|---|
| climate change | end of Holocene period | on Earth | human behavior and technology | greenhouse gases, biodiversity loss |

The climate has changed and ended the Holocene period on Earth. This change is a result of human behavior and technology. The climate has been changed by an increase in greenhouse gases and biodiversity loss.

## Pyramid Diagram

A pyramid is an effective pre-summary writing strategy that allows you to move from general to specific information. As you read or listen, begin by identifying key words. Then map out your key words in the form of a pyramid. Begin at the top by adding one word, such as the topic of the lecture or reading. As you move down the pyramid, add additional words. This allows you to build to a main idea. Look at the example:

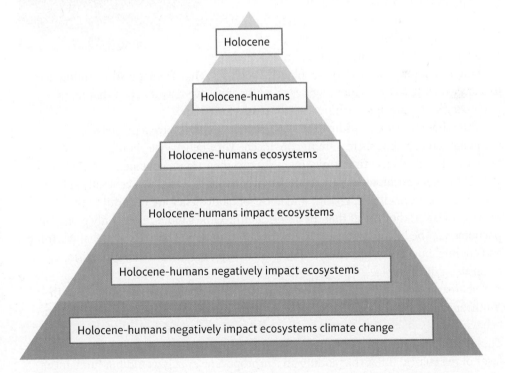

The Holocene period saw the influence of humans. Humans have negatively impacted the ecosystems on the planet. One example is our effect on the climate.

## EXERCISE 4

### A. Read the textbook excerpt.

# The Anthropocene Controversy

On the geological timetable, epochs normally begin and end based on large global events, such as ice ages, significant global warming, or other major shifts. Changes from one epoch or period to another often center on a particularly important moment, such as the meteor strike which led to a mass extinction at the end of the Mesozoic era.

Although the Holocene epoch is relatively young in geological terms—only 12,000 years old—some scientists believe it is already time to think of it as finished. As they see it, a new epoch, the "Anthropocene," is already here. Scientists who are in favor of putting the Anthropocene on the geological timetable point out the effect humans have had on the planet. They argue that humans have changed Earth so much that the Holocene is over and a brand-new epoch has begun. Industrialization and human behavior have had a damaging effect on the climate and environment of the planet. Problems range from global warming due to a large quantity of greenhouse gases to a loss of biodiversity so great that many scientists fear we are approaching a sixth "mass extinction."

While those in favor of adding the "Anthropocene" label have a persuasive argument, other scientists remain unconvinced. They believe we should not rush to modify the geological time scale. Interestingly, they are in agreement with others about humans' enormous impact on the environment. The skeptics generally agree that human-caused climate change and a loss of biodiversity are harmful to the planet. However, they think that the *geological* timetable should reflect only *geological* phenomena. The history of planet Earth contains numerous periods of global warming and cooling, but these were always effects of the type of changes that geologists examine in the first place.

Scientists against changing the geological timetable argue that deciding when the "Anthropocene epoch" actually began would be almost impossible. After all, human behavior has been altering the planet since the earliest days of agricultural practices. These practices date back nearly to the beginning of the Holocene itself. Those in favor of the change think that adding an Anthropocene epoch would put humanity's environmental impact in perspective. The skeptics, however, remain firm in their belief that the timeline should not change for the foreseeable future.

**B.** Complete one of these diagrams with the information from the excerpt.

1.

........................... EPOCH

Humans arrived

...........................

..........................

Global warming

........................... loss

2.

| What/Who? | When? | Where? | Why? | How or what? |
|---|---|---|---|---|
| Anthropocene and ................... | | | Human behavior and industry | |

3.

..........................................

↓

Effects of humanity and industry

........................... ...........................

**C.** Now listen to a short lecture on the same topic. Add to your diagram.

**D.** Work with a partner. Discuss the similarities and differences in your diagrams and summarize the key ideas from the reading and lecture.

Go to MyEnglishLab to complete a skill practice.

## LANGUAGE SKILL

### USING MODALS FOR POSSIBILITIES AND PROBABILITIES

**WHY IT'S USEFUL**  By identifying and utilizing modals for possibility and probability, you can clearly understand and communicate your certainty and reliability.

Go to MyEnglishLab for the Language Skill presentation and practice.

# VOCABULARY STRATEGY

## LEARNING VOCABULARY THROUGH WORD PARTS

**WHY IT'S USEFUL** By identifying word parts and their meanings, you can more accurately determine and retain the meaning of new words.

In academic disciplines like science, the difficulty and complexity of new vocabulary can interfere with your overall understanding of the course content. To help you understand the content better, you need to use strategies to determine the meanings of new words. One effective strategy is using word parts to establish the meaning or form of new words. This involves identifying root words, which are the basic form of a word, and the prefixes and suffixes that modify the root word.

**Prefixes** are a small group of letters added to the beginning of word. Adding a prefix to the word modifies its meaning. Many of prefixes come from languages other than English. In the field of science, many prefixes are from Greek or Latin.

Paleo – remotely     Paleocene – in the remote past

Holo – wholly     Holocene – in the present

**Suffixes** are also a small group of letters, but they are added to the end of the word. While prefixes alter the meaning of the word, suffixes generally alter the meaning and the part of speech. Look at the examples:

Crystal        Crystallize (-ize changes the noun to a verb)

Geology       Geologist (-ist changes the noun from a subject area to a person)

A good understanding of English prefixes and suffixes can help you develop your vocabulary. The charts on the next page highlight common prefixes and suffixes.

## PREFIXES

| Prefix | Meaning | Example |
|---|---|---|
| Ab/abs- | apart, away from | abnormal |
| Agri- | soil, field | agriculture |
| Ante- | before | anterior |
| Anthro- | man | Anthropocene |
| Ceno- | recent | Cenozoic |
| Creta- | chalky | Cretaceous |
| Epi- | upon, over | epicenter |
| Geo- | Earth | geology |
| Holo- | whole | Holocene |
| Hydro- | water | hydrology |
| Litho- | stone | lithography |
| Macro- | large | macrophage |
| Meta- | change or transformation | metabolize |
| Paleo- | ancient | Paleozoic |
| Thermo- | heat | thermometer |

## SUFFIXES

| Suffix: Noun | Meaning | Example |
|---|---|---|
| -age | act of/state of action | forage |
| -ion | act of | lithification |
| -ism | condition or manner | catastrophism |
| -ist | person | geologist |
| -ite | connected with | meteorite |
| -oid | like | asteroid |
| -ology | study/ science | geology |
| -sis | state or condition | analysis |

| Suffix: Verb | Meaning | Example |
|---|---|---|
| -ate | become | eradicate |
| -ize | to make or become | categorize |

| Suffix: Adjective | Meaning | Example |
|---|---|---|
| -al | having the form of | structural |
| -ic/-ical | characteristic of | Mesozoic geological |
| -cene | new or recent | Pleistocene |

## EXERCISE 5

**A. Read the lecture excerpt. Circle all the prefixes and underline all the suffixes.**

Welcome back! Last week we looked at how geologists study Earth's history, and the geological time scale. We spent time going over the idea of the Anthropocene and why it is such a controversial idea. Does the importance of human influence on the environment necessitate a change in the geological timetable, or should that timetable only reflect particular phenomena?

**B. Use the prefixes and suffixes in these words to determine their meanings and forms.**

|  | Meaning | Part of speech |
|---|---|---|
| 1. thermodynamic | .................................... | .................................... |
| 2. paleolithic | .................................... | .................................... |
| 3. geocentric | .................................... | .................................... |
| 4. metamorphosis | .................................... | .................................... |
| 5. breakage | .................................... | .................................... |
| 6. anthropology | .................................... | .................................... |

**C. Work with a partner. Brainstorm other words you have learned in this unit that have prefixes and suffixes.**

## APPLY YOUR SKILLS

**WHY IT'S USEFUL**  By applying the skills you have learned in this unit, you will be able to understand and participate in extended discourse in an academic setting.

**ASSIGNMENT**
Prepare a presentation on a geological time period. Research changes that occurred during that time period, and outline those changes by organizing your presentation in time frames, so that you can easily summarize those events for your audience.

### BEFORE YOU LISTEN

**A. Before you listen, discuss the questions with one or more students.**

1. What changes have occurred on Earth? Which of those changes do you think are related to humans' presence?

2. How does the world culture today impact our planet? Consider both positive and negative influences.

3. What could be done to change the effects of humans on the planet?

**B. You will listen to a lecture on the scientific debate surrounding the term "Anthropocene epoch." As you listen, think about these questions.**

1. Why do some geologists argue that we are in a new epoch?

2. Why is the current situation of extinction and evolution different from past situations?

3. Why do other scientists disagree with the new era?

4. What role does politics play in this controversy?

C. Review the Unit Skills Summary. As you listen to the lecture and prepare for your presentation, apply the skills you learned in this unit.

## UNIT SKILLS SUMMARY

### ENGAGE IN EXTENDED DISCOURSE USING THESE SKILLS:

**Examine time phrases in discourse**

- Recognize and distinguish between time frames.
- Identify uses of time frames.

**Organize events in time frames**

- Identify and distinguish between chronological pattern and significant event or causal pattern.
- Utilize these patterns when speaking.

**Summarize a sequence of events**

- Utilize diagrams to take effective notes.
- Construct a well-organized summary of key ideas.

**Learn new vocabulary through word parts**

- Use prefixes and suffixes to identify parts of speech and probable meanings.

## LISTEN

A. Listen to a lecture on the debate about the Anthropocene epoch. Take notes.

B. Compare your notes with a partner. Do you both have the same key ideas? What skills from this unit can help you identify key ideas?

C. Review the questions from Before You Listen, Part B. Listen to the lecture again. Work with a partner and use your notes on the lecture to answer the questions.

Go to MyEnglishLab to listen more closely, and answer the critical thinking questions.

## THINKING CRITICALLY

**Discuss the questions with another student.**

1. What are the arguments for and against a new epoch? How does the professor support each argument?

2. Based on the lecture, how would you describe the speaker's opinion? In your discussion, provide examples that illustrate your understanding.

3. The professor questions when exactly the epoch would begin. What significant events does he use as potential boundaries? How certain is he that one of these events would mark a new epoch?

## THINKING VISUALLY

**A. Look at the graphic from the bottom to top. Discuss the questions with a partner.**

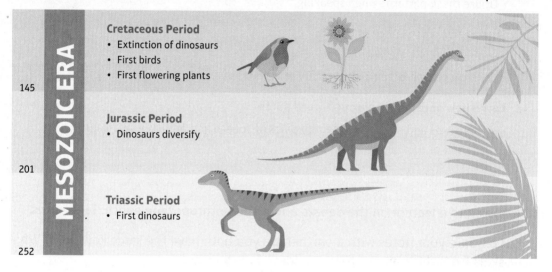

MESOZOIC ERA

**Cretaceous Period**
- Extinction of dinosaurs
- First birds
- First flowering plants

145

**Jurassic Period**
- Dinosaurs diversify

201

**Triassic Period**
- First dinosaurs

252

1. How would you summarize plant and animal life during the Mesozoic era?

2. Based on the animals in each period, what can you infer about the climate during each period?

3. How did plant and animal life change between each period? What do you think can be said about the relationship between climate and animal and plant life?

**B. Go online and investigate another geological era. Create a visual like the one above, highlighting the periods and the plant and animal life of each. Share it with your classmates. Summarize the information on the visual for your classmates.**

🔊 Go to MyEnglishLab to record your results.

## THINKING ABOUT LANGUAGE

Complete each sentence with a modal of possibility or probability.

1. You _____ find it interesting that people often confuse how long dinosaurs were alive.

2. Scientists have studied the Earth for a long time. They _____ strong evidence for the Geological timetable.

3. The Anthropocene _____ be debatable because scientists cannot seem to agree on it.

4. The professor _____ given us the reading on Holocene because it was on the test.

5. Do you think humans _____ do more to protect the plant?

6. Large mammals _____ died off because they could not adapt to the new climate.

## INDIVIDUAL PRESENTATION

A. Think about the lecture and the other information presented in the unit. Each time period has its own unique characteristics. What time period do you find most interesting?

B. You will prepare a presentation on a period on the geological timescale. Research and summarize your findings on one period. Use the questions and the visual on page 56 to help you prepare.

1. What is the period you want to research?

2. When did it occur?

3. What was the climate during this period?

4. How can you describe the biodiversity of that time?

5. What geological event brought an end to that period?

C. Listen to each presentation.

Listen carefully and take notes on each presentation. Then map each period on a timeline. Were all periods presented? Did the summaries all contain the key information?

● Go to MyEnglishLab to watch Dr. Osborne's concluding video and to complete a self-assessment.

*Present times are connected to the past*

# MEDIEVAL CULTURE

# Narratives

## UNIT PROFILE

In this unit, you will learn the meaning and history of narratives, their importance in medieval times, and how these narratives have influenced cultures, modern poetry, and songwriting. You will also become familiar with some traditional stories from different societies that recount well-known legends.

**You will prepare an individual presentation of a culturally important narrative, employing prosodic features to highlight all the key elements.**

## OUTCOMES

- Utilize spider maps to improve your note-taking skills
- Recognize and utilize prosodic features to relate narratives
- Identify elements of a narrative
- Distinguish time frames and aspects used in storytelling
- Recognize common collocations from fiction

For more about **MEDIEVAL CULTURE**, see ❷ ❸.

See also [R] and [W] **MEDIEVAL CULTURE** ❶ ❷ ❸.

# GETTING STARTED

⊙ Go to MyEnglishLab to watch Professor Galvez's introductory video and to complete a self-assessment.

## Discuss these questions with a partner or group.

1. Do you like stories? What kind of stories do you like?

2. Can you think of a story that has been passed down to you from previous generations, for example, from your parents or grandparents? Tell a partner the story.

3. According to Professor Galvez's introduction, what was incorporated into medieval literature?

# FUNDAMENTAL SKILL

## IDENTIFYING NARRATIVES

**WHY IT'S USEFUL** By identifying narratives, you are better able to determine the sequence of events of a story or an experience. Understanding narratives can also help you determine the speaker's purpose or message.

Throughout your college career and life, you will often be called upon to recount a series of events. When relating the events of an experience, story, movie, or book, this is known as narration. When narrating, speakers tell the story, or experience, from their point of view. Some simply relate facts, such as who, what, when, where, why, and how, while other speakers may utilize literary elements like establishing a plot, describing characters, and building suspense. These types of narratives often deeply engage listeners, create memorable stories, and even elicit emotional responses. Many of these memorable stories have been passed down from one generation to the next for the purposes of teaching, advising, or helping preserve cultural identity.

Being able to **identify the key elements of a narrative** is critical for understanding the speaker's purpose and the overall message of the narrative. In more dramatic narratives, speakers may include several characters, events, and actions. Identifying each element, its purpose, and the overall message can be challenging. One strategy to aid you in deciphering this information is a **spider map**. A spider map is a graphic organizer that is commonly used in literature. It allows the note-taker to distinguish the key narrative elements and record their details efficiently. A spider map also allows listeners to visualize the various elements of the narrative.

In addition to mapping out the key elements of a narration, it is also important to pay careful attention to a speaker's voice. As you probably have noticed, lectures on science might be more direct, with a steady and more controlled use of voice. In contrast, a lecture on literature might be less direct, contain more dramatic language, and have poetic voice patterns, with frequent variation in speaking speed and intonation. In many narratives, the main ideas are not always stated directly, so determining the key ideas requires more interpretation of the content. Paying careful attention to **prosody** and non-verbal cues is one strategy that can help you determine key ideas.

Music and poetry have distinguishable features, such as intonation, stress, tone, and rhythm of phrases. These features in speech are known as *prosody*. Prosody refers to the intonation, stress, tone, and rhythm of phrases. Identifying the characteristics of how language is spoken, as well as non-verbal cues, can help you determine a speaker's purpose and main ideas. Additionally, by employing these features in your own speech, you will be able to deliver your own message more effectively.

## VOCABULARY PREVIEW

**Read the vocabulary items. Circle the ones you know. Put a question mark next to the ones you don't know.**

| ancestors | recite | diminish | transcribe | oral tradition | rhyme |
| --- | --- | --- | --- | --- | --- |

## EXERCISE 1

### A. Work with a partner. Discuss the questions.

1. Are you familiar with any legends? Share a legend with your partner.

2. Are you familiar with any myths? Share a myth with your partner.

3. What do you think are the purposes of legends and myths? Why do you think many legends and myths have survived hundreds, or even thousands of years?

## Glossary

**Legend:** an old, well-known story, often about brave people, their adventures, or magical events

**Myth:** an ancient story that was invented to explain an event or a practice

**Epic poem:** a long, narrative poem about a heroic event, often significant to a culture

**Millennium:** a period of 1000 years, such as 1 to 1000 or 1001 to 2001

**Medieval period/Middle Ages:** the time period from the 5th century to the 15th century in Europe, beginning with the end of the Roman Empire

B. **Listen to the lecture on the history of storytelling. Choose the ideas you hear.**

1. People have been sharing stories since ancient times.

2. Stories evolved when writing evolved.

3. You were considered knowledgeable in ancient times if you could memorize legends or myths.

4. Written language reduced our desire to hear stories.

5. The rhyme and characters in stories and poems helped people to remember the story.

6. When books became popular, and as people began to read, oral storytelling slowed.

### CULTURE NOTE

Homer was a poet in Ancient Greece who is thought to be the author of the two best-known Greek epic poems: *The Iliad* and *The Odyssey*. Like many troubadours, or musicians, his epic poems contained musical elements, indicating that at one time, they may have been sung. *The Iliad* and *The Odyssey* are still studied today, and have greatly impacted Western culture and education.

C. **Listen again. Work with a partner. Discuss the questions.**

1. Who do you think the presenter is speaking to? How do you know?

2. What do you think the purpose of the lecture is?

3. How do you think the content, or information in the lecture, affects the speaker's voice?

4. How would you describe the speaker's voice? Is it poetic and lively? Or is it direct and more controlled?

D. **Imagine you need to retell the story to a classmate. How would your speaking style differ from the professor's? Why do you think your speaking style would be different?**

🔊 E. Now listen to a conversation between two students. Choose the key ideas that you hear.

☐ 1. Oral storytelling continued even after stories were written.

☐ 2. Being able to tell a story was a sign of intelligence.

☐ 3. Only kings and rulers told stories.

☐ 4. Many myths illustrated bravery and good behavior.

☐ 5. Storytelling songs later became poetry and prose.

**CULTURE NOTE**

Modern storytelling often includes folktales, or folklore. Folklore is a group of stories that reflect a cultural group. These tales may involve traditional events like weddings, births, or holiday celebrations. In the United States, many folktales are related to spirits and the connection between the physical world and the non-physical world. This is common with Native Americans whose stories are rich in myths and legends.

## VOCABULARY CHECK

A. Review the vocabulary items in the Vocabulary Preview. Write the definitions and add examples. Use a dictionary if necessary.

B. Complete the paragraph with the vocabulary items from the box.

| ancestors | diminish | oral traditions | preserve | recite | transcribe |

Legends and myths have been around a long time. During the ancient times, scholars would ........................stories in front of large crowds. These ........................helped to preserve the culture, values, and beliefs of people during that time. Once writing became a common practice, these stories that were once shared orally, were ........................ or written down for everyone. Our ........................ helped to continue the traditions of early scholars, and shared these stories with family members. Many believe that our ancestors did not want to ........................ the value of these stories, or their moral messages. So, while the time was different, the messages remained constant. Because of their ........................ , many of these early myths and legends became poems and songs.

↑ Go to MyEnglishLab to complete a listening and vocabulary practice and to join in collaborative activities.

# SUPPORTING SKILL 1
## UTILIZING SPIDER MAPS

**WHY IT'S USEFUL** By utilizing spider mapping, you can better identify its key elements, which makes the story easier to understand and to retell.

Note-taking during a lecture can be especially challenging if you do not have a clear method of organizing your notes. One successful method of note-taking is **spider mapping**. Spider mapping is especially effective in courses where stories are shared or told. Spider mapping is a graphic organizer which looks like a spider. In the center is the main topic, and its "legs" are the supporting elements.

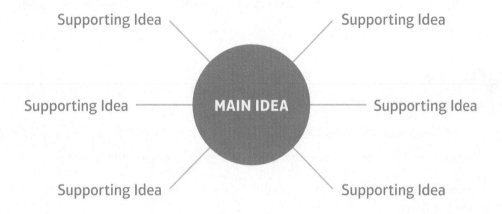

Look at the example of spider mapping containing notes from the listening in Exercise 1.

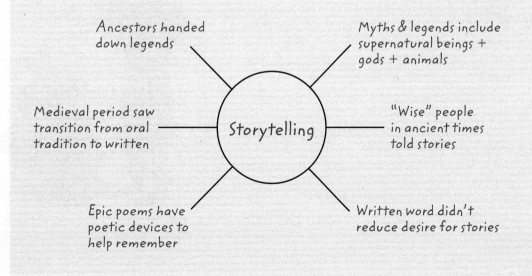

In the completed spider map, storytelling is the main idea of the lecture. The supporting ideas are represented by the "legs" of the spider. We can easily see the relationship between the main idea and each supporting idea. Graphically representing the key ideas is not only an effective note-taking strategy, but can also help you when you are studying for a test or quiz.

## VOCABULARY PREVIEW

Read the vocabulary items. Circle the ones you know. Put a question mark next to the ones you don't know.

| evolution | improvised | aristocrats | royalty | outweigh | asset |
|-----------|-----------|-------------|---------|----------|-------|

## EXERCISE 2

### A. Brainstorm with a partner.

1. What do you know about medieval times? How did the people live? Who led people?

2. What types of entertainment do you think existed during that time?

3. What do you think were some common themes of storytelling, songs, and poems during this time? Why?

### Glossary

**Skalds:** medieval Norse composers and reciters of poems

**Troubadour:** a composer and musical performer of lyrical poetry during the Middle Ages

**Chivalry:** behavior that is honorable, kind, and generous—especially men's behavior towards women

**Vellum:** a material used for covering books or writing on, made from prepared calf skin

**Parchment:** a material used in the past for writing on, made from the skin of animals

**The Renaissance:** the period of time in Europe between the 14th and 17th centuries, when art, literature, philosophy, and scientific ideas became very important

**B. Listen to two speakers on a panel discuss medieval times and storytelling. Write *M* (main idea) and *S* (supporting idea).**

............ 1. Songbooks varied by culture.

............ 2. During medieval times, books were rare due to their cost.

............ 3. Storytelling, poetry, and music were all common entertainments for aristocrats.

............ 4. Storytelling styles differed, and focused on different issues.

............ 5. As time passed, storytellers created songbooks to preserve their traditions.

............ 6. Present day poets, musicians, and storytellers have most likely been influenced by these early stories.

**C. Listen to the panel discussion again. Complete the spider map.**

Traditional storytellers influenced future ........................, authors, and ........................

Each country had different traditions and ........................

Medieval Times (5th- ........................ centuries) Performers: ........................, poets and ......................... .

Making a book costly due to ........................

Nordic skalds recorded stories of kings while European troubadours often told stories of ........................ an chivalry

In 11th century, emergence of ........................

Styles of storytelling were similar

## VOCABULARY CHECK

**A.** Review the vocabulary items in the Vocabulary Preview. Write the definitions and add examples. Use a dictionary if necessary.

**B.** Choose the best meaning for the underlined vocabulary items in each sentence.

1. In early stories, knights and other nobility were known for their bravery. Being brave was an <u>asset</u> then, just as it is now.

   a. a beneficial quality

   b. something extra

   c. a caring behavior

   d. a dangerous behavior

2. Actors need to be able to <u>improvise</u> on stage to make the scene more authentic.

   a. to practice a performance

   b. to perform without preparation

   c. to manage effectively

   d. to become better

3. <u>Aristocrats</u> during medieval times included kings, queens, and lords.

   a. governing body

   b. middle class

   c. counselors

   d. highest social class

4. The <u>evolution</u> of writing and the printed word meant that reading and writing became more commonplace.

   a. beginning

   b. entrance

   c. development

   d. increase

5. When making a decision, we often ask ourselves if the benefits <u>outweigh</u> the disadvantages.

   a. have more distinction than

   b. are more isolated than

   c. have more value than

   d. have less value than

6. <u>Royalty</u> during the medieval times led communities, and granted land to commoners.

   a. kings and knights

   b. knights and other nobility

   c. storytellers, poets, and musicians

   d. king, queen, or a member of their immediate family

> Go to MyEnglishLab to complete vocabulary and skill practices and to join in collaborative activities.

# SUPPORTING SKILL 2
## IDENTIFYING PROSODIC FEATURES

**WHY IT'S USEFUL** By identifying prosodic features in speech, you can better determine a speaker's key idea, and how he or she feels about the topic. By incorporating prosodic patterns in your own speech, you can keep the attention of your listeners and help them better comprehend your key points.

**Prosody** refers to aspects of speech that provide some additional meaning or feeling to what is being said; they are not related to individual sounds, but to the way the sounds are being made. Every language has its own distinct sound and flow. In English, speaking is similar to singing a song. Both singing and speaking involve **rhythm** and **melody**. In speech, *rhythm* refers to how long, and how clearly vowels are pronounced in each syllable. Notice that certain syllables in words are longer (said more slowly) than others. That is because these are key words and contain important ideas in the sentence. Look at the line markers that show length and vowel clarity in the example:

The sad old woman walked out into the storm.

*Melody* refers to two things in speech: the joining of words into meaningful groups, and their intonation. We pause between meaningful groups of words, and raise the pitch on stressed syllables to emphasize key words, to clarify, express surprise, or show our agreement. Look at the intonation and pause markers in the example:

The monk was afraid, / but he was also pure of heart.

Rhythm and melody are only two prosodic features of speech. Two more prosodic features are *tempo* (speaking rate) and *volume* (loudness or softness). These elements, along with non-verbal cues such as facial expressions and gestures, add important meaning to the message. These prosodic features differ according to the situation, who we are talking to, and how we feel about the message.

**CULTURE NOTE**

In many cultures, we can determine someone's emotions based on the tempo, pitch, and volume of speech. If someone is excited, the tempo and volume of speech will usually increase, and the general pitch level will become higher. If someone is very sad, the tempo will often become slower, the volume will decrease, and the pitch will be at a lower level.

Look at the chart.

| Speaking Situation | Rhythm | Melody | Tempo | Volume | Non-Verbal Cues |
|---|---|---|---|---|---|
| Presentation or lecture | Longer, clearer stressed syllables on new terms and key words | Longer pauses after new ideas are introduced | Normal speaking rate with slight variations | Higher volume on new terms | May use gestures when a new term is introduced; no characteristic facial expressions |
| Making an appeal | Longer, clearer stressed syllables on emotionally loaded words | Pitch rises on emotionally charged words | May slow down rate during supporting ideas and counter-argument | Higher volume on words that express emotions | Direct eye contact; strong stance and gestures |
| Telling an exciting or scary story | Longer, clearer stressed syllables on important story elements | Clear, distinct pitch rises and falls; few pauses | Faster rate during climactic events of story | Higher volume on key elements/ events of the story | Dramatic facial expressions and gestures showing characters' emotions |
| Reading poetry or singing a song | Longer, clearer content words (nouns and verbs) and shorter function words (articles, prepositions, etc.) | Longer pauses between thought groups | Slower rate | Steady volume | Dramatic facial expressions |

## VOCABULARY PREVIEW

Read the vocabulary items. Circle the ones you know. Put a question mark next to the ones you don't know.

| | | | |
|---|---|---|---|
| heroism | wizard | fierce | drew |
| disguise | prophecy | crafted | reign |

## EXERCISE 3

**A. Work with a partner. Discuss the questions.**

1. Are you familiar with any legends about kings and knights?

2. If so, who are the characters and where does it take place? If not, what do you think might be in these legends?

3. How are these legends often told? Do the storytellers act it out? Do they use different voices for different characters? How do you decide what the important parts are?

🔊 **B. Listen to a story. Choose the prosodic features you hear.**

☐ 1. Important words are given long syllables with clear vowels.

☐ 2. There are clear pitch rises and falls.

☐ 3. Key elements are spoken at a much faster or slower rate.

☐ 4. There is increased volume during surprising or exciting elements.

## C. Listen to these sentences. As you listen, notice how the prosodic features in the box are used.

1. Uther was so in love with Igraine that he was willing to risk his life to be with her.

2. So, one dark and magical night, he snuck into her bedroom disguised as her husband.

> ### Prosodic Features
>
> Rhythm: phrases that have long syllables
>
> Melody: phrases where you hear distinct pitch rises and falls
>
> Tempo changes: phrases where the speaking rate is faster or slower
>
> Volume: phrases where loudness is increased

3. The Duke suspected that baby Arthur was not his own son, so, he gave the baby to another man to raise.

4. Merlin developed young Arthur's powers and taught him how to be brave, heroic, and knightly, while preparing the young boy for greatness.

5. As time passed, the knights of the land grew impatient and began arguing about which of them was worthy of that seat at the great knight's table.

6. According to Merlin, only the most moral man in the land could pull a mysterious sword out of the stone, and that man would be the next king.

7. As news of this spread, knights began arriving from all over the land to try to take the sword out of the stone, but they could not.

8. One day, while Arthur was returning home, he suddenly came upon the sword in the stone.

9. Arthur quickly grabbed the sword, easily drew it out of the stone and ran to take it to his brother.

10. The people who saw this could not believe their eyes. They informed Arthur of the prophecy, and rejoiced when Arthur was proclaimed the new king!

### TIP

During exciting tales, like a supernatural story, storytellers will help the story come alive by using their voices and facial expressions. During exciting moments, the speakers may raise their eyebrows and widen their eyes. When there is strange, or confusing behavior in the story, storytellers may narrow their eyes, indicating their confusion.

**D. Work with a partner. Retell the story. As you listen to your partner, use the list to check your partner's prosody and facial expressions.**

☐ Rhythm: pronouncing some syllables longer and with very clear vowels

☐ Melody: clear and distinct rises and falls in pitch

☐ Tempo: increased speaking speed during exciting events

☐ Volume: increased volume during surprising events

☐ Eyes open wider or close somewhat to look smaller.

☐ Facial expressions change with the text

## VOCABULARY CHECK

**A. Review the vocabulary items in the Vocabulary Preview. Write the definitions and add examples. Use a dictionary if necessary.**

**B. Complete the sentences with the correct vocabulary items.**

1. A ........................... is someone who has special, magical powers.

2. Kings often ........................... over a country or territory until they die.

3. During medieval times, performers often ........................... themselves as the characters in the story.

4. Knights must demonstrate acts of ........................... and bravery.

5. They fought a ........................... battle, and many knights died.

6. Arthur was unaware of the ........................... about the sword, but Merlin was.

7. When two knights have a sword fight, they must ........................... their swords at the same time.

8. The magical sword was ........................... by the powerful wizard.

🔾 Go to MyEnglishLab to complete vocabulary and listening practices and to join in collaborative activities.

# INTEGRATED SKILLS

## IDENTIFYING NARRATIVE ELEMENTS

**WHY IT'S USEFUL** By identifying the key elements of a narrative, you can better understand its contents, make logical inferences, and draw effective conclusions.

Academic lectures have clear organizational patterns with a topic, main ideas, supporting ideas, and examples. However, narratives work differently; therefore, being able to **identify narrative elements** is especially critical for comprehension. These elements are: the **setting**, **characters**, **plot**, **conflict**, **resolution**, and **theme**.

The setting describes the time and place in which the story takes place. Listening for cues, such as a description of the scenery (forest, mountains, lakes), weather, and time of day will help you determine the setting. The setting also creates a mood. Mood refers to the feelings the storyteller is trying to provoke, such as happiness, sadness, awe, or fear.

The characters are the people, animals, or supernatural beings that the story is built around. In most stories there is a *protagonist*, also known as the hero or heroine. The protagonist is the character who is good and honorable and whose behavior provides an example of moral values. In contrast, an *antagonist* is the character who opposes the protagonist, and is an example of bad or dishonorable behavior and values.

The structure of the story, or its sequence of events, is known as the plot. These events lead to the climax, or the point of most excitement in the story, and often takes place in the middle or toward the end of the events.

Every story has a conflict, or problem. Conflicts in stories are generally either external or internal. An *external* conflict is a visible or physical obstacle, such as a fight, a robbery, or a disappearance. Conversely, an *internal* conflict is a personal challenge that a character has to struggle against mentally, such as loving another man's wife, or being tempted to steal a great treasure. The resolution of the conflict is the end of the story that answers all questions the listener or reader may have had.

Finally, there is the theme, which is the key message, the controlling idea, or practical lesson to learn from the story. Themes often describe how we should behave or how to live a better life.

Look at the chart on page 91 for the elements of the story you heard on page 87.

| Setting | Characters | Plot | Conflict/Resolution | Theme |
|---|---|---|---|---|
| Long, long ago, in Cornwall | Arthur<br>Merlin<br>Duke of Cornwall<br>Uther<br>Igraine | Arthur unaware of his true parents, is tutored by the wizard Merlin. Merlin's prophecy: Only the next true king will be able to remove the magic sword from its stone | Powerful knights fail to remove the sword from its stone, but young Arthur removes it easily and becomes king. | Be heroic, loyal, and compassionate and you will be rewarded. |

## EXERCISE 4

### A. Work with a partner. Discuss these questions.

> **TIP**
>
> In folktales, the theme is often a moral lesson teaching ethical behavior. Stories that feature animals with human characteristics are known as fables. Fables are often introduced by set phrases, such as *A long time ago, Once upon a time*, and *There once was a …*

1. The characters in fables are animals with human characteristics. What are some animals that regularly occur in stories?

2. Think of a story where the main character is an animal. Are there other characters? Where does it take place? Is there a problem that is being solved? How does it get solved? Does the story teach a lesson?

3. Why do you think writers use animals to teach moral lessons? Look at the two animals below. What traits do you associate with each one?

A hare

A hedgehog

**B. Read the fable. Complete the story elements chart on page 94.**

## The Tale of the Hare and the Hedgehog

Once upon a time, a prideful hare was being quite mean to a little hedgehog. Mr. Hedgehog had a small farm hidden away in the forest, whereas Hare simply wandered around all day bothering the other woodland creatures. Hare would repeatedly say cruel things before running off. "Oh, you poor thing! I don't know how you survive, being so slow! Don't your spines get all tangled up in the leaves?" Now, Mr. Hedgehog was normally a patient fellow, but after days and days of this behavior, he had finally had enough.

"Oh, you think you're so fast! I'm sure I could beat you in a race if I really wanted to." The hare laughed and laughed. "Is that so? Well, why don't we have a race, then?"

"Perhaps we should," the poor hedgehog yelled.

"Well then, we could race right now! I'll bet you a gold coin and a bushel of asparagus that I'll win." The cruel Hare was delighted, as he knew Mr. Hedgehog dearly loved asparagus almost as much as Hare. As for the gold, well, even woodland creatures find themselves in need of money from time to time.

"Well, I agree, but only if you allow me to go home for a moment and clean up first. I've been working my fields all day and am quite dirty."

"Go ahead," snarled Hare. "Dirty or clean, I'll still win!"

Mr. Hedgehog trotted home and explained the situation to his wife. "Hare may be fast, but we both know he is quite stupid. He once spent three days arguing with a stone shaped like another hare. We should be able to trick him in some way, if only we could figure out how."

"I have an idea," said Mrs. Hedgehog. "Race out in our field, with each of you in one furrow; you will not be able to see each other. I'll stand at the other end…"

"Oh, yes, I think I see," Mr. Hedgehog said. "Excellent plan!"

A few moments later, Mr. Hedgehog and Hare were standing, each in their own furrow, next to each other. "So, you understand, don't you, Hare? We'll both race to the end, and whoever arrives first is the winner."

"Sure, sure," said Hare. "I hope you have that asparagus ready for me!"

Hare took off, not even waiting for the hedgehog to announce the start of the race, and dashed to the other end of the furrow. "Hah! We'll see," said Hare, "how long it takes that hedgehog to waddle over to this side of the furrow."

"But I was already here," said Mrs. Hedgehog. "I was wondering what took you so long to arrive!"

Hare was shocked. He peeked over the dirt separating the furrows and stared at Mrs. Hedgehog. Now, Hare, being someone who only cared about himself, rarely bothered to look at others carefully or listen to their voice, so he could scarcely tell Mrs. Hedgehog from Mr. Hedgehog even if he had tried.

"What is this? Are you some kind of hedgehog wizard? There is no possible way that you ran faster than me."

"I knew you'd be a sore loser. I tell you what, if you wager another gold coin, I'll let you try again and you can race back to the— "

Mrs. Hedgehog did not even finish speaking before Hare rushed back to the other end of the furrow.

"Aha! I know now that I've surely— "

"Oh, I'm sorry, what did you say Hare? It seems," said Mr. Hedgehog, "that I dozed off waiting for you."

"No, no, no! You could not have beaten me without some sort of supernatural trickery! Another gold coin and I'll race you to the other end."

"Suit yourself," yawned Mr. Hedgehog. "Just be careful not to tire yourself out."

The hare zipped to the end of the furrow. "First!"

"Not quite," said Mrs. Hedgehog.

"Again!" He shrieked, dashing back to the other side.

"You're going to run out of money if you keep this up," said Mr. Hedgehog.

"Never! Once more!" Hare darted back and forth, wagering another coin each time, again and again, until he finally became so tired that he collapsed, out of breath, in the middle.

A few moments passed before Mr. Hedgehog walked up, carrying a cup of water and a sprig of asparagus.

"Oh, thank you, Mr. Hedgehog," wheezed Hare. "I'm so very sorry for having doubted you. You really can be quite fast when you wish to be."

"It's no problem," said Mr. Hedgehog. "Just go back home and rest to recover your strength."

"So kind, so kind," said Hare.

"It's just that, I don't think you'll be able to pay me those ninety-nine gold pieces right away, so I'll have you work off the rest of your debt on the farm until it's settled."

"Oh, no," said the hare, who for the rest of his days was too busy working on the asparagus farm to say a cruel thing to Mr. Hedgehog, Mrs. Hedgehog, or anyone else for that matter.

**CULTURE NOTE**

The two best-known collections of fables are from Aesop, a slave and storyteller from ancient Greece, and those of Jean La Fontaine, a French author from the 17th century. La Fontaine's fables are considered classics of French literature. Other well-known fables, like the Hare and Hedgehog, appear in the works of the Grimm brothers, German authors, academics, and cultural researchers who were active in the 19th century.

## C. Use the reading to complete the story elements chart.

| Setting | Characters | Plot | Conflict/ Resolution | Theme |
|---------|-----------|------|----------------------|-------|
|         |           |      |                      |       |

## D. Use the information from the chart to complete the spider map.

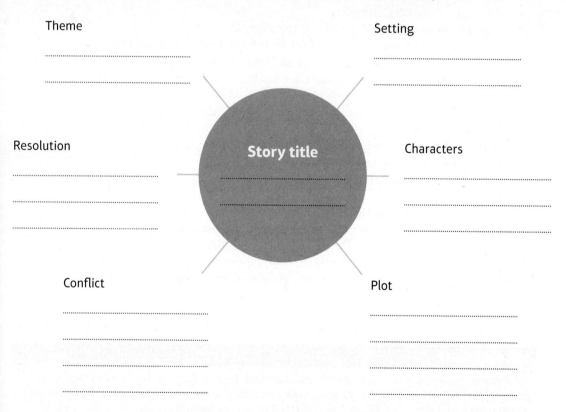

Theme

Setting

Resolution

Story title

Characters

Conflict

Plot

## E. Work with a partner. Review your spider maps and discuss what can be added.

● Go to MyEnglishLab to complete skill practices.

# LANGUAGE SKILL

## RECOGNIZING TIME FRAME AND ASPECT IN NARRATIVES

**WHY IT'S USEFUL** By identifying and recognizing time frame and aspect choices in narratives, you can better determine the underlying meaning, and how the person may feel.

🔾 Go to MyEnglishLab for the Language Skill presentation and practice.

# VOCABULARY STRATEGY

## IDENTIFYING COLLOCATIONS

**WHY IT'S USEFUL** By identifying collocations, you can more easily acquire larger groups of words and increase your vocabulary and understanding, as well as become a more fluent speaker and writer.

**Collocations** are two or more words that are frequently used together and sound natural to native speakers of a language. They are important because meaning is often determined by groups of words rather than individual words. Collocations are especially important when we look at two words that have similar meanings. The words they collocate with often help to clarify differences in meaning.

For example, look at two words that, on the surface, have a similar meaning: *rob* and *steal*. Both mean to take something that does not belong to you from a person or place. However, their collocations can help us to distinguish their difference. *Rob* and *steal* both collocate with different words. Look at the examples in the chart.

| Collocates with... | A bank | A car | money | A person | A store | A wallet |
|---|---|---|---|---|---|---|
| Rob | ✓ rob a bank | ✗ | ✗ | ✓ rob a person | ✓ rob a store | ✗ |
| Steal | ✗ | ✓ steal a car | ✓ steal money | ✗ | ✗ | ✓ steal a wallet |

Strong collocations are those words that are almost always used together. When relating stories, there are several collocations that regularly occur. Look at the examples in the chart on page 96.

| Word | Collocations | Example |
|---|---|---|
| hero | brave hero<br>gallant hero<br>the conquering hero | Arthur was a **brave hero**. |
| knight | brave knight<br>gallant knight<br>knight in shining armor | He was her **knight in shining armor**, rescuing her from the evil witch. |
| evil | evil guardian<br>evil step-mother<br>evil witch<br>the lesser of two evils | She married the prince to escape living with her **evil step-mother**. |
| legend | according to legend<br>legend has it<br>the stuff of legends | **According to legend**, young Arthur was born on a dark, stormy night. |
| prophecy | fulfill a prophecy<br>make a prophecy<br>self-fulfilling prophecy | By pulling the sword from the stone, Arthur **fulfilled the prophecy**. |
| story | tell/recount/relate a story<br>embellish a story | He **recounted the story** again for those who had just arrived. |
| warrior | band of warriors<br>mighty warrior<br>noble warrior | The **noble warrior** defended the land. |
| wizard | famous wizard<br>wise and powerful wizard | Merlin was a **wise and powerful wizard**. |

## EXERCISE 5

**A. Read the sentences. Circle the collocations related to storytelling.**

1. The gallant hero marched across the battlefield, and drew his sword.

2. Legend has it, that one day, a kindly wizard was traveling along a mountain pass.

3. Arthur's fear of losing his wife became a self-fulfilling prophecy as his jealousy drove her away from him.

4. As the young child was walking through the forest, a band of warriors charged by her on horses.

5. The evil stepmother refused to let her stepdaughter attend the prince's ball.

6. The knight in shining armor suddenly appeared to save the damsel in distress.

B. Complete each sentence with the correct collocation.

1. The young boy was playing make believe. He dressed up, and spoke like a noble
   ..................................... .

2. She really ........................... that story. I don't remember it being nearly
   that dramatic!

3. According to ........................... , there is a dragon who lives at the top of
   the mountain.

4. It is said that there are brave knights and ........................... knights.

5. The ........................... of Spiderman asserts that he was bitten by a spider as a boy.

6. He was always afraid of getting fired, so, of course they let him go. It was a
   ..................................... .

C. Work with a partner. Take turns telling one another a story from your culture.
   Be sure to use the correct collocations when you tell the story.

◐ Go to MyEnglishLab to complete a skill practice.

## APPLY YOUR SKILLS

**WHY IT'S USEFUL** By applying the skills you have learned in this unit, you will be able to distinguish key elements for a successful narration, and improve your abilities to recount stories.

### ASSIGNMENT
Prepare a presentation of a narrative that is important to your culture or community. It should contain all the elements of a story and employ prosodic features.

### BEFORE YOU LISTEN
A. Before you listen, discuss the questions with one or more students.

1. What aspects of a culture might be illustrated by stories and songs?

2. Why do many people refer to songwriters and singers as "storytellers?" What similarities do songs and stories share?

B. You will listen to a lecture on the connection between story and song. As you listen, think about these questions.

1. What is mythology?

2. How did the myth, *The Death of Balder*, originate?

3. Where did Snorri Sturluson find the tale?

4. How does the lecturer describe the relationship between song, story, and poetry?

C. Review the Unit Skills Summary. As you listen to the lecture and prepare for your presentation, apply the skills you learned in this unit.

---

## UNIT SKILLS SUMMARY

### DEVELOP YOUR NARRATIVE ABILITIES BY USING THESE SKILLS:

**Utilize spider mapping to improve note-taking**

- Determine lecture elements.
- Determine the key events from a series of events.

**Identify and utilize prosody when listening to and retelling narratives**

- Determine speaker's purpose.
- Identify signals based on rhythm, melody, tempo, and volume.
- Utilize various facial expression and gestures when telling stories.

**Analyze the elements of a story**

- Recognize characters, plot, conflict, and resolution.
- Make inferences to determine theme, or key message.

**Recognize and use appropriate time frames and aspects in narratives**

- Distinguish between the use and meaning of the present and past time frames in a story.
- Distinguish between simple, continuous, and perfect aspects in a story.

**Recognize common collocations used in myths, fables, and legends**

- Utilize collocations when recounting a story.

---

## LISTEN

🔊 A. Listen to a lecture on the relationship between stories and songs in Norse mythology. Take notes.

---

### Glossary

**Asgard:** fictional land of the gods of Norse and Icelandic mythology

**Odin and Frigg:** Odin, ruler of the Norse gods, and Frigg, the Norse goddess of wisdom

**Balder:** son of Odin and Frigg

**Loki:** a jealous god known for cheating or deceiving others

**Oath:** a serious, formal promise to do something

**Hoder:** blind son of Odin and Frigg, brother of Balder

**Snorri Sturluson:** Icelandic writer of the 13th century who collected the stories about the Norse gods

**Descendants:** related to things or people from the past

---

B. Compare your notes with a partner. Do you both have the same key ideas? What skills from this unit can help you identify key ideas?

🔊 C. Review the questions from Before You Listen, Part B. Listen to the lecture again. Work with a partner and use your notes on the lecture to answer the questions.

🔊 Go to MyEnglishLab to listen more closely, and answer the critical thinking questions.

Cuttings of Mistletoe

## THINKING CRITICALLY

**Discuss the questions with another student.**

1. Based on the lecture, what can you infer about the themes of early poems and songs?

2. What do you think served as inspiration to these early songwriters?

3. How do the themes of today's songs and poetry differ?

## THINKING VISUALLY

**A. Complete the timeline of the story with the missing events below.**

**THE DEATH OF BALDER**

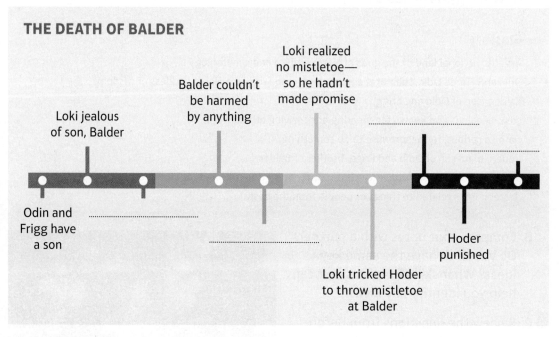

- Balder dies
- Frigg begged everyone not to harm her son
- Loki escapes punishment
- Frigg forgot the mistletoe

**B. Check your timeline with a partner. Take turns retelling the story using correct timeframes and time-order words.**

> **TIP**
>
> When describing a timeline, use transitional words of time, such as *first, second, third, next, before, after,* and *last* to let listeners know they are following a linear order.

**C. Investigate another myth online. Create a timeline of the key events like the one in Part A.**

⬆ Go to MyEnglishLab to record your results.

## THINKING ABOUT LANGUAGE

Read the excerpt from the lecture. Underline all the verbs. What is the time frame? Why does the speaker use this time frame?

Once upon a time, the chief Norse gods of Asgard, Odin and Frigg, had a son, Balder. Everyone loved Balder, except for the trickster god Loki, who was always jealous. Frigg traveled the world, asking everything in existence to swear an oath never to harm Balder. The spirits of the rocks, the trees, fires, winds, diseases—anything and everything swore an oath to never hurt her beloved son.

After, the gods in Asgard would all have fun throwing weapons and other things at Balder. Balder could be shot with arrows, but they simply bounced off. Large rocks could be dropped on Balder; he could drink cups of poison; he could stand in burning flame. Nothing harmed him, to the amusement of all.

Loki, angered at this attention, disguised himself as an old woman. Meeting with Frigg one day, he found out that Frigg had neglected to get the mistletoe plant to swear an oath, as it seemed too weak—or too young.

## INDIVIDUAL PRESENTATION

A. Discuss the questions with one or more students.

1. What are some of your favorite myths, legends, and fables? Why do you like them?

2. Is there a narrative that has been told often in your community or culture? What makes that story important? What values does it illustrate?

B. You will prepare a presentation of a narrative that is important to you or your culture. Research important myths, legends, fables, and songs. Use the questions to help you prepare.

1. What is the setting (the time period and place)?

2. Who are the main characters and how would you describe them? Who is the protagonist?

3. What are the key events in the plot?

4. Is there a clear conflict? What is the resolution of this conflict?

5. What is the theme, or moral of this story?

**TIP**

When practicing for a presentation, it is important to hear and see your delivery. To do this, consider practicing in front of a mirror, or recording yourself on video. Be sure to play back your video, and pay close attention to your use of voice, eye contact, and language choices. Make any modifications necessary.

## C. Complete the spider map with the elements of your narrative from Part B.

Theme

..................................................

..................................................

Setting

..................................................

..................................................

Resolution

..................................................

..................................................

..................................................

**Story title**

..................................................

..................................................

Characters

..................................................

..................................................

..................................................

Conflict

..................................................

..................................................

..................................................

..................................................

Plot

..................................................

..................................................

..................................................

..................................................

## D. Practice.

Work with a partner. Using your spider maps and taking turns, practice telling your story to each other. Be sure to incorporate all the narrative elements, and use prosodic features, such as rhythm, melody, speaking rate, volume, and a variety of facial expressions and gestures. Tell your story in a way that will engage your audience. For help with facial expressions and gestures, use the photos on page 102 to help you. Complete the peer review checklist for your partner.

| Peer Review: Circle the prosodic features your partner incorporates. | Yes | No | Notes |
|---|---|---|---|
| RHYTHM: Variety; long syllables with clear vowels; emphasize key words and story elements | ☐ | ☐ | |
| MELODY: Changes in intonation; strong pitch rises and falls; adds pauses between thought groups | ☐ | ☐ | |
| TEMPO: Variations in speaking rate to maintain interest; faster speaking rate during exciting or surprising events and in climax of story | ☐ | ☐ | |
| VOLUME: Variations in volume between loud and soft; louder volume emphasizes key points | ☐ | ☐ | |
| NON-VERBAL CUES: Changes facial expressions; uses body language; adds gestures; acts out the story | ☐ | ☐ | |

## E. Listen to each presentation.

Listen carefully and take notes on each presentation. Then map each story on a spider map. Which classmates were effective storytellers? Why were they effective?

🔊 Go to MyEnglishLab to watch Professor Galvez's concluding video and to complete a self-assessment.

*How the study of molecules relates to the real world*

# MATERIALS ENGINEERING

# Academic Discussions

## UNIT PROFILE

In this unit, you will learn about materials engineering and the structure of materials. You will also learn about two specific types of materials and see how their composition helps make them materials of choice for various everyday products.

**You will prepare a presentation with a partner on why a certain material produces a better and more stable product than another material.**

## OUTCOMES

- Identify organizational patterns in dense lectures
- Organize responses in complex discussions
- Compare and contrast textbooks and lectures
- Identify and utilize language for comparing and contrasting
- Utilize graphic organizers to learn new words

For more about **MATERIALS ENGINEERING**, see ❷❸.
See also R and W **MATERIALS ENGINEERING** ❶❷❸.

# GETTING STARTED

🔵 Go to MyEnglishLab to watch Professor Heilshorn's introductory video and to complete a self-assessment.

**Discuss these questions with a partner or group.**

1. Materials engineering is the study of materials. What do you think that means?

2. How do you think materials engineers determine which materials are best suited for a product?

3. In Professor Heilshorn's introduction, she mentions three materials that this section will focus on. What are they?

# FUNDAMENTAL SKILL

## PARTICIPATING IN ACADEMIC DISCUSSIONS

**WHY IT'S USEFUL** By utilizing strategies to increase your participation in academic discussions, you can engage more in your courses and retain more information.

College classrooms in North America involve a lot of give and take. That is, there is often a great deal of two-way communication in the classroom. Professors lecture, but they also expect students to engage or interact with the content. **Participating in academic discussions** is the first step to engaging with the content. Participating can take many forms: there is class participation, small group participation, and pair or partner participation. Each of these offers you an opportunity to increase your learning, and actively engage with your classmates and professor.

In order to be successful with these forms of participation, you need to be well-prepared. This involves having a basic understanding of the lesson material before you enter the classroom. Because many new technical terms and much of the new material will be presented in a lecture, understanding and extracting key terms and information from dense lectures is critical. There are several **strategies** that you can use to help you **understand dense lectures**. First, listening for cues and signal words can help you understand the overall organization. Next, paying close attention to the lecturer's voice and pace can aid you in identifying key words and terms. Finally, developing your own note-taking system can help you organize the material in a way that is clear and memorable for you.

After you have a clear understanding of the course content, the next step is organizing the ideas you want to share with your class, group, or partner. It can be challenging to share your thoughts on complex material in a cohesive, understandable manner. In the same way that using strategies to help you comprehend dense lectures, there are also several effective **strategies** you can use to **organize your responses**. First, consider using signal words in your responses. Signal words can help your listeners follow your idea, and can help you organize your overall response. Next, predict questions or comments your listeners may have. Be prepared to respond to any questions or comments with effective response techniques. For example, if you agree with someone's idea, be sure to acknowledge your agreement, but also add to the idea presented. If you disagree with someone's idea, be clear as to which element of their idea you disagree with, and offer your counter-position in a clear, concrete, and concise way.

## VOCABULARY PREVIEW

Read the vocabulary items in the box. Circle the ones you know. Put a question mark next to the ones you don't know.

| relate to | compound | critically | bond | floating around | ideal |
|---|---|---|---|---|---|

## EXERCISE 1

### A. Work with a partner. Discuss the questions.

1. In terms of chemistry, what is an *element?* Can you list a few examples?

2. Which two elements are in the compound molecule $H_2O$? Are you familiar with other molecular compounds? Give examples.

3. Why do you think materials engineers need to understand the composition of a material?

---

Glossary

Atoms:  the smallest part of an element that can exist alone or can combine with other substances to form a molecule

Elements:  substances that cannot be reduced to other substances; for example: iron or gold

Molecules:  two or more atoms bonded together

Alloy:  a metal that consists of a mixture of two or more metals

Nitrogen:  a gas that has no color or smell, and forms most of the Earth's air

Properties:  the chemical characteristics or attributes of a substance

---

B. Listen to a lecture that introduces basic chemistry and how it relates to materials engineering. Look at the topics below. Write *M* for main idea, *S* for supporting idea, and *D* for detail or example.

1. .............. Understanding basic chemistry is necessary for materials science.

2. .............. Iron is an element that cannot be melted down.

3. .............. Atoms bond together to form a molecule.

4. .............. Water is the most famous bonded molecules, or compound.

5. .............. Creating biomaterials requires planning to select appropriate materials.

6. .............. Contact lenses could damage the human eye if the wrong material is used.

**Nitrogen**

$N_2$

**Water**

$H_2O$

C. Listen again. Listen carefully for how the speaker defines each new term. Circle the cues you hear when each term is defined.

| | | | |
|---|---|---|---|
| Elements: | slower | higher pitch | repeated |
| Atom: | slower | higher pitch | repeated |
| Molecules: | slower | higher pitch | repeated |
| Compound: | slower | higher pitch | repeated |

**TIP**

Listening to a dense lecture can be even more confusing when many new terms are used. While taking notes, highlight, circle, or annotate unfamiliar vocabulary during the lecture. After the lecture, be sure to check your textbook, or other course materials, for the meanings of the terms you wrote down.

D. Why does the speaker give definitions at a slower rate, and higher pitch? In addition to giving definitions, in what other situations might a professor speak more slowly and have a noticeable pitch rise? Share your ideas with a partner.

E. Now listen to a conversation in which a confused student asks a tutor for advice. What advice does the tutor offer the student?

## VOCABULARY CHECK

A. Review the vocabulary items in the Vocabulary Preview. Write their definitions and add examples. Use a dictionary if necessary.

B. Choose the sentence that correctly describes the underlined vocabulary item.

1. a. When two things attach, they form a <u>bond</u>.

   b. When two things detach from one another, they are a <u>bond</u>.

2. a. One substance is a <u>compound</u>.

   b. Two or more elements make a <u>compound</u>.

3. a. She always thinks <u>critically</u> about her work; she's quite analytical.

   b. She always thinks <u>critically</u> about her work; she's quite illogical.

4. a. When dust moves, it can often be seen <u>floating around</u> in air.

   b. When dust is settled, it can often be seen <u>floating around</u> an object.

5. a. The conditions for the experiment were <u>ideal</u>; we heard everyone's opinion.

   b. The conditions for the experiment were <u>ideal</u>; they were just perfect.

6 a. Marta can <u>relate to</u> the challenges you face with science class; Marta thinks it's easy.

   b. I can <u>relate to</u> the challenges you face with science class; I have them, too.

Go to MyEnglishLab to complete a vocabulary and skill practice and to join in collaborative activities.

# SUPPORTING SKILL 1

## IDENTIFYING ORGANIZATIONAL PATTERNS IN DENSE LECTURES

**WHY IT'S USEFUL** By recognizing organizational patterns when listening to a dense lecture, you can better detect the main ideas, key words and phrases, and comprehend the information being presented.

College lectures can be challenging. Lecturers often present a lot of information, in a short period of time. Some speakers may be fast-paced and blend words together while others may speak slowly, with little or no inflection. Adjusting to diverse classroom styles may take time. However, there are several strategies you can employ to help you to adapt to a wide variety of lecture styles, and better organize the dense content being presented.

First, identify the **organizational pattern** of the lecture. The organizational structure is the framework of the entire lecture. There are several different organizational patterns, and each pattern has a unique purpose, and signal words that can help you determine the pattern. Look at the chart.

| Pattern | Purpose | Signal words/phrases |
| --- | --- | --- |
| Cause-Effect | to illustrate either the cause or effect | an effect, a reason, as a result, in order to, this is due to, for this reason, because of, the cause of this, a consequence |
| Compare-Contrast | to show what is similar and what is different about two or more things | like, similarly, unlike, different from, characteristics |
| Descriptive | to describe a topic deeply. This usually includes a definition, characteristics and even advantages and disadvantages. | describe, define, the first characteristic, another trait, attribute, advantage, disadvantage, benefit, downside |
| Historical | to outline events/actions by time periods | first, next, secondly, not long after, initially, finally |
| Problem-Solution | to outline a problem, and possible solutions to the problem | a problem, a solution, a challenge |

Once you have identified the organizational pattern, the number of main ideas may be clearer to visualize. Keep in mind that lecturers will repeat new technical vocabulary and **key ideas**. Any repeated ideas or terms are most likely critical for the overall comprehension of the lecture. Last, listen for **phrases that summarize** or conclude an idea. These words and phrases give you a clue that the key ideas are going to be restated, but also that a new idea will soon be introduced.

| Words/phrases to summarize | Words/phrases to conclude |
|---|---|
| To briefly highlight/summarize, | Given these points, |
| In summary, | In the final analysis, |
| In short, | Ultimately, |
| To sum up, | Before I end, |
| By and large, | |

For examples of different lecture patterns refer to these units: cause and effect, see Earth Sciences, Part 1; compare and contrast, see Linguistics; descriptive, see Business Ethics, Part 2 , or Materials Engineering, Part 2; historical, see Earth Sciences, Part 1; problem-solution, see Materials Engineering, Part 1.

## VOCABULARY PREVIEW

Read the vocabulary items in the box. Circle the ones you know. Put a question mark next to the ones you don't know.

| | | | | | |
|---|---|---|---|---|---|
| characteristic | distinguish | deform | conductor | vanish | distinct |

## EXERCISE 2

A. Work with a partner. Look at the slide from the lecture on the next page and complete the tasks.

1. Predict the organizational pattern of the lecture based on clues from the slide.

2. Circle the technical terms on the slide that you think the professor will define.

## Metals

- **Definition**
- **Characteristics**
  - ○ Malleability, ductility, elasticity, hardness
- **Properties**
  - ○ Heat conductors, melting ability, reforming ability
- **Metallic bonding**
- **Purposes**

**B. Listen to a lecture on the material properties of metals. Circle the key words that you heard. Was your prediction in Part A correct?**

| define | describe | characteristics | trait |
| --- | --- | --- | --- |

**CULTURE NOTE**

Table salt is a common seasoning around the world. The salt we have on our tables is a compound of sodium chloride and other minerals. Freshly mined salt, and salt from the sea have slightly different chemical compositions. While these types of salt are used in many things from the manufacturing of plastics to paper, they are also consumed. Sea salt is a coarser salt, and is popular for cooking and seasoning.

**C. Listen again and match each new technical term with its definition.**

1. Metals are .............
2. Malleability refers to .............
3. Ductility is .............
4. Elasticity is .............
5. Hardness refers to .............
6. Metallic bonding is .............

a. how metals can be deformed.

b. the ability to withstand friction.

c. solid elements that are distinguished by bonding properties.

d. a form of molecular bonding.

e. how flexible a metal is.

f. how metals have the ability to return to their original shape.

**D.** Work with a partner. Complete the slide by adding a definition of metals, metallic bonding, and list various purposes of metals.

## Metals

● **Definition** ...................................................................................................................................

● **Characteristics**

    ○ Malleability, ductility, elasticity, hardness

● **Properties**

    ○ Heat conductors, melting ability, reforming ability

● **Metallic bonding** .......................................................................................................................

● **Purposes** .....................................................................................................................................

## VOCABULARY CHECK

**A.** Review the vocabulary items in the Vocabulary Preview. Write their definitions and add examples. Use a dictionary if necessary.

**B.** Complete the sentences with the correct vocabulary items.

1. A ........................... is a material that allows electrons to move freely.

2. There are several things that ........................... electrons from protons.

3. First, one notable ........................... is that electrons have a negative charge.

4. Heat can cause materials to change their shape or ........................... .

5. There are several ........................... or marked features of conductors and insulators.

6. During the experiment, electrons seemed to ........................... and then reappear.

❖ Go to MyEnglishLab to complete vocabulary and skill practices and to join in collaborative activities.

# SUPPORTING SKILL 2
## ORGANIZING RESPONSES IN COMPLEX DISCUSSIONS

**WHY IT'S USEFUL** By organizing your responses in complex discussions, you can present your ideas coherently and cohesively. This will aid your listeners' understanding and allow for a more productive conversation.

In many college classrooms, part of your overall grade involves participation: in-class participation, partner work, and small group work. These all require that you listen to your professors and classmates, and respond to them. To respond clearly, you will need to **organize your responses**, especially when the class or group discussions involve complex topics. There are several factors you need to consider when organizing your responses.

First, consider your language style. Your language varies depending on the situation you are in (setting), who you are talking to (relationship), and what you are discussing (subject). How you would respond in a classroom might be very different than how you would respond while in a study group at someone's dormitory. The relationship you have with your listeners also impacts how you respond. You may respond more formally when answering a question from a professor, but respond very informally to a question from a friend or peer. Finally, the subject you are discussing influences the language used. When discussing an academic topic, your language will be more formal than while talking about an everyday topic like what the cafeteria is serving for lunch. The setting, the relationship you have to the listeners, and the subject determine the formality of the language you use.

> **Formal**: I'm very sorry, but I didn't quite understand what you said about the conductivity of ceramics.

> **Informal**: Sorry, I missed something. What'd you say about ceramics and electrical properties?

Next, you need to formulate organized responses. Using the **Triple A method:** *acknowledge, agree (or disagree)*, and *add to* can help you. In the first step, you acknowledge by restating or paraphrasing what you hear to confirm that you understood it correctly. In the second step, you agree or disagree with the information that you have acknowledged. Finally, in the third, you add to your statement by giving the reasoning behind your position. Look at the chart.

| Function | Formal signal words/phrases | Formal examples | Informal signal words/phrases | Informal examples |
|---|---|---|---|---|
| Acknowledge (restate) | I understand what you're saying | I understand what you're saying about ceramics having favorable mechanical properties. | I see what you mean. | I see what you mean about ceramics being great insulators. |
| Agree/ Disagree | Ways to agree: I agree. I definitely agree. I completely agree. Ways to disagree: I'm afraid I don't agree with you. I'm not sure I agree with you. I see your point, but… | I understand what you're saying about ceramics having favorable mechanical properties; however, I'm not sure I agree with you about their strength. | Ways to agree: Good point. I see what you mean. Ways to disagree: Well, even so… Yes and no… Yes, but the thing is… Don't you think that…? | Yes, ceramics are great insulators, but the thing is, metals are even better. |
| Add to | I'd like to add… The reason I agree/disagree is… | I understand what you're saying about ceramics having favorable mechanical properties; however, I'm not sure I agree with you about their strength. The reason is glass is a ceramic, and it breaks quite easily. | What's more, On top of that, As a matter of fact, In any case, At any rate, Not to mention… | At any rate, both ceramics and metals have beneficial properties. |

## VOCABULARY PREVIEW

Read the vocabulary items in the box. Circle the ones you know. Put a question mark next to the ones you don't know.

| | | | |
|---|---|---|---|
| stiff | efficient | insulator | apply to |
| brittle | radiate outward | shatter | evenly |

## EXERCISE 3

A. Look at the list of everyday products. Write *M* next to those that you believe are made of metal. Write *C* next to those that you believe are made of ceramics, and write *MC* next to those that can be made of both metal and ceramics.

.............. alarm clock                      .............. cookware

.............. ear buds                          .............. computer

.............. oven                              .............. vases

.............. televisions                       .............. cutlery (knives, forks, spoons)

.............. vacuum cleaner

B. Compare your list with a partner's. Are they similar? Discuss why some products might have a metal version and a ceramic version.

C. Listen to a study group discussion on ceramics and metals. Answer the questions.

> **Glossary**
>
> Silicone: a synthetic compound
>
> Crystalline molecular structure: a structure of ions, molecules or atoms held together in a three-dimensional arrangement
>
> Conductivity: the ability or power to conduct or transmit heat, electricity, or sound

1. Where do you think these two students are?

2. What do you think their relationship is?

3. What is the topic of their conversation?

4. Do you think their language style is formal or informal? Give examples from the listening to support your idea.

🔊 **D. Listen again. How does each student employ the Triple A method? Fill in the blanks.**

1. "I hear that televisions have a lot of ceramic material in them."

   Acknowledge: ......................................................................................................

   Agree or disagree: ..............................................................................................

   Add to: ................................................................................................................

2. "These ceramics form hard, stiff crystalline molecular structures that are very strong and they're supposed to be excellent insulators for heat-proofing."

   Acknowledge: ......................................................................................................

   Agree or disagree: ..............................................................................................

   Add to: ................................................................................................................

3. "If those stoves conducted heat so efficiently that most of it radiated outward, how were those metal stoves able to cook effectively?"

   Acknowledge: ......................................................................................................

   Agree or disagree: ..............................................................................................

   Add to: ................................................................................................................

**E. Work with a partner. Discuss the everyday products from Part A. Take turns giving an opinion, and using the Triple A method for responding.**

A: I can see why metals are so popular in the production of cookware. They're great conductors of heat.

B: I see why you would say that, and I agree that they heat very well. To add to that, they also hold heat for a long time, making them great servingware as well.

## VOCABULARY CHECK

**A. Review the vocabulary items in the Vocabulary Preview. Write their definitions and add examples. Use a dictionary if necessary.**

**B. Complete the sentences with the correct vocabulary items.**

1. Glass breaks easily. When it hits the floor, it can just ..................... .

2. If something is ..................... it does not bend easily.

3. We learned a new theory about steel in class, and I'm not convinced it will ..................... all types of steel.

4. They've added new curtains to their living room, and they act like an
..................... ; they help keep the cold out.

5. New microwave ovens are very ..................... ; they use little energy.

6. Ceramics are very ..................... , so they're easily broken.

7. During the experiment, the students need to apply a substance ..................... to
glass plate.

8. Heat from artificial sources tend to ..................... , or extend from the center.

⊙ Go to MyEnglishLab to complete vocabulary and skill practices and to join in
collaborative activities.

## INTEGRATED SKILLS
### COMPARING AND CONTRASTING TEXTBOOKS AND LECTURES

**WHY IT'S USEFUL**  By identifying the differences and similarities between how
information is organized in a textbook and how it is organized in a lecture, you can
better identify and retain key information.

Textbooks and class lectures are two ways in which new information is communicated
in college. Each has a unique purpose, organizational style, and benefits. Becoming
familiar with their differences can help you fully comprehend the course content.

Compare the excerpt below with the excerpt on page 118.

Textbook Excerpt

## Ionic and Covalent Bonds

**Ionic bonds** are a type of chemical bond which occurs when a metal atom "loans"
one or more electrons to another atom. This results in both atoms having a full outer
shell of electrons, with the metal becoming a positively-charged ion and the nonmetal
becoming a negatively-charged ion. **Covalent bonds** are similar in many ways, but
involve two atoms sharing electrons, without altering the atom's charge.

"First, let's discuss metallic bonds. Uh, be sure to write down a definition of metallic bonding, and maybe even a diagram of how it works. This will come up again and again in future classes! Anyway, in practical terms, the way that metal atoms link with each other in metallic bonding, along with a metal's numerous unconnected electrons, is the reason that metals can be manipulated in so many ways."

## Textbooks

As you have probably noticed, the textbook excerpt has a heading, and words in bold. Textbooks often arrange information by headings, making the overall organization of the information quite clear. If you removed all the text that is not a heading, or a word in bold, you would probably see a clear outline of the information. In addition, textbook readings are often dense; they contain a lot of information with few examples. However, a great advantage with a textbook is that you can read it again and again to extract information. To successfully identify and extract that information, consider using the **P2R method**.

P2R stands for: **preview**, **read**, and **review**. The first stage, *previewing*, involves scanning through the assigned pages, and noticing the headings, words in bold, images, and other visual elements. While you are previewing, ask yourself questions about the headings and bold words. For example: What are ionic and covalent bonds? How are they similar? How are they different?

You may even use the heading and bold words to construct an outline, such the one below.

I. Ionic and covalent bonds
   a. Ionic:
   b. Covalent:

The next stage in the P2R method is *read*, and it involves reading through the information several times. The first time you read, focus on answering the questions you asked yourself in the preview stage and on filling in the outline you created.

The final stage is *review*. In this stage, you read the information again in order to check and add to your information. This may mean filling in gaps in your outline or simply verifying the information you wrote down.

## Lectures

In contrast, lectures have no visual cues, such as headings or words in bold to help you, and the language is often less concise and formal. Although the language and the environment may be more informal, professors often have their own method of emphasizing important ideas. They may begin by introducing the topic and giving an overview of the entire lecture. They often draw attention to key words and ideas by repeating them. Lecturers offer explanations, give concrete examples, and repeat or paraphrase difficult concepts. Most importantly, lectures, unlike textbooks, are interactive. They provide an opportunity in real time to ask the professor for clarification on any questions you have about the material.

In order to prepare for the lecture, it is best to read the textbook material before class and take notes. Using your reading notes in the lectures can help to make complex readings clearer by adding authentic examples and explanations. Bring your reading notes to the lecture, and fill in any gaps you may have in them.

## EXERCISE 4

**A. Use the P2R method. Preview the excerpt from the textbook. Then write four questions and an outline.**

### Glossary

**Proton:** a very small piece of matter with a positive electrical charge that is in the central part of an atom

**Neutron:** a part of an atom that has no electrical charge

**Nonmetal:** a chemical element that does not have the properties of a metal

**Charge:** the physical property of matter that causes it to experience a force when placed in an electromagnetic field

**Ductile:** the adjective form of *ductility*; can be stretched without breaking

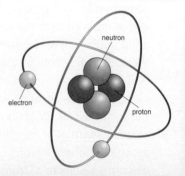

# CHEMICAL BONDING

Atoms contain electrons, protons, and neutrons. Electrons are found in the shell that surrounds the nucleus of an atom. **Valence electrons** are those in the outermost ring of an atom's electron cloud, making the atom reactive. This reactivity contributes to atoms bonding with other atoms. These bonds are referred to as chemical bonds. **Chemical bonds** are the ways in which different atoms bond, or connect with, each other. There are two main categories: **primary bonding** and **secondary bonding**. This section covers primary bonding; secondary bonding is covered in Chapter 6.

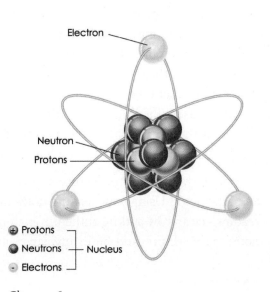

Electron

Neutron

Protons

⊕ Protons
● Neutrons ⎱ Nucleus
- Electrons ⎰

## Primary Bonding

**Primary bonding**, strong in nature, occurs when atoms join, or bond together, by sharing or transferring electrons. There are three main types of primary bonding. **Ionic bonds** are a type of chemical bond which occurs when a metal atom "loans" one or more electrons to another atom, a nonmetal. This results in both atoms having a full outer shell of electrons, with the metal becoming a positively-charged ion and the nonmetal becoming a negatively-charged ion. **Covalent bonds** are similar to Ionic bonds, but involve two atoms sharing electrons, without altering the atom's charge. Covalent bonds occur between a pair of nonmetals, and the electrons are shared between the pair. Water is an example of a covalent bond. **Metallic bonds** involve electron sharing. In metallic bonding, the valence electrons are not localized on one atom, but rather clouding over a large number of surrounding atoms. This sharing of electrons results in a strong, high-elastic, high-ductility, high-conductivity material.

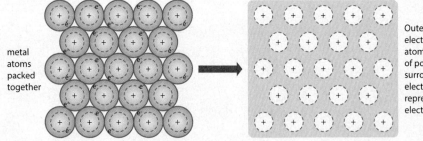

metal atoms packed together

Outer energy level (shell) electrons are lost from atoms leaving a lattice of positive metal ions surrounded by delocalized electrons. The shaded area represents the delocalized electrons.

B. Now carefully read the excerpt on page 120 and answer your questions from Part A. Then complete the outline.

Topic: Chemical Bonding

I.

    A. Valence electrons make atom reactive; part of chemical bonding

II. Two types of bonding

    A.

       1. strong

       2.

       3. Three types:

          a.

             i. metal atom loans electrons to another atom, nonmetal

          b. Covalent bonds

             i.

             ii. Ex:

          c.

             i. involve electron sharing

    B. Secondary bonding

C. Listen to a short lecture on the same topic. Take notes.

D. Work with a partner. Compare your notes and discuss what you can add to your outline.

Go to MyEnglishLab to complete a skill practice.

For more about **MATERIALS ENGINEERING**, see [R] 1 and [W] 1.

## LANGUAGE SKILL

### USING LANGUAGE OF COMPARISON AND CONTRAST

**WHY IT'S USEFUL** By identifying and utilizing language for comparing and contrasting, you can differentiate between the similarities and differences of things.

Go to MyEnglishLab for the Language Skill presentation and practice.

# VOCABULARY STRATEGY

## LEARNING VOCABULARY THROUGH GRAPHIC ORGANIZERS

**WHY IT'S USEFUL** By utilizing a graphic organizer to learn vocabulary, you can better understand new terms, their characteristics, and how to use them successfully.

The fields of science and engineering contain difficult and complex terms. Learning this vocabulary is like learning a new language. Simply memorizing these terms is not an option since what you really need to understand is their application in the field. Using a graphic organizer can help you "visually" understand the word. You can also use the graphic to understand attributes or characteristics, examples, relationships to other key terms, and even non-examples.

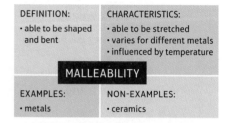

| DEFINITION: | CHARACTERISTICS: |
|---|---|
| • able to be shaped and bent | • able to be stretched<br>• varies for different metals<br>• influenced by temperature |
| **MALLEABILITY** | |
| EXAMPLES: | NON-EXAMPLES: |
| • metals | • ceramics |

A popular vocabulary graphic, the Frayer model, contains the key word or phrase, its definition, its characteristics or attributes, and examples and non-examples. A non-example is something that has some of the same characteristics as an example, but is missing its most important characteristic. Non-examples are important because they can help you make connections to other terms, and clearly state what is similar and what is different. Graphic organizers are not only a great way to learn key vocabulary, but they can be helpful study aids.

## EXERCISE 5

### A. Read the excerpts and circle the key terms being discussed.

**Excerpt One**
Ionic Bonds are a type of strong chemical bond which occur when a metal atom "loans" one or more electrons to another nonmetal atom—for instance, sodium chloride (table salt). This results in both atoms having a full outer shell of electrons, with the metal becoming a positively-charged ion and the nonmetal becoming a negatively-charged ion.

**Excerpt Two**
Covalent bonds are similar to ionic bonds, but involve two atoms *sharing* electrons, without altering the atom's charge. Covalent bonds occur between a pair of nonmetals, and the electrons are shared between the pair. Water is an example of a covalent bond.

**Excerpt Three**
Metallic bonds involve electron sharing. In metallic bonding the valence electrons are not centered on one atom, but rather they cloud over a large number of surrounding atoms. This sharing of electrons results in a strong, highly-elastic, highly-ductile, and highly-conductive material, like iron.

**B. Complete each graphic organizer using the key terms from the excerpts in Part A.**

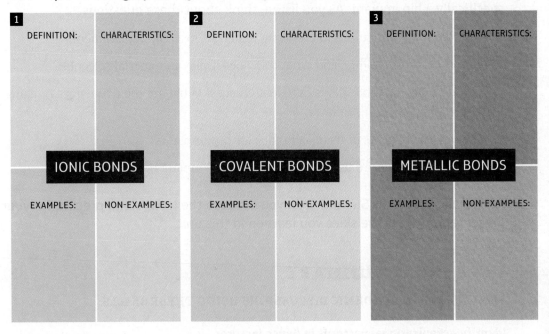

**1**

DEFINITION:   CHARACTERISTICS:

IONIC BONDS

EXAMPLES:   NON-EXAMPLES:

**2**

DEFINITION:   CHARACTERISTICS:

COVALENT BONDS

EXAMPLES:   NON-EXAMPLES:

**3**

DEFINITION:   CHARACTERISTICS:

METALLIC BONDS

EXAMPLES:   NON-EXAMPLES:

**C. Work with a partner. Compare and contrast your graphic organizers.**

## APPLY YOUR SKILLS

**WHY IT'S USEFUL**  By applying the skills you have learned in this unit, you will be able to understand and participate in academic discussions in college-level courses.

**ASSIGNMENT**
Prepare a presentation with a partner comparing and contrasting the advantages of using a metal or ceramic in the production of an everyday product.

### BEFORE YOU LISTEN

**A. Before you listen, discuss the questions with one or more students.**

1. Biomaterials engineering is a combination of biology and materials engineering. Biomaterials engineers study how materials interact with living organisms like humans. Can you think of some examples of materials that interact with humans?

2. What are some medical uses for materials created with ceramics and metals? How do they support human health and well-being?

3. What are some disadvantages, or problems, associated with artificial materials used in the human body?

B. You will listen to a lecture on how materials are chosen for medical implants, specifically a hip implant. As you listen, think about these questions.

1. What are some difficulties in choosing materials for a hip replacement?

2. What is biocompatibility, and what role does it play in material selection?

3. Why are biocompatible alloys excellent choices? What are the downsides of using these alloys?

4. What are the benefits of using ceramics for hip implants?

5. What are materials are used in current-day hip implants? Why?

C. Review the Unit Skills Summary. As you listen to the lecture and prepare for your presentation, apply the skills you learned in this unit.

## UNIT SKILLS SUMMARY

### PARTICIPATE IN ACADEMIC DISCUSSIONS USING THESE SKILLS:

**Identify organizational patterns in dense lectures**

• Listen for key words to detect the organizational pattern.
• Recognize signal words that indicate a summary or conclusion.

**Organize responses in complex discussions**

• Determine the language style by considering the setting, the relationship, and the subject.
• Employ the Triple A method: *acknowledge, agree/disagree, add to.*

**Compare and contrast textbooks and lectures**

• Build background knowledge with the P2R method: *preview, read, review.*
• Extract details and examples from a lecture to synthesize content.

**Utilize language for comparing and contrasting**

• Distinguish between similarities and differences.
• Utilize comparatives, superlatives, and words and phrases of comparison and contrast.

**Utilize a graphic organizer to learn new words**

• Determine the meaning of new words by identifying their definitions, characteristics, examples, and non-examples.

## LISTEN

A. Listen to a lecture on how materials are chosen for medical implants, specifically a hip implant. Take notes.

B. Compare your notes with a partner. Do you both have the same key ideas? What skills from this unit can help you identify key ideas?

C. Review the questions from Before You Listen, Part B. Listen to the lecture again. Work with a partner and use your notes on the lecture to answer the questions.

Go to MyEnglishLab to listen more closely, and answer the critical thinking questions.

## THINKING CRITICALLY

Discuss the questions with another student.

1. Based on the lecture, what is the primary concern with products that will be placed in a human body? What problems could arise if the wrong materials were used?

2. When making products like hip implants, the right material may be the difference between life and death. In what other products are the choice of material so important?

3. The professor brings up polymers. What can be inferred about their use?

## THINKING VISUALLY

A. Look at the diagram. Discuss the questions with a partner.

1. Why is ceramic used for the parts labeled ceramic?

2. Why is metal used for the parts labeled metal?

3. What might happen if all the parts were metal?

Metal

Ceramic

Metal

> **TIP**
>
> To describe a diagram, move from one part of the diagram to the other. For the diagram in Part A, begin with the largest part, the metal piece that is angled, then move up to the other pieces. For example, "Here is an image of the parts of a hip replacement. The largest piece is angular and is made of metal. It is attached to two ceramic pieces, which are attached to a final metal piece."

B. Go online and investigate another implant. Then create a diagram like the one above, noting what components are made from. Share your diagram, summarizing the information for your classmates.

Go to MyEnglishLab to record your results.

## THINKING ABOUT LANGUAGE

Complete each sentence with signal words for making comparisons or contrasts.

1. There are .................... between hip implants from the 20th century and hip implants from the 21st century. Today, we use a combination of materials.

2. Ceramics are used in the production of electronics. .................... , metals are used in the production of electronics.

3. Doctors and materials engineers .................... must take into account how a product will affect a human body.

4. Ceramics lack elasticity. .................... , metals are flexible.

5. Putting the wrong material in the human body is .................... poisoning someone.

6. A shoulder joint is not load-bearing; .................... , a hip joint is load-bearing.

## PAIR PRESENTATION

A. Work with a partner. Think about the lecture, and the other information presented in the unit. There are definite benefits to using metals or ceramics to produce certain products. Brainstorm the characteristics of these materials.

B. You and a partner will prepare a presentation on an everyday product and the materials used to produce it. Consider microwaves, ovens, stoves, car tires, airplane parts, computers, and televisions. You will research and summarize your findings about why a certain material was chosen for that product. Think about these questions as you research and prepare.

1. What are some everyday products that you would like to learn more about?

2. What materials is the product made of? Why?

3. Why were other materials not appropriate for the product?

C. Listen to each presentation.

Listen carefully to each presentation and take notes. Then, use your notes to discuss the questions. Use the Triple A method to organize your responses during your discussion.

1. Which materials are used more frequently? Why?

2. What are specific advantages to using that material?

⬆ Go to MyEnglishLab to watch Professor Heilshorn's concluding video and to complete a self-assessment.

# Critical Thinking Skills

*Part 2 moves from skill building to application of the skills that require critical thinking. Practice activities tied to specific learning outcomes in each unit require a deeper level of understanding of the academic content.*

*Language communicates who we are*

# LINGUISTICS

# Facts and Opinions

## UNIT PROFILE

In this unit, you will learn about the differences between accents and dialects. You will also investigate variations of accents and dialects across the United States.

**You will prepare a class debate on the advantages and disadvantages of having and using a single, "official" national dialect throughout the country.**

## OUTCOMES

• Recognize phrases that signal a fact or an opinion

• Utilize idioms to add emphasis and variety in discussions

• Detect bias in listening texts

• Identify and utilize change-of-topic signals

• Create an idiom journal to learn useful new idioms and their usage

For more about **LINGUISTICS**, see ① ③ . See also R and W **LINGUISTICS** ① ② ③ .

# GETTING STARTED

⟩ Go to MyEnglishLab to watch Professor Podesva's introductory video and to complete a self-assessment.

**Discuss these questions with a partner or group.**

1. Do all speakers of your native language sound the same? What are some differences?

2. What influences, or changes, the way a particular language is spoken from one place to another?

3. In Professor Podevsa's introduction, he states that accents and dialects are different. What do you think the difference might be?

# CRITICAL THINKING SKILL

## DISTINGUISHING FACTS FROM OPINIONS

**WHY IT'S USEFUL**  By distinguishing a fact from an opinion, you can determine what is simply a belief and what is real, or based on evidence. This aids in identifying a speaker's position and evaluating the reliability of the speaker's information.

Typically, in North American college classrooms, students must listen carefully to class discussions and presentations in addition to lectures from the professor. While listening in these situations, students need to be able to **distinguish facts from opinions**. A *fact* is information that can be proven, whereas an opinion represents someone's viewpoint. An *opinion* can be discussed and debated; however, it cannot be proven. It is not always easy to determine which information is a fact, and which is an opinion. Speakers can subtly include opinions in ways that can make them sound like facts.

To determine if something is a fact or an opinion, pay close attention to the words and phrases the speaker uses. Speakers often introduce a fact with a phrase that lets you know the information is supported by evidence and can be proven. Many of these phrases include the word *fact*; however, some do not. Speakers often introduce an opinion with a phrase. Many times these phrases are descriptive. Descriptive phrases appeal to our emotions and are subjective.

Paying close attention to the phrases used to introduce information can help you determine if the information is a fact or an opinion. However, be aware that speakers often use a mix of facts and opinions when presenting information. Differentiating between the two involves listening closely and evaluating word choice.

## VOCABULARY PREVIEW

Read the vocabulary items in the box. Circle the ones you know. Put a question mark next to the ones you don't know.

| | | |
|---|---|---|
| set the record straight | variations | corrupt |
| get in the way of | authentic | forceful |

## EXERCISE 1

🔊 **A.** Listen to a lecture about the difference between a dialect and an accent. Answer the questions.

1. What facts does the professor use to show the difference?

2. How do you know these are facts?

🔊 **B.** Listen again. Answer the questions.

1. What opinion does the professor offer regarding dialects?

2. How do you know it is an opinion?

**C.** What phrases could you use to introduce a fact? How about an opinion? Compare your phrases with a partner.

🔊 **D.** Now listen to a conversation between two students after the lecture. Note the phrases they use to introduce their opinions on the topic.

## VOCABULARY CHECK

A. Review the vocabulary items in the Vocabulary Preview. Write their definitions and add examples. Use a dictionary if necessary.

B. Complete the sentences with vocabulary items from the box.

| | | |
|---|---|---|
| authentic | forceful | get in the way of |
| corrupted | variations | set the record straight |

1. Mike told me what really happened. He felt that he needed to ..................... .

2. We have heard many ..................... of the New England accent, but the most unique one is the Boston accent.

3. There is a ..................... file on my computer, and it just happens to be my research paper for Linguistics.

4. There is a comedian I like to watch who imitates all kinds of accents; I wonder which is his ..................... accent.

5. Jami can be pretty ..................... when she wants to be, she expressed some strong, powerful feelings in that meeting.

6. Please don't ..................... of our work right now; we don't want to be interrupted.

⊙ Go to MyEnglishLab to complete a vocabulary and skill practice and to join in collaborative activities.

# SUPPORTING SKILL 1

## USING SIGNAL PHRASES TO STATE FACTS AND OPINIONS

**WHY IT'S USEFUL** By recognizing signal words and phrases that indicate a fact or opinion, you can better evaluate whether the content can be proven or is simply a belief. By incorporating signal words and phrases into your own speech, you can clarify which statements are facts and beliefs for your own listeners.

Speakers use a combination of facts and opinions to present content. Distinguishing between the two is critical to understanding the content and a speaker's position. A fact is supported by evidence, has been proven true, and is measurable. Some facts are common knowledge. Opinions, on the other hand, are beliefs; they are subjective, and are often used to make an emotional appeal. Opinions may be believed by many people, but that alone does not make them true. It is critical to make the distinction between facts and opinions to have a clear understanding of the information.

The words and phrases used by a speaker can often help distinguish between the two. While opinions are easily identifiable by the use of *I believe* and *I think*, there are many other phrases that also mark an opinion. The same is true for a fact. Dates, numbers, and statistics are easily identifiable as facts. Speakers also use phrases prior to stating the fact that help listeners know the information is true, and has been proven. We call these phrases **signals**.

| Signals for a fact | Signals for an opinion |
|---|---|
| In fact | Personally speaking |
| As a matter of fact | As far as I'm concerned |
| The fact is | From what I know/from my point of view |
| It's a known fact that | It has been my experience |
| It is certain that | My interpretation of this is |
| It has been determined that | It's likely that |

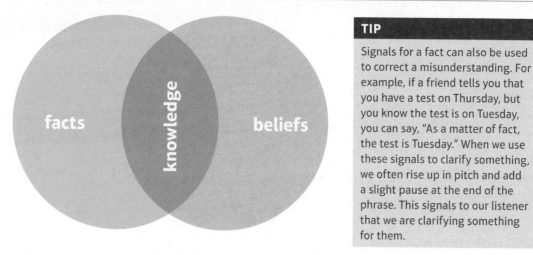

**TIP**

Signals for a fact can also be used to correct a misunderstanding. For example, if a friend tells you that you have a test on Thursday, but you know the test is on Tuesday, you can say, "As a matter of fact, the test is Tuesday." When we use these signals to clarify something, we often rise up in pitch and add a slight pause at the end of the phrase. This signals to our listener that we are clarifying something for them.

In addition to listening for signals, it is also important to ask yourself a few questions. Because facts can be proven, ask yourself if the information is verifiable. Since opinions indicate beliefs, ask yourself if the statement indicates how someone feels, thinks, or believes.

## VOCABULARY PREVIEW

**Read the vocabulary items in the box. Circle the ones you know. Put a question mark next to the ones you don't know.**

| | | | | | |
|---|---|---|---|---|---|
| prestige | prosperous | the cutting edge | criticized | stereotype | trickled down |

## EXERCISE 2

**A. Brainstorm with a partner. Think of a dialect that is particularly unique or different. What are three things that make it unique?**

> ### Glossary
> **Sociolect:** the dialect used by a certain social class
> **Discourse marker:** words or phrases that help us organize and connect our speaking and writing

**B. Listen to three students discussing a unique dialect of American English. Answer the questions.**

1. What dialect is being discussed?

2. Where did it originate?

3. Who speaks this dialect?

4. What are two of its features?

**C. Listen again and choose the phrases you hear that signal a fact or an opinion.**

**Signals for facts**

☐ It's a fact
☐ In fact
☐ As a matter of fact
☐ It's a known fact
☐ It is certain

**Signals for opinions**

☐ Personally speaking
☐ As far as I'm concerned
☐ From my point of view
☐ It has been my experience
☐ My interpretation of this is

> **CULTURE NOTE**
> Valspeak, or the Valley Girl dialect, became very well-known in the 1980s when a popular movie about that area, entitled *Valley Girl*, was released. The movie's influence spread across the United States, and many young people began adding the discourse marker "like" to their speech.

Even without signal phrases, you can often tell just by listening if someone is stating an opinion by the way they speak. Because opinions involve our emotions, they are often stated with a more emphatic tone. That is, opinions are stated more forcefully or louder, longer, and clearer. A good way to identify an opinion without a signal is to listen closely to the emotion in the speaker's voice. Speakers who are passionate about their beliefs indicate it by using a stronger voice with a greater pitch rise.

D. Work with a partner. Practice giving your opinion about Valspeak. Be sure to use a signal phrase to indicate your opinion.

E. Work with a small group. Share features of unique dialects within your native languages. Be sure to give both facts and opinions and use appropriate signal phrases.

## VOCABULARY CHECK

A. Review the vocabulary items in the Vocabulary Preview. Write their definitions and add examples. Use a dictionary if necessary.

B. Complete the paragraph with vocabulary items from the box.

| | | |
|---|---|---|
| criticized | prosperous | the cutting edge |
| prestige | stereotype | trickled down |

Language is so interesting, but is also a way in which people make judgments about others, or _____ them. Some accents are _____—looked down or disapproved of. While there are other accents that carry a certain amount of _____ . This respect can make some _____ because it results in a high-paying job. However, many tech companies on _____ are not concerned how their employees speak, but are focused on their technological skills. This trend seems to have _____ to other industries as well, as we can hear diverse accents spoken by many corporate executives.

⬡ Go to MyEnglishLab to complete vocabulary and skill practices and to join in collaborative activities.

# SUPPORTING SKILL 2
## UTILIZING IDIOMS IN DISCUSSIONS

**WHY IT'S USEFUL**  By utilizing idioms in your discussion, you can add emphasis and variety to your speech.

Idioms are phrases that include two or more words that are not used literally. Idiomatic speech is commonly used in informal settings, including the college classroom. They often communicate a strong feeling, and add variety to a conversation. Understanding idioms is a critical part of participating in classroom discussion. When someone gives their opinion, idioms can provide an indicator of how strongly they may feel about something. Look at these examples:

A: I didn't complete the assignment for today. What did we have to do?

B: You're kidding! Professor Wills is going to go through the roof. He told us to be sure to complete it before class.

A: Oh, no! What should I do?

In this example, *go through the roof* indicates that someone is going to be very, very angry. This creates a strong feeling for anyone who hears it. Compare it to this example:

A: I didn't complete the assignment for today. What did we have to do?

B: You're kidding! Professor Wills is going to be upset. He told us to be sure to complete it before class.

A: Oh, so it's not a big deal.

You can see in the second example that the reaction is not nearly as strong as it was in the first. Using idioms makes a greater emotional appeal, which in turn often creates a greater reaction from the listeners.

Many idioms are formed by a verb + a phrase like *go through the roof*. In this case, it is a verb + a prepositional phrase. For examples of more idioms, see the chart on page 136.

| Idiom | Meaning |
| --- | --- |
| be on the same wavelength | in agreement |
| be on your last legs | tired; near the end of one's life |
| bear in mind | consider; think about |
| beat around the bush | avoid; not stating something directly |
| bent out of shape | angry; upset |
| cross your mind | to think about something; consider |
| draw a blank | to be unable to remember |
| draw a line | to put a limit on or stop to |
| give (someone) a hand | to help someone |
| give something a shot | try something |
| give the benefit of the doubt | to choose to believe something |
| have an open mind | be open-minded |
| leave no stone unturned | to do everything possible |
| make a long story short | get to the main point |
| run with an idea | go in that direction |
| read between the lines | find the hidden meaning or inference |
| speak your mind | say what you think |

## VOCABULARY PREVIEW

Read the vocabulary items in the box. Circle the ones you know. Put a question mark next to the ones you don't know.

| | | | |
| --- | --- | --- | --- |
| constitute | broad | minor | distinctive |
| classification | lose touch | subdivision | organically |

## EXERCISE 3

A. Work with a partner. How many dialects do you think exist in North America? What are some dialects you have heard in movies, TV, or in your daily life?

B. Listen to the academic discussion on North American dialects. Choose the ideas you hear.

☐ It's difficult to draw the line between a full dialect and a minor variation.

☐ There are seven dialects in California.

☐ There are several variations of dialects in England.

☐ Dialects from unknown areas can become known through a single person.

☐ Regions adopt dialects to sound different from others.

☐ New York City's dialect has changed since the early 20th century.

C. Listen again and choose the idiomatic expressions you hear.

| | | | |
|---|---|---|---|
| bear in mind | make a long story short | draw the line | have an open mind |
| draw a blank | read between the lines | ring any bells | speak your mind |

D. Work with a partner. Discuss an interesting dialect you have heard in a movie, online, or on TV. Use two to three idiomatic phrases when describing the dialect.

E. Share your ideas from Part D with the class.

## VOCABULARY CHECK

A. Review the vocabulary items in the Vocabulary Preview. Write their definitions and add examples. Use a dictionary if necessary.

B. Choose the sentence that correctly paraphrases the meaning of each underlined vocabulary item.

1. a. A distinctive accent is one that has distinguishing features or characteristics.

   b. A distinctive accent is one that represents a certain group of people.

2. a. Speakers of English in the United States constitute, or are equal to, a wide variety of accents.

   b. Speakers of English in the United States constitute, or consist of, a wide variety of accents.

*(Continued)*

3. a. There is a system of <u>classification</u>, or branding, of accents.

   b. There is a system of <u>classification</u>, or grouping, of accents.

4. a. There are wide-ranging, or <u>broad</u>, risks of stereotyping people by their accents.

   b. There are clear, or <u>broad</u>, risks of stereotyping people of their accents.

5. a. There are some <u>minor</u>, or little, differences between those two accents.

   b. There are some <u>minor</u>, or large, differences between those two accents.

6. a. Phonology is a <u>subdivision</u>, or different field, from Linguistics.

   b. Phonology is a <u>subdivision</u>, or a smaller part of, Linguistics.

7. a. It seems that the best ideas come up <u>organically</u>, or synthetically.

   b. It seems that the best ideas come up <u>organically</u>, or naturally.

8. a. I promised my friend that we would always stay connected, and not <u>lose touch</u>.

   b. I promised my friend that we would always live nearby one another, and not <u>lose touch</u>.

🔊 Go to MyEnglishLab to complete vocabulary and skill practices and to join in collaborative activities.

## INTEGRATED SKILLS

### DETECTING BIAS

**WHY IT'S USEFUL**  By detecting bias in reading and listening texts, you can determine how accurate and complete the information is. You can also identify the author's point of view, and the purpose of the text.

All speakers have their own opinions and sometimes these opinions directly affect the content being presented. This is known as **bias**. Bias involves making a judgment, or showing a preference towards or against something. Presenting information with a bias makes the information subjective. In other words, feelings influence how information is reported, which makes the accuracy of information uncertain.

Being aware of bias and knowing how to identify it are very important critical thinking skills. There are several things you can look for to determine what biases an author may hold.

## Generalizations

Generalizations are broad statements. They categorize something under one broad heading, and may include words like *all, every*, and *everyone*. Certain verbs also signal a generalization. These verbs are often non-specific verbs like *feel, believe, think*. In these cases, it is quite difficult to verify, or identify, if the information is proven.

**Everyone feels** English is a very difficult language to learn.

The words *everyone* and *feels* make the statement a generalization.

## Exaggerations

Exaggerations are when something is overstated, making it better or worse than it really is. Exaggeration is often used for effect.

He gave us enough homework **for a year**.

## Loaded Words

Loaded words are words that are emotionally charged. In other words, language that creates a strong emotion when heard. The purpose of using loaded words is to gain support, or sway someone's opinion about something. Many idiomatic phrases are loaded because they produce strong emotions in the listener.

He was really **bent out of shape** when I told him we needed to read long research articles for class tomorrow.

## Purposes

Frequently, the purpose of a presentation or piece of writing is to persuade. If the purpose is to persuade, then presenting your opinion is an essential tool. While it is important to make an emotional appeal, avoid using generalizations and exaggerations. These are not considered effective tools when persuading or making an argument in an academic context. However, because you still want to emotionally appeal to your listeners, strong loaded words can be used. In order to persuade without using biased language, present your opinion but support it with a fact.

Our accents are **an integral part** of our identities. This is proven by the research.

## EXERCISE 4

### A. Work with a partner. Write two examples under each heading.

| Generalizations | Exaggerations | Loaded Words |
|---|---|---|
| | | |
| | | |

B. Read the letter to the editor from a local newspaper. Then complete the tasks below.

# One nation, one dialect

**To The Editor:**

This nonsense surrounding dialects, and our leniency regarding them, simply must come to an end. How can the United States, as a nation, be expected to work towards common goals when we cannot even agree on the proper way to speak?

I recognize that dialect variations were an unfortunate reality for many years, but today all of us have the benefit of broadcast television and public education; if we so choose, we can set and enforce a national standard.

The benefits of this standardization would be numerous. I believe that the clear, easily-understood Midwestern dialect spoken by newscasters and many television personalities is easily learned and can be understood by all immigrants. I am 100 percent certain that using the Midwestern dialect would make it easier for everyone to learn English and assimilate in record time to the American way of life. Our school children would have clear goals and there would never be any doubt whatsoever surrounding grammar or speech.

At the very least, we should heavily promote the adoption of the perfect Midland dialect which we all agree to be the de facto standard. If we all spoke the same English, the playing field would be more level—fairer—when we apply for a job or entrance into a prestigious school. We wouldn't be unfairly judged by the accent we have. In the United Kingdom, dialect variation is still present, but everyone knows and agrees that the "Received Pronunciation" is the proper, prestigious way of speaking. Any dialects remaining are widely recognized as being inferior to this form of speech and are avoided in settings where clarity and good diction are valued.

The United States has an opportunity to take a greater step towards linguistic unity than even the United Kingdom! By naming and legislating a national dialect, we will improve both education and our sense of civic identity.

*David Kelley*
*Riverdale*

1. Circle the generalizations.

2. Underline the exaggerations.

3. Put a star next to loaded words.

**C.** Now read a response to the letter in Part B and answer the questions below.

# Diverse dialects celebrate our history and complexity

**To The Editor:**

In response to Mr. Kelley's letter on dialects, I would like to offer a concise explanation as to why the idea of "one nation, one dialect" is flawed—especially when discussing the United States. First, and this should be obvious to any student of history, there has never been one dialect of English which truly dominated the American landscape. Since it was formed in 1776, the nation we call the United States has always been home to not just multiple languages but also to multiple dialects. Settlers from particular areas of England, Scotland, and Ireland each brought their own vibrant forms of speech to the United States; these went on to become the dialects we know and use today.

Second, while modern broadcast and print media may create the illusion of a "standard" dialect, this is merely something mutually agreed upon for the sake of convenience. The broadcast standard of the early 20th century was far different than what we hear on the television today; it is only reasonable to expect that the broadcast standard heard a century from now will also be radically different. Dialects change, and this change is inevitable.

Finally, dialects are richly expressive and a source of enjoyment for many. Dialects lend authenticity to fiction and allow us to hear and appreciate the delightfully idiosyncratic speech of our fellow citizens in serious broadcasts. Presidents since the invention of radio, for example, were memorable because of their unique dialects and accents. How dreadfully dull would the world be if everyone spoke exactly the same!

*Susan Hunter Saldivar*
*Fordham*

1. What is the writer's position? How does it differ from the position of the writer of the first letter?

2. How does the writer persuade?

3. Is there biased language in the letter? What type of bias?

**D. Work with a partner. Compare and contrast the two letters. Use the questions to complete the Venn diagram below.**

1. What is the key argument in the first letter? How does the writer support this argument?

2. What is the key argument in the second letter? How does the writer support this argument?

3. Do the authors provide benefits for their positions? If so, what are they?

4. Which letter do you think makes a better argument? Why?

Letter One                    Letter Two

**E. Now work in small groups. Share your diagrams and discuss the questions.**

⬇ Go to MyEnglishLab to complete a skill practice.

# LANGUAGE SKILL
## USING CHANGE OF TOPIC SIGNALS

> **WHY IT'S USEFUL**  By identifying and utilizing signals that indicate a change in topic, you can easily follow what someone is saying, and make it easier for your listeners to follow your ideas.

⬇ Go to MyEnglishLab for the Language Skill presentation and practice.

# VOCABULARY STRATEGY
## CREATING AN IDIOM JOURNAL

> **WHY IT'S USEFUL**  By identifying and recording new idiomatic expressions, you can build your vocabulary and better comprehend colloquial English.

Idioms are a common part of spoken English. Native speakers use idioms in all types of settings because they provide vivid descriptions and create powerful images in the listeners' minds. Understanding idioms helps you to develop and better understand colloquial English. Colloquial English refers to the language that is commonly spoken in informal and everyday situations. When you are working with a group of students, listening to class discussions, or participating in a study group, you are likely to hear colloquial English.

One effective strategy to understand and acquire more idioms is to keep an idiom journal. An idiom journal is a place to record the new idiom, the sentence you heard it in, its meaning, and your own sentence. By doing so, you will have a collection of vocabulary that can easily be incorporated into your own speech.

| Idiom | Context idiom heard in | Meaning | My own sentence |
|---|---|---|---|
| read between the lines | To fully understand the author's position, you need to **read between the lines**. He didn't state it directly. | Find the implied meaning | I sometimes have to **read between the lines** when I am working with José. He doesn't always say exactly what he is thinking. |

## EXERCISE 5

**A. Read the conversation and underline all the idioms.**

**Chen:** Have you heard if you were accepted into the honors program yet?

**Alla:** No, I've been keeping an eye out. I can't wait to hear.

**Chen:** Maybe you should drop them a line. Have you thought about that?

**Alla:** I'm not sure writing them would speed things up. So, how about you? What's new with you?

**Chen:** Nothing much. I gave Darin a hand the other day. He moved to a new place, and he was trying to talk me into applying for the science scholarship.

**Alla:** You know, you should really give it a shot.

**Chen:** Do you really think so? I started the essay, but I was drawing a blank, so, I had a change of heart.

**Alla:** Why? You would love working with the science department. Go for it!

**B. Use the chart to start an idiom journal. Add the new idioms from above.**

| Idiom | Context Idiom Heard | Meaning | My Own Sentence |
|-------|---------------------|---------|-----------------|
|       |                     |         |                 |
|       |                     |         |                 |
|       |                     |         |                 |
|       |                     |         |                 |
|       |                     |         |                 |

**C. Work with a partner. Share an experience where you had a hard time understanding a dialect or accent. Incorporate two or three new idioms.**

# APPLY YOUR SKILLS

**WHY IT'S USEFUL** By applying the skills you have learned in this unit, you will be able to distinguish facts and opinions and determine the reliability of information in college-level courses.

## ASSIGNMENT
Prepare a class debate on the proposition of adopting and enforcing one dialect as the national standard. You and your group members will prepare an argument to either support or refute the proposition. You will use both facts and opinions to make your argument.

## BEFORE YOU LISTEN

A. Discuss the questions with one or more students.

1. Do you think it is easy to adopt a new dialect? Why or why not?

2. Why would someone want to change their speech?

3. Do you think the dialect you speak affects your success in life? Why or why not?

B. You will listen to a lecture on the differences between accents and dialects. As you listen, think about these questions.

1. How do dialects differ from accents?

2. How are dialects or accents recognizable to others?

3. How many dialects exist in the United States?

4. Does Standard American English really exist? Why or why not?

C. Review the Unit Skills Summary on page 146. As you listen to the lecture and prepare for your group presentation, apply the skills you learned in this unit.

## UNIT SKILLS SUMMARY

### DISTINGUISH FACTS AND OPINIONS USING THESE SKILLS:

**Identify facts and opinions**

- Identify phrases that signal a fact or an opinion.
- Recognize statistics and dates that indicate a fact.
- Listen for descriptive or emotive phrases that indicate an opinion.

**Recognize bias in listening and reading texts**

- Identify generalizations, exaggerations, and loaded vocabulary.
- Determine a speaker's purpose.

**Increase your benefit from lectures and class discussions**

- Recognize and utilize topic shifters.
- Utilize idioms in discussions to add variety to discussions.

**Learn new idioms by keeping a journal**

- Determine meaning from context.

## LISTEN

A. Listen to the lecture on accents and dialects. Take notes.

B. Compare your notes with a partner. Do you both have the same key ideas? What skills from this unit can help you identify key ideas?

C. Review the questions from Before You Listen, Part B. Listen to the lecture again. Work with a partner and use your notes on the lecture to answer the questions.

Go to MyEnglishLab to listen more closely and answer the critical thinking questions.

## THINKING CRITICALLY

Discuss the questions with another student.

1. How does the speaker feel about the need to recognize different dialects? How do you know?

2. Based on the lecture, how would you describe the speaker's opinion? In your discussion, provide examples that illustrate your understanding.

3. The professor makes the point that there is really no true Standard American English. How does she support his point? How does she feel about the wide variations of dialects?

## THINKING VISUALLY

**A.** Look at the graphic. Discuss the questions with a partner.

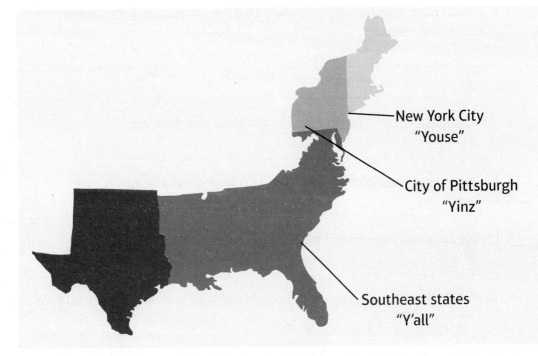

New York City
"Youse"

City of Pittsburgh
"Yinz"

Southeast states
"Y'all"

1. Which of the "you" terms have you heard before?

2. How do you think each variation developed?

3. What impact do you think speakers have on a language?

**B.** Go online and investigate dialects in your own country. How does language differ from one area to another? Create a map and highlight the differences. Share your map with your classmates. Discuss the differences. What could be responsible for the differences?

🔘 Go to MyEnglishLab to record your results.

## THINKING ABOUT LANGUAGE

**Read the sentences. Replace the underlined phrase with an idiom.**

1. Rav and I <u>have been searching</u> for the differences in dialects across parts of the United States.

   .................................................................................

   .................................................................................

2. We <u>are in agreement</u> regarding how many variations there are.

   .................................................................................

3. It's important to <u>consider</u> that language is constantly changing.

   .................................................................................

4. I really can't study anymore! I have to <u>stop</u> at the 10 hours we have been working.

   .................................................................................

5. You <u>have a chance</u> at winning the research grant. Your work is really ground-breaking.

   .................................................................................

6. We <u>are in the same situation</u>. I have a lot of research to complete before the due date.

   .................................................................................

## GROUP DEBATE

**A. Think about the lecture and the other information presented in the unit. Consider how having one officially accepted dialect or accepting several dialectics might impact education and the workplace. What do you think are the benefits and drawbacks of each? Complete the chart.**

|  | Benefits | Drawbacks |
|---|---|---|
| Accepting a variety of dialectical differences | | |
| Allowing only one standard dialect | | |

B. Share your chart with your classmates. Divide into two teams—in favor of a variety of dialects and in favor of one standard dialect. Follow these steps:

1. Alone, or with your team, research language practices in other countries to support your team's position.

2. Develop your position, using evidence from reliable sources.

3. Integrate your opinion with facts using signal phrases and idioms where possible.

4. Prepare for your debate against the other team.

C. Debate the issue. Follow these steps:

1. Establish the rules of your debate.

2. Each team takes a turn presenting its claims.

3. As the opposing team speaks, take notes.

4. Once the opposition has presented their argument, ask questions to ensure you understand the implications of their argument.

5. After the debate, take a class vote to determine which team supported their opinions best.

◉ Go to MyEnglishLab to watch Professor Podesva's concluding video and to complete a self-assessment.

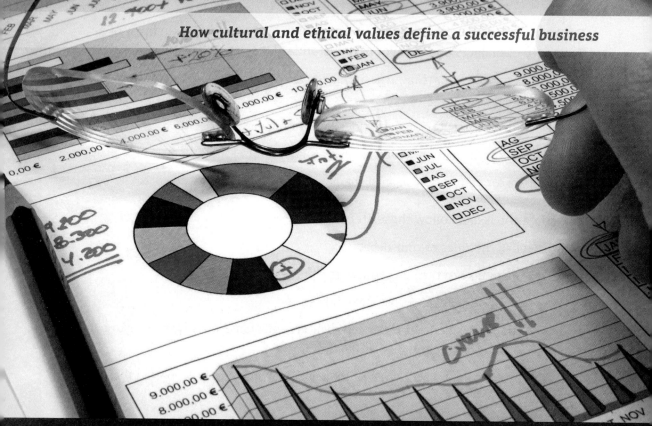

*How cultural and ethical values define a successful business*

## BUSINESS ETHICS

# Implications and Inferences

## UNIT PROFILE

In this unit, you will learn how businesses advertise and market their products. You will also investigate the issue of corporate social responsibility and government regulations that ensure that responsibility.

**You will give a persuasive presentation with a partner arguing how one global corporation is socially responsible.** You will integrate evidence into your presentation to support your position.

## OUTCOMES

- Recognize and interpret hesitations
- Assess your audience
- Select appropriate evidence
- Utilize noun clauses to clarify
- Determine connotative meanings

For more about **BUSINESS ETHICS**, see ❶ ❸.
See also ⬛R and ⬛W **BUSINESS ETHICS** ❶ ❷ ❸.

## GETTING STARTED

⊙ Go to MyEnglishLab to watch Dr. McLennan's introductory video and to complete a self-assessment.

**Discuss these questions with a partner or group.**

1. What responsibilities do corporations have to ensure their advertisements are accurate? Why?

2. What other obligations do corporations have to consumers and their communities?

3. In Dr. McLennan's introduction, he introduces ends-based ethics and virtue-based ethics. How are they different?

## CRITICAL THINKING SKILL

### DETECTING IMPLICATIONS AND INFERENCES

**WHY IT'S USEFUL** By making inferences, you can determine someone's meaning when it is not stated directly.

Attending lectures, collaborating with your peers, and participating in class discussions are regular requirements of higher learning institutions. In each of these scenarios, you need to determine a speaker's key point in order to fully understand the content and respond appropriately. In many cases, speakers will state their main point in a straightforward manner. However, perhaps equally as often, speakers will subtly **imply** their idea rather than stating their meaning directly. In order to determine their meaning, you need to make an **inference**. You make inferences by using your observations and experience, as well as the information that has been presented, to arrive at a likely meaning. We do this all the time. For example, when you observe a fire truck, you use your experience with firetrucks to make the inference that there must be a fire somewhere.

Look at the photo on page 152. Based on the picture, what can you infer about the man, the man's feelings, and what what has just happened?

Although we have not heard anything, we can use our observation of the man's expression and our own experiences with facial expressions to infer that he is angry about something connected with his phone; perhaps the phone isn't working or he might have just had an upsetting phone conversation. Being able to make inferences during lectures, conversations, and other academic activities where meanings are implied will help you grasp the information on a deeper level.

There are several cues that can help us to determine the implied meaning. First, it is important to **recognize and interpret hesitations** in speech. Hesitations are pauses that often indicate the speakers' lack of certainty about what they are saying. Hesitations can also indicate that a speaker is looking for a word, or the best way to express their idea. By recognizing these, we can determine how decisive or conclusive someone may be.

Additionally, it is important to identify the audience the speakers are addressing. If speakers are addressing a room full of experts, or those who have studied the topic in depth, the speakers can safely assume their listeners have a lot of background knowledge on or experience with the subject. In these circumstances, speakers are more likely to imply their meaning and expect the audience to make inferences. On the other hand, if the audience is a group of people new to the topic, the speakers will probably be more direct because of the audience's lack of background information.

Another important strategy is listening carefully for the phrases that are used to describe relationships. In addition to their literal, dictionary meaning, these phrases often have connotative meanings, or connotations. Connotations indicate positive and negative feelings meanings that are associated with a word, in addition to the explicit meaning you find in a dictionary. We can easily infer how someone feels about something, and make an accurate inference by identifying and understanding the connotative meaning.

You will have more practice with connotative meanings in the Language Skill section in MyEnglishLab. Refer to page 168.

## VOCABULARY PREVIEW

Read the vocabulary items. Circle the ones you know. Put a question mark next to the ones you don't know.

| | | | | | |
|---|---|---|---|---|---|
| extensive | disreputable | diluted | corrupt | manipulate | perceptions |

## EXERCISE 1

**A. Work with a partner. Discuss the questions below.**

1. Have you ever bought a product because of its advertisement? What was it?

2. How do advertisements persuade? What kind of ads are the most effective? Why?

3. Do you think the federal government should be involved in advertising? If so, what should its role be? If not, why not?

**B. Listen to the lecture on advertising. Choose the topics the professor discusses.**

### Glossary

Unscrupulous: having no morals or ethics

Patent medicine: medicines sold in the 1800s that claimed to be able to cure everything, but had no medicinal effects

........... 1. Changes in advertising practice over the years

........... 2. Making false claims as a common business practice

........... 3. Consumer protection laws in previous centuries

........... 4. Manipulation of consumers by advertisers

### CULTURE NOTE

Snake oil was just one product companies produced in the early 1900s that promised cures for everything from calming a crying baby to cancer. In 1914, US President Woodrow Wilson established the Federal Trade Commission Act. This act gave government agencies the right to enforce and prevent unfair methods of competition in business.

🔊 C. Listen again. Choose the statements that cannot be inferred from the lecture.

1. Advertising is persuasive.

2. The government established regulations because of the false promises made in advertising.

3. Advertisers were once allowed to say things that they knew were not true.

4. One goal of government regulation is to penalize companies.

5. Medical and pharmaceutical companies commonly attempt to persuade customers.

6. The professor believes government regulations are unnecessary.

🔊 D. Listen to a conversation between two students who attended the lecture. How certain is each speaker? How do you know?

> **TIP**
>
> When listening to a conversation, pay close attention to how people state their ideas. When speakers pause between phrases, or clearly stress key words, they are expressing assertiveness. You can infer that they are quite certain about what they are saying. If pauses are longer, and occur between words rather than phrases, this may indicate the speaker is feeling less certain or assertive.

## VOCABULARY CHECK

A. Review the vocabulary items in the Vocabulary Preview. Write their definitions and add examples. Use a dictionary if necessary.

B. Complete sentences with vocabulary items from the box.

| corrupt | diluted | disreputable | extensive | manipulate | perception |
|---------|---------|--------------|-----------|------------|------------|

1. Some consumers have a negative ............................. of some large, profitable corporations.

2. Customers expect medicines to be full strength, not ............................. .

3. There is satisfaction in seeing ............................. leaders of corporations going to jail, or paying huge fines for their unethical behavior.

4. Advertisements often ............................. the truth to help sell a product.

5. If a large business closes down, it can have ............................. consequences for the city it is located in.

6. When a business has a scandal, consumers lose respect for the ............................. corporate leaders.

🔊 Go to MyEnglishLab to complete a vocabulary and skill practice and to join in collaborative activities.

## SUPPORTING SKILL 1
### RECOGNIZING AND INTERPRETING HESITATIONS

**WHY IT'S USEFUL** By identifying and interpreting hesitations in conversations, lectures, and discussions, you can determine a speaker's certainty. You can also assess the validity of someone's argument or position.

Hesitations refer to short pauses while speaking. Generally, native speakers speak in thought groups. They organize their speech in chunks of words rather than individual words or full sentences. A pause between a thought group has a falling intonation, and pauses often are placed strategically to allow the listeners to absorb the speaker's key points.

Hesitations, on the other hand, are short pauses with rising intonation that do not come at the end of a thought. Hesitations can be quite common when you are first learning a language; you often need to stop speaking to think of the correct word or decide what you want to say. They also occur in other types of situations. For example, a lecturer may hesitate when giving a lecture, a classmate may hesitate when working in a group, or a speaker may hesitate during a discussion.

There are several ways you can identify a hesitation in speech. Native speakers will either fill or not fill the pause. These generally occur when there is a change in topic. Look at the example:

> The government needs to regulate advertising more… [pause] Remember that advertisement on herbal supplements?

A filled pause uses a *filler*. A filler is a sound, or short word, that is used to fill the empty space, or silence. Speakers use fillers with rising intonation to let listeners know that they are not finished speaking, and that they may just be thinking of what to say next. There are several common patterns of fillers in spoken American English. Look at the chart.

| Patterns | Fillers | Examples |
|---|---|---|
| Sound fillers | Ah<br>Uh<br>Um | Regulations need to be in place for consumers. **Um** ... well, advertising tries to manipulate consumers. |
| Word or phrase fillers | Like<br>Right<br>Well<br>You know<br>You see | **Well** ... I think companies invest too much money into advertising, and not enough money into product research. |
| Sound fillers + word repetition | Ah<br>Uh<br>Um | It's likely ... **uh** ... likely that the government won't get involved. |

Why do speakers hesitate and how can you interpret their hesitations? Speakers may hesitate for two distinct reasons. First, a speaker may hesitate to take more time to think and to let you know that they are not finished speaking. They may fill the space with a sound, so you understand that they still have the floor. You can often determine this by not only the filler, but also the intonation pattern of that filler, or what was last said. If the speaker has a rising intonation pattern before their pause, or on the filler, they are just letting you, the listener, know that they have more to say. Look at these examples:

Advertising practices today are... are more just than in the past.

Advertising practices today, well, are more just than in the past.

In both these cases, the speaker had a rising intonation pattern—indicating they have more to say. The hesitation can be filled with a filler, or just a short pause.

Secondly, a speaker's hesitation often tells you about his or her certainty. If a speaker hesitates, he or she may not be 100 percent certain about what is being said. Hesitations are usually followed by words or phrases that may show a lack of certainty, such as certain verbs, modals, and adverbs.

| Signal words to express uncertainty | | |
|---|---|---|
| Verbs | Modals | Adverbs |
| Well … I **think** companies need to try to trick consumers.<br><br>Like … I **believe** consumers know that companies do this. | Uh … you **could** try to research past practices.<br><br>All right … we **may/might** want to incorporate that into our presentation. | Like … they **probably** understand.<br><br>Um … it's **likely** they do this to try to make more money. |

## VOCABULARY PREVIEW

Read the vocabulary items. Circle the ones you know. Put a question mark next to the ones you don't know.

| consultant | fundamentally | driven by | generate | innovative | intangible |
|---|---|---|---|---|---|

## EXERCISE 2

A. Work with a partner. You will listen to a guest lecturer talk about fundamental marketing techniques. Predict which ideas you might hear.

............ 1. Why companies invest in marketing

............ 2. Benefits marketing products

............ 3. How marketing decisions are made

............ 4. An example of a product that is marketed

B. Listen to the guest lecturer. Which of your predictions were correct?

### CULTURE NOTE

The US Congress voted to ban the advertising of cigarettes on television and radio in 1970. This was part of the anti-smoking initiative of the early 1970s, and was a direct outcome of a report released by the Surgeon General of the United States. His report detailed the health dangers of smoking. As a result, the FCC (Federal Communications Commission) required TV networks to give "fair time" to anti-smoking advertising for every cigarette ad aired.

C. These statements occur in the listening. Listen again. As you listen, choose how certain the speaker is. If the speaker is not 100 percent certain, write the reason you think so next to the box.

|  | 100% | Not 100% | Reason |
|---|---|---|---|
| 1. Everyone here wants to make a million dollars. | ☐ | ☐ | ............................................ |
| 2. All business is fundamentally driven by profit. | ☐ | ☐ | ............................................ |
| 3. Everything comes down to brand recognition. | ☐ | ☐ | ............................................ |
| 4. A marketer's job is to generate profit. | ☐ | ☐ | ............................................ |
| 5. The practices are the same for something healthy and something unhealthy. | ☐ | ☐ | ............................................ |
| 6. Selling the concept is the magic bullet. | ☐ | ☐ | ............................................ |

D. Work with a partner. Take turns giving your ideas about the statements. Hesitate and use signal words to help your partner understand when you are not 100 percent certain.

1. Companies shouldn't deceive consumers in their advertisements.

2. Companies that deceive consumers should face some penalty.

3. Making money is the goal of a business, and companies should be able to do whatever they can to meet that goal.

4. The advertising of dangerous products should be banned.

5. Governments should create stronger advertising regulations.

6. Consumers need to be made aware of advertising practices.

**TIP**

When participating in discussions, conversations, and debates, a good way to prevent long hesitations is to repeat what was said. You can use the time it takes to state the repetition to form your ideas. By repeating the key words, you have more time to formulate your own response.

## VOCABULARY CHECK

**A.** Review the vocabulary items in the Vocabulary Preview. Write their definitions and add examples. Use a dictionary if necessary.

**B.** Complete the paragraph with vocabulary items from the box.

| | | |
|---|---|---|
| consultant | fundamentally | intangible |
| driven by | innovative | generate |

My cousin works as a ............................ for a large corporation. Her role is to help the company increase their profits, or ............................ more income. While she does not get a bonus for an increase in profits, she gets many ............................ rewards, like extra vacation days and more potential work. She is really ............................ her desire to help companies be ............................ successful. She looks for ways in which they can produce new, ............................ products for consumers while at the same time keeping costs down for the company. She loves her work, but it is definitely not for me!

⊙ Go to MyEnglishLab to complete vocabulary and skill practices and to join in collaborative activities.

## SUPPORTING SKILL 2

### ASSESSING YOUR AUDIENCE

**WHY IT'S USEFUL** By assessing your audience, you can determine what kind of information you need to present and the style of language you need to use in order to communicate most effectively.

During your college career, you will experience many different speaking situations, such as working with your peers, speaking in front of a class, or in front of a panel of professors. For each situation you find yourself in, you need to frame your language and style around your **audience**. *Audience* simply refers to people who are listening to you. Your audience could be a roommate, classmates, or a professor. Identifying your audience and how to best address them leads to successful communication.

You can assess your audience by determining the characteristics of the group. What is their knowledge base on the topic you are presenting? Are you educating them on a topic, or are you demonstrating *your* understanding and knowledge on a topic? Are your audience members part of your peer group, or are do they represent a broader group of listeners?

Once you have assessed who your listeners are, you can better frame your presentation. Look at the flow chart.

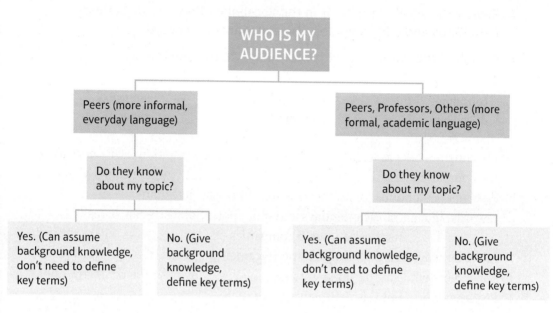

If you are presenting to your immediate peers, such as your classmates, in an informal situation, you can use more informal and idiomatic language. However, if you are giving a formal presentation to colleagues or a broader group, you will want to use more formal, academic language. Look at the examples.

Advertisers will try to suck you in, and get you to buy their products.

Advertisers lure consumers with tempting ads in order to generate more sales.

Also, for both groups you need to consider the background knowledge they may or may not have on the topic. Background knowledge refers to what the audience may already know about the topic. If they have background knowledge, you will not necessarily need to define key terms, or offer a broader prospective. However, if the topic is new to your listeners, you will need to define key terms, and present a clear context for your comments.

## VOCABULARY PREVIEW
**Read the vocabulary items. Circle the ones you know. Put a question mark next to the ones you don't know.**

| | | |
|---|---|---|
| outbreak | undertaken | human concerns |
| monitor | dire situations | (don't) buy it |

# EXERCISE 3

**A. Look at the statements. Determine if the information is *BK* (background knowledge), *D* (definition), or *NI* (new information).**

............ 1. We live in an era of clearly defined regulations that seem to limit advertising and favor consumer protections.

............ 2. Virtue-based ethics encourage a focus on living up to ethical ideals instead of arguing over trivialities.

............ 3. The core concept of consequentialist ethics is that the *correct* decision is whatever action leads to the best outcome for all involved.

............ 4. Polls regularly indicate that the average citizen is aware of the dangers facing the environment; from global climate change to the harmful effects of pollutants.

............ 5. You have to understand that fiduciaries have two main responsibilities to their clients: first, a duty of loyalty. Secondly, fiduciaries have a duty to care.

............ 6. The main idea of the virtue framework can be a bit difficult for some people to understand—essentially, virtue ethics requires that a person or business work to *become* a virtuous, ethical entity that acts appropriately in all situations.

**B. Work with a partner. Look at two presenters' notecards on the virtue-based ethics framework. Complete the tasks.**

---

### Presenter One

Why companies are not only concerned with profits

— Corporate social responsibility—how companies protect public

— Example: fast-food company
  • Background: e. coli outbreak
  • New technologies

— Virtue-based ethics—making best ethical decisions, and living up to those decisions

---

Why companies are only concerned with profits

— Only want to make themselves look good

— Example: cigarette
  • Selling death sticks, killing our environment
  • Feel zero responsibility

— Not ethical; concerned with making money

1. Underline each presenter's main topic.

2. Predict who the audience is for each presenter.

3. Circle key words that help you determine who the audience is.

4. Put an asterisk (*) by any terms the presenter plans to define.

🔊 **C. Listen to two short presentations on social responsibility and corporations. Complete the chart for each presentation. Were your predictions correct?**

|  | Presentation One | Presentation Two |
|---|---|---|
| 1. Who is the audience and why do you think so? |  |  |
| 2. What are two examples of formal or informal language used by the speaker? |  |  |
| 3. What background knowledge or definitions of key terms are provided by the speaker? |  |  |

**D. Work with a partner. Take turns stating your opinions on the topics to different types of audiences. Use the chart to vary your language according to your audience.**

Topic One: Governments should regulate advertisers more.

Topic Two: All businesses need to be more ethical when it comes to the environment.

Topic Three: Large corporations need to establish ethical policies for their employees.

| Formal vocabulary | | Informal equivalent | Formal vocabulary | | Informal equivalent |
|---|---|---|---|---|---|
| a large number of | = | lots of | postpone | = | put off |
| apologize | = | say sorry | represent | = | stand for |
| authorize | = | give the go ahead | retain | = | keep |
| considerable | = | huge | wealthy | = | loaded |
| increase | = | go up | | | |

## VOCABULARY CHECK

**A. Review the vocabulary items in the Vocabulary Preview. Write their definitions and add examples. Use a dictionary if necessary.**

**B. Choose the best synonym for each underlined vocabulary item.**

............ 1. When I first began at the company, I <u>undertook</u> many tasks that were not part of the job, but someone had to do the work.

a. assumed

c. made

b. completed

d. followed

............ 2. This is a <u>dire situation</u> for the company. They may lose everything.

a. terrible state

c. deadly circumstance

b. tiring state

d. costly circumstance

............ 3. The medical center said there has been a real flu <u>outbreak</u> this semester. Everyone seems to be getting it.

a. outside area

c. problem

b. burst

d. issue *(Continued)*

............. 4. They're saying that their company is really broke? Sorry, I just <u>don't buy it</u>.

a. refuse to shop at that store

c. refuse to make purchases

b. refuse to accept it

d. refuse to believe them

............. 5. The doctor said they're going to wait and <u>monitor</u> my condition before doing surgery.

a. screen

c. inspect

b. observe

d. display

............. 6. I can't understand why those tobacco companies keep making cigarettes. They need to think more about <u>human concerns</u> and less about money.

a. anxieties

c. feelings

b. enterprises

d. judgments

⬆ Go to MyEnglishLab to complete vocabulary and skill practices and to join in collaborative activities.

## INTEGRATED SKILLS

### SELECTING APPROPRIATE EVIDENCE

**WHY IT'S USEFUL** By understanding how to select appropriate resources, you can better prepare for presentations by providing valid evidence and gaining a greater understanding of your topic.

Preparing for a presentation can be a daunting task. However, with the proper preparation, it can be a rewarding, educational experience. After topic selection, you will need to map out your main points and supporting ideas. As you map these out, consider your audience. Will you need to build background knowledge? Will you need to define key terms? To effectively build background knowledge, define key terms, and support your ideas, you will need to select evidence.

**Selecting appropriate evidence** involves navigating through a wide range of materials, and utilizing your digital literacy skills. You will need to distinguish between valid evidence and evidence that has not been proven or validated. To select the best evidence for your presentation, begin by determining the purpose of the evidence you are searching for. There are three main purposes for incorporating evidence into your presentations:

1. To clarify your argument or position. If you need to define key terms, or provide background knowledge on your topic, you are clarifying.

2. To add authority to your position. If you are making a claim, argument, or establishing your position, you need an expert, or the authority of a person or organization to make your argument stronger.

3. To add interest to your presentation. If your presentation is dry, or boring, you may want to make it more appealing by adding interesting information, or color.

Once you have determined its purpose, you will have a better idea of what kind of evidence you can use. Look at the chart for types of evidence classified by purpose.

| To clarify | To add authority | To add interest |
|---|---|---|
| • Encyclopedia<br>• Professor's lecture<br>• Textbook | • Interview with professor or expert<br>• Quote or paraphrase from reliable journal | • Famous image<br>• Popular quote<br>• Short video clip<br>• Survey |

**EXERCISE 4**

A. Work with a partner. Imagine giving a presentation on how the government protects its citizens from corporations that are not environmentally-friendly. What type of evidence will you need? Fill in each blank in the outline with the type of evidence you could use.

Topic: The government protects citizens against corporations that are not environmentally-friendly.

I. Introduction: get attention of audience ........................................

II. Body
    1. Background information on how harming environment ........................................
    2. Background information on government regulations ........................................
    3. Current regulations ........................................
    4. More needs to be done ........................................
    5. What will happen if more is not done ........................................

III. Conclusion: Final thought, if we don't act now, our children may not have an Earth ........................................

B. Now read the textbook excerpt carefully. What evidence can you use from this article? Where would you put it on your outline?

The average citizen is aware of the dangers facing the environment; from global climate change to the harmful effects of pollutants, and opinion polls regularly indicate that the state of our environment remains a pressing issue for many. Most successful businesses recognize this and many companies have taken steps to make environmental stewardship a cornerstone of their operations. Some companies, however, frequently work against the common good for the sake of a quick buck. In response, various world governments have implemented measures meant to discourage practices that enrich a handful of people at the cost of environmental stability.

First and foremost among these measures are strict regulations on the use and disposal of certain toxic chemicals. Famously, the pesticide known as DDT has been highly regulated over the last century and remains outlawed in a variety of countries because of the harmful effect it has on humans. Disposal of toxic byproducts is also regulated and companies that violate these laws face severe repercussions. Even manufacturing processes that are not immediately harmful to the surrounding area are highly controlled to avoid exacerbating larger problems; manufacturing that contributes to carbon emissions, for example, is frequently taxed to discourage the overuse of fossil fuels.

Of equally great importance is the issue of sustainability; the Earth has a limited amount of resources available and businesses in all sectors of commerce need to use these resources in a non-exploitive manner which will not negatively impact the environment. To promote sustainable practices, organizations like the Environmental Protection Agency of the United States maintain several projects aimed at promoting sustainability in a variety of fields and raising awareness of relevant laws. Merely raising awareness can only do so much, though, so other resources available to the EPA are allocated towards the inspection of businesses and the enforcement of existing regulations.

C. Listen to an interview with an environmental law expert. Take notes. Decide what you can add to your presentation and where to place your additions.

D. Work with a partner. Using the information from the reading and from the interview, finalize your outline from Part A. Is there any evidence missing? What might you need to look for?

Go to MyEnglishLab to complete skill practices.

# LANGUAGE SKILL

## USING NOUN CLAUSES TO CLARIFY

**WHY IT'S USEFUL** By utilizing noun clauses to clarify your ideas, you can describe them with more precision and sophistication.

⊙ Go to MyEnglishLab for Language Skill presentation and practice.

# VOCABULARY STRATEGY

## DETERMINING CONNOTATIVE MEANING

**WHY IT'S USEFUL** By identifying connotative meanings in English, you can better understand how a speaker feels about an event, or situation. Additionally, when you understand how a speaker feels, you are able to make accurate inferences. When you are persuading, choosing words with strong connotative meanings can help make you a more persuasive speaker.

Words have both connotative and denotative meanings. **Connotations** refer to the cultural meaning of a word, specifically the positive, neutral, or negative meaning a culture might attach to a word. The explicit meaning of the word, or the meaning you might learn from a dictionary, is referred to as the denotative meaning.

Speakers who want to appeal to their listeners' emotions will select language that creates a feeling in their listeners. If you want to make your listeners feel positive about something, you choose words that create a very positive emotion for your listeners. Consider these two examples:

I really miss my **house**.

I really miss my **home**.

The word *home* communicates more than just a physical structure. It creates a feeling of warmth and nostalgia in listeners reminding them of family, or a special place where they belong. It has a positive connotation. Whereas the word *house* really just represents a building or structure that people live in; there is no thought of family, friends, or special memories. It has a neutral connotation.

The same is true when making a negative emotional appeal. Look at these two examples:

Environmentalists organized a **demonstration** to bring attention to global warming.

Environmentalists organized an **uprising** to bring attention to global warming.

Here the word *demonstration* is neutral while *uprising* has a negative connotation. The choice of the word *uprising* creates a negative image of revolt and probable violence for the listeners.

When speakers restate their ideas, they may use a synonym. The synonym they choose often communicates not only how they feel about the topic, but also how they would like their listeners to feel about it. Learning these positive and negative connotations can better help you infer how the speaker feels. Look at the examples in the chart.

| Positive connotation | Neutral connotation | Negative connotation |
|---|---|---|
| charm | attract | lure |
| entice | persuade | con into |
| extraordinary | impressive | intimidating |
| painstaking | thorough | pedantic |
| speedily | quickly | hastily |
| stimulating | challenging | daunting |

Learning the connotations of a word can be difficult. However, there are several strategies that can help you. First, think about the context. That means consider the statements the speaker has made before and after. Second, consider the overall tone of the presentation, lecture, or discussion. Is the speaker trying to point out negative aspects of something? If so, the language used probably conjures up a negative connotation. Next, consider the body language of the speaker. You can often tell by someone's face if they feel positive or negative about something. Last, listen to *how* it is said. A speaker often stresses words with negative meanings. That means, they may say the word at a higher pitch and lengthen the syllables.

## EXERCISE 5

### A. Use a dictionary or thesaurus to add synonyms to the chart.

| Positive connotation | Neutral connotation | Negative connotation |
| --- | --- | --- |
| | deal (n) | |
| | duty (n) | |
| | occupation (n) | |
| | powerful (adj) | |
| | supervise | |

### B. Work with a partner. Read the short presentation. Replace the words in parentheses with a synonym. How does the emotional tone of the presentation change?

In the advertising business, advertisers have the (challenging) ................................ task of creating ads that will (persuade) ................................ buyers to purchase their products. Those who work in the field must follow (standards) ................................ ; however, the client helps to drive decision-making. Once a (deal) ................................ is made, the (thorough) ................................ planning begins. The manager who (supervises) the ad team feels he or she has a (duty) ................................ to deliver the best ad ever to the client without considering how it might misinform customers.

🔘 Go to MyEnglishLab to complete a skill practice.

# APPLY YOUR SKILLS

**WHY IT'S USEFUL** By applying the skills you have learned in this unit, you will be able to make accurate inferences when listening to discussions and presentations, as well as successfully prepare for and give presentations in a college-level course.

## ASSIGNMENT

Prepare a persuasive presentation with a partner on how a global corporation of your choice is acting socially responsible. You will select appropriate evidence, identify your audience and utilize connotative meanings, words, and phrases to make your claim that this corporation acts in a socially responsible manner.

## BEFORE YOU LISTEN

### A. Before you listen, discuss the questions with one or more students.

1. People today are increasingly concerned with the environment. However, at the same time, consumers are demanding more products that make their lives easier. These products often are produced in factories that add to environmental problems. How can these two work together? What can be done to ensure we are not harming our environment, and still have access to new products?

2. In recent years more companies are claiming to be "green" to help protect our environment. Are you familiar with any companies? What do they produce? Do you feel they are actually helping the environment?

3. Historically, producing and driving automobiles has been especially harmful to the environment. What can the automobile industry do to be more socially responsible? How can they become more "green"?

B. The upcoming lecture is on corporate responsibility, specifically focusing on trends in the automotive industry.

1. What are corporations doing to demonstrate their commitment to the environment?

2. Are you familiar with any large automobile companies that are demonstrating a commitment to the environment?

3. What challenges might companies face who are attempting to be more socially responsible?

4. How can a company be both socially responsible and profitable?

C. Review the Unit Skills Summary. As you listen to the lecture and prepare for your presentation, apply the skills you learned in this unit.

## UNIT SKILLS SUMMARY

### MAKE INFERENCES AND DETERMINE IMPLIED MEANINGS USING THESE SKILLS:

**Recognize, interpret, and use hesitations in speaking**

- Identify and utilize appropriate fillers.
- Determine a speaker's level of certainty.

**Assess your audience**

- Identify the background knowledge of your audience.
- Determine needed definitions and the context of your speech.

**Select appropriate resources**

- Distinguish and use resources that will clarify and add authority and interest to your topic.

**Utilize noun clauses**

- Identify and make use of noun clauses to clarify ideas.
- Use noun clauses to add precision to your speech.

**Determine connotative meanings**

- Identify connotations to make more accurate inferences.
- Utilize connotations to become a more persuasive speaker.

## LISTEN

A. Listen to a panel discussion on corporate social responsibility. Take notes.

B. Compare your notes with a partner. Do you have the same key ideas? What skills from this unit can help you identify key ideas?

C. Review the questions from Before You Listen, Part B. Listen to the lecture again. Work with a partner and use your notes on the lecture to answer the questions.

Go to MyEnglishLab to listen more closely, and answer the critical thinking questions.

## THINKING CRITICALLY

Discuss the questions with another student.

1. Based on the lecture, how successful do you think automobile companies will be in the future? Do you think there will be more or less automobile manufacturers that produce electric cars? Why or why not?

2. Why do you think the professor does not mention exactly how profitable these companies have or have not been?

3. What can you infer regarding other companies investing large amounts of money into solar power?

## THINKING VISUALLY

A. Work with a partner. Look at the graphics and discuss the questions.

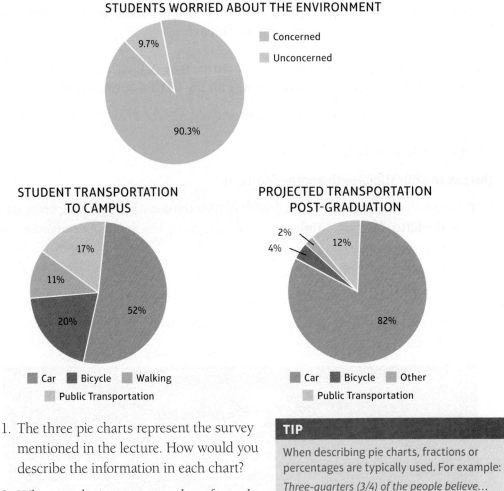

STUDENTS WORRIED ABOUT THE ENVIRONMENT

9.7%
90.3%

Concerned
Unconcerned

STUDENT TRANSPORTATION TO CAMPUS

17%
11%
20%
52%

Car ■ Bicycle ■ Walking
Public Transportation

PROJECTED TRANSPORTATION POST-GRADUATION

2%
4%
12%
82%

Car ■ Bicycle ■ Other
Public Transportation

1. The three pie charts represent the survey mentioned in the lecture. How would you describe the information in each chart?

2. What conclusions can you draw from the three graphics? What impact do these conclusions have on the environment?

3. In your opinion, what will the pie charts look like in 2020? 2025?

> **TIP**
>
> When describing pie charts, fractions or percentages are typically used. For example:
>
> *Three-quarters (3/4) of the people believe…* or 75 percent of the people believe…
>
> *One-half (1/2) report that…* or 50 percent report that…
>
> *One-quarter (1/4) feel that…* or 25 percent feel that…

B. Go online and investigate modes of transportation in your community. Create a pie-chart like the ones above. Share it with your classmates. Summarize the information on the visual for your classmates.

◐ Go to MyEnglishLab to record your results.

## THINKING ABOUT LANGUAGE

Circle the noun clauses in each item.

1. How this car company is failing is a mystery. I see their cars everywhere.

2. It is critical that innovative American businesses adopt eco-friendly policies.

3. The professor asked me why I wanted to go into advertising and not marketing.

4. Many consumers believe that large corporations only care about profits.

## PAIR PRESENTATION

A. Work with a partner. Think about the lecture, and the other information presented in the unit. There are definite benefits for a corporation that adopts socially responsible business practices. Brainstorm a list of benefits.

B. You and your partner will prepare a persuasive presentation on a business that demonstrates concern for the environment by either adopting sustainable practices, or creating sustainable goods. Use the questions to help you prepare.

1. What is the name of the company, and what do they produce?

2. What guides their socially responsible practices? Does their mission include a statement regarding their desire to be more socially responsible?

3. Are they a profitable company? Provide appropriate evidence.

C. Listen to each presentation.

Listen carefully and take notes on each presentation. Pay close attention to the word choices of the speakers. After all the presentations, discuss the language used, and each of the companies.

D. Discuss these points with the class.

1. Consider the language that was used. Which words and phrases had strong connotative meanings? Were noun clauses used to clarify meaning?

2. Which company demonstrates the most socially responsible actions? Why?

Go to MyEnglishLab to watch Dr. McLennan's concluding video and to complete a self-assessment.

# EARTH SCIENCE

# Processes

## UNIT PROFILE

In this unit, you will investigate climate changes from across the geologic time scale and how climate change has affected the projected survival rates of a variety of living things.

**You will participate in a roundtable discussion about increased greenhouse gases in the atmosphere.** You will also summarize a process for reducing greenhouse gases and improving the planet's sustainability.

## OUTCOMES

• Identify descriptions of a process in a discussion

• Clarify steps and stages of a process

• Recognize definitions in written and spoken texts

• Identify boosting words

• Recognize and utilize collocations

For more about **EARTH SCIENCE**, see ❶ ❸. See also ⌈R⌉ and ⌈W⌉ **EARTH SCIENCE** ❶ ❷ ❸.

## GETTING STARTED

➊ Go to MyEnglishLab to watch Dr. Osborne's introductory video and to complete a self-assessment.

**Discuss these questions with a partner or group.**

1. There is a lot of talk these days about climate change and global warming. How has the climate changed over the last 100 years? What caused these changes?

2. How does climate change affect plant and animal life?

3. In Dr. Osborne's introduction, he states that our planet is under threat. What three threats does he mention?

## CRITICAL THINKING SKILL

### IDENTIFYING A PROCESS

**WHY IT'S USEFUL** By identifying a process in lectures and discussions, you can better understand the key events or developments that lead to a specific outcome. You can also be better prepared to deliver clear, organized process presentations.

What is a process? A process outlines the steps or stages of something's development or how something can be done. **Identifying a process** during a lecture or academic discussion helps you better understand the overall content.

Identifying a process is similar to listening for directions on how to get from point A to point B. Just like directions, presenters outline key actions or events. Many of these key actions or events are marked by signal words and phrases. When introducing a new step or stage of development, the presenter often uses sequence signals such as *First, Second, Next, Then, Last, Finally,* or *Eventually.* These signals help listeners to understand the order of events.

In addition to listening for sequence signals, it is important to listen for markers that **clarify the step or stage**. These clarification markers help break down complex information by presenting it in more detail. When presenting a process, it is important to include these markers in order to help your audience better understand complex events, steps or stages. Look at the examples:

Clarification Markers: In other words; Simply put; By X, I mean …

Another common, but non-verbal, clarification technique is to provide visual reinforcement by physically pointing something out on a slide or other image. These visuals can help listeners "see" a process.

## VOCABULARY PREVIEW

Read the vocabulary items in the box. Circle the ones you know. Put a question mark next to the ones you don't know.

| | | | | | |
|---|---|---|---|---|---|
| hypothetical | sustainability | advocate | average | fossilized | fern |

## EXERCISE 1

### Glossary

**Basin:** a large area of land that is lower than the land around it; sometimes covered by an ocean or ice

**Eocene epoch:** an epoch during the Paleogene period of the Cenozoic era, which lasted from about 58 million to 33 million years ago

**Greenhouse gases:** gases such as carbon dioxide that absorb radiation and trap heat in the Earth's atmosphere

🔊 **A. Listen to a lecture about how Azolla ferns and greenhouse gases dramatically changed the climate during the Eocene Epoch. Number the events 1–5 in the order they occurred.**

............. There was a decrease in greenhouse gases.

............. Azolla ferns removed carbon dioxide from the atmosphere.

............. Warm temperatures increased the growth of Azolla ferns.

............. The planet became cooler.

............. The temperatures decreased.

Azolla ferns

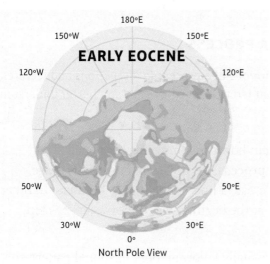

**EARLY EOCENE**

180°E
150°W
150°E
120°W
120°E
50°W
50°E
30°W
30°E
0°
North Pole View

🔊 B. Listen to a conversation between the professor and a confused student. How does the professor clarify the confusing information?

**VOCABULARY CHECK**

A. Review the vocabulary items in the Vocabulary Preview. Write their definitions and add examples. Use a dictionary if necessary.

B. Complete the sentences with vocabulary items from the box.

| advocate | average | ferns | fossilized | hypothetical | sustainability |
|---|---|---|---|---|---|

1. Our professor often presents a ............................ situation and has us give feedback and an analysis of the unreal situation.

2. The ............................ temperatures have risen greatly in the last 100 years.

3. While ............................ is about the future, it is important to change our behaviors now before it is too late.

4. My mother loves gardening, and ............................ are her favorite plant.

5. Geologists look for ............................ rock because that helps them date events.

6. Many geologists ............................ for a change in the way we live our lives. Humans should not be creating so much non-biodegradable garbage.

🔼 Go to MyEnglishLab to complete a vocabulary and skill practice and to join in collaborative activities.

# SUPPORTING SKILL 1

## IDENTIFYING DESCRIPTIONS OF A PROCESS

**WHY IT'S USEFUL** By identifying descriptions of a process in discussions and lectures, you can recognize the steps or stages that led to a specific result and better understand the overall content.

In academic study, it is common to explain how something has happened. This explanation often involves **describing a process**, step-by-step, or stage-by-stage. Effective descriptions of processes often create a linear timeline for listeners. In other words, reports of processes usually start at the beginning and move step-by-step towards the end.

When speakers describe a process, they usually follow an organizational pattern that can help listeners determine and distinguish each step or stage. First, the speaker gives background information on the topic, describing the significance of it, and defining key terms. Next, the speaker generally begins with the oldest event, or first step, and then moves to the next step or event. Transitional words link each step or event, and are often signposted. In other words, the speaker will signal each new step or event with a transitional word or phrase that indicates the sequence in which they occur.

| Words and phrases to signal the first step | Words and phrases to signal any further steps | Words and phrases to signal the last step |
| --- | --- | --- |
| First | Following | Eventually |
| Initially | Next | Finally |
| To begin with | The second/third/fourth stage/step | Last |
| To start with | Subsequently | Ultimately |
|  | Then |  |

In addition to linking or connecting each step with a signal word or phrase, speakers will generally highlight the importance of each step or event, and add details to help the listener understand its specifics.

When planning to describe a process, an outline can be helpful to ensure that you include each step, as well as the important details of each one.

I. What is it? Azolla Event

   A. Occurred in Eocene epoch

   B. Azolla—type of fern

   C. Example of how greenhouse gases can change climate

II. How did it occur? What are the events that led to it?

   A. One: Warmer temperatures in Arctic Basin, caused ferns to grow and flourish

      a. Rapid and constant growth

   B. Two: Ferns removed carbon dioxide from air

      a. green plants remove toxic gases

   C. Three: Decrease in greenhouse gases

      a. direct result of reduction of carbon dioxide

   D. Four: Temperatures decrease

      a. with removal of greenhouse gases

## VOCABULARY PREVIEW

Read the vocabulary items from the box. Circle the ones you know. Put a question mark next to the ones you don't know.

| terrestrial life | atmosphere | landmass | evolve | graze | buildup |
|---|---|---|---|---|---|

## EXERCISE 2

A. Brainstorm with a partner. What is an "ice age"? What events could have led to an ice age?

### CULTURE NOTE

Pangaea was a supercontinent made up of all present-day continents. It was one large landmass that existed during the Late Paleozoic and Early Mesozoic eras (roughly from about 300 million to 200 million years ago).

PANGAEA

## Glossary

Vertebrates: animals that have backbones

Carboniferous period: part of the Paleozoic era that lasted from about 358 to 298 million years ago

Oxygenate: supply with oxygen

Circulatory system: blood vessels, heart, and lymph nodes that move blood and lymph fluid around the body

**B.** Listen to two students giving a presentation on the Karoo Ice Age. Number the events 1–5 in the order they occurred.

............. Ice increased and reflected the sun, making it cooler and producing more ice.

............. Oxygen increased, and carbon dioxide decreased.

............. Plants continued to grow rapidly because they were not the food source for anything.

............. Plants spread easily over all the land.

............. Temperatures decreased, as greenhouse gases decreased.

> **CULTURE NOTE**
>
> The Karoo Ice Age (360–260 million years ago) is only one of five major ice ages that have occurred on Earth. The oldest ice age is the Great Ice Age, or the Huronian. It occurred over 2 billion years ago. The most recent was the Quaternary. A popular animated film, *Ice Age*, is set during the Quaternary Ice Age.

**C.** Listen again. Choose the words and phrases you hear that signal a new step or stage in the process.

| | | | |
|---|---|---|---|
| Finally | Initially | Subsequently | To begin with |
| First | Last | The second event | To start with |
| Following | Next | Then | Ultimately |

**TIP**

When listening to a description of a process, pay attention to words and phrases showing cause and effect. The steps of an event are generally the result of the previous event. Listen for words and phrases like *as a result, in turn, resulting in, this caused,* and *this led to.* This can help you see the relationship between each stage. Look at the cause-and-effect chain diagram. You can see how one stage causes another stage. This is often referred to as the domino effect—one event causing many others.

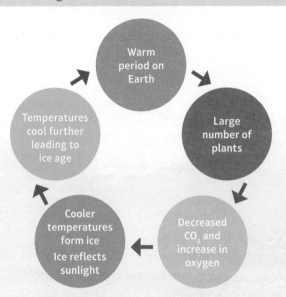

D. Work in a small group. Brainstorm recent environmental events.

E. Work with a partner. Select one event from your list in Part D. Outline the process (or stages) of the event using a cause-and-effect diagram. Compare your outline with your partner.

## VOCABULARY CHECK

A. Review the vocabulary items in the Vocabulary Preview. Write their definitions and add examples. Use a dictionary if necessary.

B. Complete each excerpt with vocabulary items from the box.

| | | | | | |
|---|---|---|---|---|---|
| atmosphere | buildup | evolved | grazed | landmasses | terrestrial life |

### Excerpt One

A geologist's work can vary greatly. While many focus on the studying of rocks and other _____ , others focus on the planet's changes. This may involve watching the _____ of dangerous toxins in the air, or _____ . They pay close attention to how there may be a collection of gases, which could affect the temperature, and overall well-being of the planet.

### Excerpt Two

Life has existed on this planet for a long time. When we think of early life, pictures of dinosaurs may come to mind. However, we may want to direct our mind to the ocean. According to recent research, aquatic life arrived before _____ . We also know that many aquatic animals _____ into land animals. Those images we see of large dinosaurs who _____ alongside man, may be just the stuff of movies.

⟐ Go to MyEnglishLab to complete vocabulary and skill practices and to join in collaborative activities.

## SUPPORTING SKILL 2

### CLARIFYING STEPS AND STAGES IN A PROCESS

**WHY IT'S USEFUL**  By clarifying steps and stages in a process, you can break down complex events, making it easier for your listeners to understand. Identifying clarifications can also aid in your overall comprehension of a detailed process.

Scientific processes are often quite complex. While understanding the order of events might be clear with the aid of transitional words and phrases, understanding the specifics of each step or stage may be difficult. In order to make the content comprehensible, it is important to **clarify each step or stage of the process** for your listeners. Clarifying involves restating, adding detail, and creating a picture for the listeners.

First, you can clarify by restating. Restating involves rephrasing what was said in simpler terms. There are several ways to introduce a restatement:

| Ways to Introduce a Restatement |
| --- |
| By that I mean |
| In other words |
| Simply put |
| To simplify that |

Geologists have constructed the geologic time scale by placing events in a sequence. This is done by applying several principles, including the law of superposition. **In other words**, geologists can understand the events by looking at layers of sedimentary rocks or lava flows.

**Adding specific details** can also help clarify by describing, explaining, expanding, and illustrating complex information for listeners. There are several techniques that can be used to add specific details. Consider these techniques in the chart:

| Technique | Example |
| --- | --- |
| Answer the *WH* questions (*who, what, when, why, where,* and *how*). | The Karoo Ice Age, which primarily occurred during the Carboniferous period, is one of the first instances where terrestrial life altered the planet's climate. |
| Compare or contrast information to previously presented information. | We often think of the entire Mesozoic era as being the time of the dinosaurs, but this only became true after the Triassic-Jurassic Extinction Event, which occurred part way through the Mesozoic. Unlike the later Cretaceous-Paleogene Event there is no single, obvious cause. |
| Add numerical information (dates, statistics). | About 49 million years ago, during the Eocene epoch—this is relatively recent, geologically speaking—the climate was *generally* quite warm. |
| Refer to a visual. | If you take a look at the image in your texts, you can see that the warm Arctic Basin was nearly closed off from other water sources and almost surrounded by other landmasses. |

**CULTURE NOTE**

How exactly did the dinosaurs disappear? Many geologists advocate the theory now known as *K-T*. K-T refers to the catastrophic event of an asteroid hitting Earth at the end of the Cretaceaous Period. K-T wiped out the dinosaurs and changed Earth's environment.

## VOCABULARY PREVIEW

Read the vocabulary items in the box. Circle the ones you know. Put a question mark next to the ones you don't know.

| sufficient | disrupt | pin down | starvation | niche | theory | trigger | bacteria |
|---|---|---|---|---|---|---|---|

## EXERCISE 3

A. Work with a partner. A *mass extinction* is an event where the majority of living things die or go extinct. What are some possible causes of a mass extinction?

### Glossary

Methane: a colorless gas that can be burned for fuel

Sulfates: salts that contain sulfuric acid

Ozone layer: a layer of oxygen high in the Earth's atmosphere that protects the Earth from the Sun's radiation

B. Listen to a study group's discussion. Choose the ideas you hear.

☐ During the Permian-Triassic Extinction Event, 96 percent of all marine life vanished.

☐ During the Permian-Triassic Extinction Event, 76 percent of all other living things vanished.

☐ The Permian-Triassic Extinction Event and Cretaceous-Paleogene Extinction Event experienced nearly the same loss.

☐ There are many theories as to the cause of the climate change during the Permian-Triassic event.

☐ One theory relates to a dangerous gas, methane, buried in the ocean floor.

☐ One theory relates to rising temperatures creating dangerous gases.

☐ Another theory relates to the displacement of oxygen.

☐ Gases released during a volcanic eruption could harm marine life.

☐ The ozone layer damage caused the mass extinction.

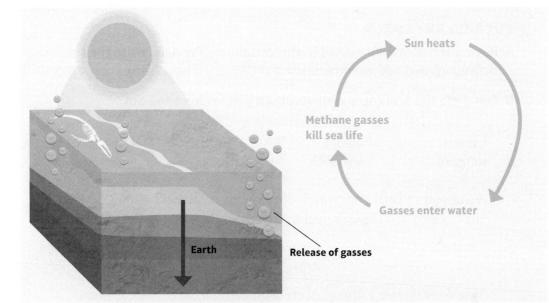

Sun heats

Methane gasses kill sea life

Gasses enter water

**Earth**

**Release of gasses**

🎧 **C. Listen again. Choose the techniques used to clarify information.**

☐ Uses a restatement word or phrase

☐ Adds details by giving numerical information

☐ Adds details by referring to a visual

☐ Adds details by comparing or contrasting to something similar

☐ Adds details by including who, what, where, when, or how

---

**TIP**

Note-taking during a lecture can be challenging, especially when many events or actions are cited. Professors often present information in the order in which things occur. Timelines are especially effective in taking notes when the material is presented in this way. Timelines are straight lines that move from the oldest event to the newest.

---

| Permo-Triassic | Triassic-Jurassic | | | Cretaceous-Paleogene | |

| Carboniferous | Permian | Triassic | Jurassic | Cretaceous | Paleogene | Neogene |

| Paleozoic | | Mesozoic | | | Cenozoic | |

| -350 | -300 | -250 | -200 | -150 | -100 | -50 | 0 |

**in millions of years**

**D. Create a timeline of the Permian-Triassic Extinction Event. Use the information from the discussion and the visual above to help you.**

**E. Work with a partner. The study group discussed two theories. Retell the methane theory using your timeline. Be sure to clarify each step by restating and adding details.**

## VOCABULARY CHECK

A. Review the vocabulary items in the Vocabulary Preview. Write their definitions and add examples. Use a dictionary if necessary.

B. Complete the sentences with vocabulary items from the box.

| | | | |
|---|---|---|---|
| bacteria | disrupt | niche | pin down |
| sufficient | starvation | theory | trigger |

1. Because the planet once was frozen over, food sources for many animals disappeared and those animals died of ..................... .

2. I really am trying to ..................... what Armando wants, but he is not being very cooperative.

3. Whenever there is a geological event on Earth, it can ..................... many living beings.

4. Many wonder what could cause, or ..................... another mass extinction.

5. Geologists can form a ..................... based on what they find in rocks and other sediments.

6. Before she took geology class, she hadn't found her ..................... . Now she knows exactly what she wants to study.

7. Geologists study the ..................... on Earth, and how it can impact changes on the planet.

8. Do we have a ..................... amount of materials to conduct this experiment? It doesn't look like we have everything we need.

⬥ Go to MyEnglishLab to complete vocabulary and skill practices and to join in collaborative activities.

# INTEGRATED SKILLS
## RECOGNIZING DEFINITIONS

**WHY IT'S USEFUL** By recognizing definitions in written and spoken texts you can become a more critical reader and listener. You can also increase your overall comprehension.

Studying in an academic discipline like science can sometimes feel like you are learning a new language. Lectures, textbooks, and other learning tools are filled with new words. However, many times these new words are defined for you within the lecture or reading; you just need to be a good detective and find the meaning.

In reading, **punctuation** can give clues to a new term's definition. Information contained between commas, dashes, and parentheses are often clarifications or definitions.

> Many climate scientists believe that the cooling effect of the Azolla ferns started the downward trend, decrease, in temperatures that would lead to cooler epochs in the future.

> Many climate scientists believe that the cooling effect of the Azolla ferns started the downward trend—decrease—in temperatures that would lead to cooler epochs in the future.

> Many climate scientists believe that the cooling effect of the Azolla ferns started the downward trend (decrease) in temperatures that would lead to cooler epochs in the future.

In each of the above examples, you can see how the punctuation marks the definition of *downward trend*.

As in readings, in lectures and discussions there are often clues to definitions as well. One common clue to a definition is a **defining verb**. Defining verbs are linking verbs that show a state rather than an action. The verb *be* is the most common defining verb. However, speakers may also use *mean, can be defined, indicate,* or *involve*.

> Mass extinction **involves** a large number of species dying within a short period of time, due to a catastrophic event.

> Mass extinction **is defined as** a large number of species dying within a short period of time, due to a catastrophic event.

Another common way speakers define technical vocabulary is through **example**. Speakers will give examples that help listeners decipher new words.

The high-oxygen atmosphere allowed animals with open circulatory systems to grow increasingly massive. So a variety of things like enormous spiders, insects, crabs, shrimp, and scorpions, evolved in this high-oxygen environment.

"Massive" things may be unknown to you. However, when the speaker gives examples of what a massive thing is, you can probably determine what type of animal is being referred to.

> **TIP**
>
> In North American colleges and universities, most professors will write new terms on the board, or repeat them. Both the writing and the repetition of the new term is usually followed by the definition.

## EXERCISE 4

**A. Read the editorial. Complete the tasks.**

### Sustainability – it's now or never

As the world moves forward into the Anthropocene—a new geological epoch characterized by man-made climate change—environmentally friendly practices must be developed and applied on a global scale. Sustainability, which is the protection of biodiversity, must be an increasingly important factor in the political and economic decisions of all nations. Environmental preservation is no longer the problem of the Everglades or the panda. It is now the most important factor to ensure humanity's safe survival.

Because they survived previous mass extinctions, humanity's ancestors seemed both lucky and determined. During the Cretaceous-Paleogene Extinction Event, when an enormous asteroid impact led to environmental catastrophe, humankind's tiny mammalian ancestors managed to survive extremely difficult times. However, this does not mean that humans should be fearless and unprepared for the Anthropocene. Our concerns need to move beyond mere survival and instead focus on both protection and preservation.

There are those who argue with the idea that none of our current problems are the fault of any one individual. Global warming—the heating of the Earth due to greenhouse gases—is simply the result of our modern way of life. This attitude misses the grand opportunity before us; it can become not our burden but our privilege to guard and preserve the planet's ecosystem. By doing so, we will find ourselves responsible for not just the survival of future generations of humans, but the ecosystems we hope they shall inhabit.

1. Circle the three words that are defined.

2. Underline each definition.

**B. Listen to a short excerpt from a lecture. Write the definitions of the terms.**

1. sustainability ...................................................................................................................................................

2. perished .............................................................................................................................................................

3. dire situation ..................................................................................................................................................

4. altered .................................................................................................................................................................

5. environmental stewardship ...................................................................................................................

**C. Work with a partner. Take turns defining the terms.**

| ancestors | dinosaurs | ecosystem | environment | extinction |

**D. Work in a small group and discuss this question: Was it easier to identify definitions in the reading or in the listening? Why?**

Go to MyEnglishLab to complete a skill practice.

## LANGUAGE SKILL
### NOTICING BOOSTING LANGUAGE

**WHY IT'S USEFUL**  By noticing boosting language, you can determine the intensity of a speaker's statement. You can also determine how certain the speaker is about the information being presented.

Go to MyEnglishLab for the Language Skill presentation and practice.

# VOCABULARY STRATEGY

## RECOGNIZING COLLOCATIONS

**WHY IT'S USEFUL** By being able to recognize and utilize collocations, your language is more natural and easily comprehensible.

Collocations are recurrent combinations of words. These combinations pair either the same part of speech (noun + noun) or different parts of speech (adjective + noun). Learning collocations takes time, and practice. While traditional vocabulary methods like flashcards can be effective, it is most effective to chart your newly learned collocations on a grid. Begin your grid by first identifying the combination you will chart. For example: adjective + noun. Second, as you read, listen and interact in English, identify the collocations that occur.

|  | survey | event | formations | warming | temperatures | vision |
|---|---|---|---|---|---|---|
| geological | ✓ | ✓ | ✓ | ✗ | ✗ | ✗ |
| global | ✗ | ✓ | ✗ | ✓ | ✓ | ✓ |

Many collocations are strong, and if you replace a word in the collocation, it will lose its strength, and perhaps its meaning. For instance, take *global warming*. If a synonym replaces *global* like *worldwide*, it becomes *worldwide warming*. However, to a native speaker of English, both the meaning and strength are now affected.

## EXERCISE 5

**A. Read the excerpt. Underline all adjective + noun combinations.**

The Cretaceous-Paleogene Extinction wiped out over 70 percent of living things on Earth. What about the surviving life? Survival of the fittest? What conditions existed that killed an entire group of animals, but did not kill everything? Let's break it down. An asteroid crashed into Earth. That asteroid hit over million years ago creating a crater in the Earth, a huge hole. Dirt, dust, and debris all were thrown into the atmosphere. That small impact throws up dirt and other debris. However, in this case, there was so much debris, that was happened next was it blocked the sun. The climate changed dramatically, causing a mass extinction. With plants and animals dying off, the food chain collapsed. It wasn't exactly the asteroid that killed off all the dinosaurs, it was the dramatic change in the climate which affected food supply.

## B. Complete the chart.

|  | change | increase | difference | measurement | regulation | shift |
|---|---|---|---|---|---|---|
| dramatic |  |  |  |  |  |  |
| temperature |  |  |  |  |  |  |

## C. Work with a partner. Choose one of the words below and create your own collocation chart.

| environment | volcanic | extinct |
|---|---|---|

# APPLY YOUR SKILLS

**WHY IT'S USEFUL** By applying the skills you have learned in this unit, you will be able to identify processes, clarify steps and events, and engage in college-level courses.

## ASSIGNMENT

You will participate in a roundtable discussion. A roundtable discussion is an academic discussion where participants prepare individually, and then discuss and debate a specific topic in a group. You will contribute by outlining the steps that have led to an increase in greenhouse gases in Earth's atmosphere. Additionally, you will outline a process of how greenhouse gases can be reduced to improve the planet's livability.

## BEFORE YOU LISTEN

### A. Before you listen, discuss the questions with one or more students.

1. What do you think can be done to reverse climate change?

2. Is the human impact on climate greater now than in previous periods of climate change? Why or why not?

3. How can we change our lifestyles to increase the sustainability of our planet?

### B. You will listen to a lecture on sustainability and climate change. As you listen, think about these questions.

1. What can be done to reverse climate change?

2. What is a central problem with sustainability?

3. How would converting to clean energy impact sustainability?

4. What do you think slows our progress with sustainability?

C. Review the Unit Skills Summary. As you listen to the lecture and prepare for your roundtable discussion, apply the skills you learned in this unit.

## UNIT SKILLS SUMMARY

**IDENTIFY PROCESSES BY USING THESE SKILLS:**

**Identify descriptions of a process**

- Identify words and phrases that signal steps in a process.
- Determine stages of a process.

**Recognize clarifications of a process**

- Identify and utilize restatements for clarity.
- Break down details of complex steps with details using comparisons, data, examples, and visuals.

**Increase your understanding of new terms from lectures and reading**

- Recognize definitions in reading.
- Utilize cues in a lecture that introduce new vocabulary.

**Identify a speaker's certainty**

- Recognize boosting language.
- Communicate your enthusiasm and interest by using boosting language.

**Recognize collocations**

- Identify words that naturally occur together.

## LISTEN

A. Listen to a class discussion on sustainability and climate change. Take notes.

B. Compare your notes with a partner. Do you both have the same key ideas? What skills from this unit can help you identify key ideas?

C. Review the questions from Before You Listen, Part B. Listen to the lecture again. Work with a partner and use your notes to answer the questions.

Go to MyEnglishLab to listen more closely, and answer the critical thinking questions.

## THINKING CRITICALLY

### Discuss the questions with another student.

1. The professor does not explicitly lay out steps to resolve this issue. Using the information in the lecture, what are some key steps that must happen?

2. One student refers to the use of solar energy. Why do you think the student feels it is a viable option?

3. Based on the lecture, how would you describe the speaker's opinion regarding the public's desire to change their behaviors? Support your answer with specific examples.

**CULTURE NOTE**

Advocacy is a large part of North American and European culture. Advocacy involves publicly supporting a particular cause, issue, or policy. Climate change and sustainability are two causes that have large advocacy groups. Advocacy can bring about great change. For example, Greenpeace, an international organization that peacefully protests to bring awareness to environmental issues, protested the deforestation of Brazil's rainforest. They provided evidence that this deforestation was impacting climate change, and government officials changed their policies.

## THINKING VISUALLY

A. Work with a partner. Look at the diagram and complete the tasks.

1. **Solar radiation passes through Earth's atmosphere**
2. **Some radiation is reflected back into ..............**
3. **Some of reflected .............. is trapped by .............. gases**
4. **Greenhouse gases send radiation back to ..............**
5. **The extra .............. further warms the Earth**
6. **The warmer .............. melt the ice caps**
7. **Less ice means less .............. radiation, warming Earth further**

1. Complete the missing information on the cause-and-effect graphic.

2. What process does it describe?

3. Using the information in the graphic, restate the events to your partner.

B. Go online and investigate gases, like methane and nitrous oxide. Create a graphic like the one above. Share it with your classmates. Are there any differences in the trends?

🔼 Go to MyEnglishLab to record your results.

# THINKING ABOUT LANGUAGE

Read the sentences below. Add a boosting word or phrase from the chart to express your interest, enthusiasm, or certainty.

| Adverbs that intensify and emphasize | Definitive phrases | It + is + adjective |
|---|---|---|
| certainly<br>definitively<br>emphatically<br>incredibly<br>inevitably<br>obviously<br>surely<br>unquestionably | of course<br>with certainty<br>without a doubt | It is certain<br>It is clear<br>It is evident<br>It is obvious<br>It is uncontestable<br>It is definitely |

1. If we don't make a change now, there could be another mass extinction.

   ........................................................................................................................

2. Governments need to create incentives for people to use alternative energy sources.

   ........................................................................................................................

   ........................................................................................................................

3. Nations working together is the only option to resolve this global crisis.

   ........................................................................................................................

4. Mass extinctions have occurred throughout our geological history.

   ........................................................................................................................

5. The climate on our planet is changing.

   ........................................................................................................................

6. Dinosaurs vanished due to a large asteroid strike that affected the planet's climate and their food sources.

   ........................................................................................................................

   ........................................................................................................................

## ROUNDTABLE DISCUSSION

A. Think about the lecture, and other information presented in the unit. Answer the questions and complete the chart.

1. What are some events that led to increased greenhouse gases and climate change?

2. What suggestions were presented in the lecture and elsewhere for reducing fossil fuel use and improving the sustainability of the planet?

| Events causing increase of greenhouse gas | Suggestions on sustainability |
|---|---|
| | |

B. Work in a small group. Share your chart and brainstorm other ideas for improving the sustainability of the planet.

C. Your group will participate in a roundtable discussion. To prepare for the roundtable, you will research your ideas individually. Follow the steps:

1. Research the steps that have led to an increase in greenhouse gases, and the resulting change in our climate.

2. Using the ideas from Parts A and B, develop a plan on how to reduce these gases and improve our planet's sustainability.

3. Outline the steps of your plan.

## D. Establish the rules of your roundtable discussion.

Return to your group. Before you begin your discussion, determine:

- how much time each person has to speak
- the order in which each group member will speak
- how much time there will be for questions and discussion after each speaker

## E. Discuss the issue.

As you discuss, follow these steps:

1. One person begins by outlining the first step that led to an increase in greenhouse gases.

2. Other members of the roundtable take turns outlining other steps, or events.

3. After each step in the increase has been presented with details, each participant suggests ideas on ways to deal with the issue and improve the planet.

4. After each participant has spoken, be sure to ask questions about that person's information, such as asking for clarification or specifics.

⬤ Go to MyEnglishLab to watch Dr. Osborne's concluding video and to complete a self-assessment.

# MEDIEVAL CULTURE

# Style and Genre

## UNIT PROFILE

In this unit, you will learn about life during medieval times. You will also investigate how the values of that period are reflected in poetry, song, and story.

**You will prepare a persuasive appeal on the meaning behind a song, poem, or short story.**

## OUTCOMES

- Distinguish between different types of appeals
- Utilize the language, or rhetoric, of appeals
- Recognize and utilize descriptive imagery
- Distinguish between metaphors and similes
- Recognize idioms based on medieval culture

For more about **MEDIEVAL CULTURE**, see ❶ ❸.

See also R and W **MEDIEVAL CULTURE** ❶ ❷ ❸.

## GETTING STARTED

◐ Go to MyEnglishLab to watch Professor Galvez's introductory video and to complete a self-assessment.

**Discuss these questions with a partner or group.**

1. *Style* refers to the characteristics of something written or spoken. These characteristics include syntax and grammar. What are some common words and phrases used to make an appeal, in other words, to persuade someone?

2. *Genre* refers to the categorization of fiction, music, and movies. What are some common genres of books, movies, or music?

3. In Professor Galvez's introduction, she talks about medieval values. Which values does she mention?

## CRITICAL THINKING SKILL

### IDENTIFYING STYLE AND GENRE

**WHY IT'S USEFUL** By identifying the style and genre of oral and written text, you can better understand the speaker's intention, as well as recognize important rhetorical devices that cause an emotional response in listeners.

Each academic discipline has its own distinct characteristics, as does each speaking situation. Thus, the ways we present information varies from one situation to the next. The purpose behind what we are saying, who we are speaking to, and the circumstances influence how we deliver information. This is often referred to as *speaking style*. Imagine you are asked to give a presentation to a group of professors on an academic topic, how might you style your presentation? Now, imagine you need to give a presentation to a group of your peers on an everyday topic. How would that presentation differ? In these two situations, your speaking style would vary in the words and expressions you use, as well as how you use your voice. This is **style**.

Style refers to the linguistic characteristics of what is being said or read. Syntax (how words are arranged in a sentence) and grammar help us to determine the style being used. Common styles include: descriptive, narrative, and persuasive. A descriptive piece will probably contain many different adjectives or adjective phrases. A narrative tells a story, and would include story elements as well as signals for time order. Last, a persuasive style makes an appeal, and tries to convince the audience to do or think about something differently.

**Genre** refers to its categorization, or specific type of content. In literature, there are five main genres: poetry, drama, prose, fiction, and non-fiction. Within each of these genres, there are sub-genres, or smaller categories. For example, a fictional story may be a piece of science fiction, crime, fantasy, horror, or romance. Style and genre work together to provide the audience with a context for what they will hear or read.

In persuasive pieces, speakers and writers use **rhetorical devices** to help make an **appeal**. Rhetorical devices are techniques for using language in a way that influences the audience. They often involve using figurative language, words, and phrases that have a meaning different from their dictionary meaning and such things as **similes and metaphors**. The use of figurative language makes an appeal more vivid.

## VOCABULARY PREVIEW

Read the vocabulary items. Circle the ones you know. Put a question mark next to the ones you don't know.

| | | | |
|---|---|---|---|
| distinguished | peasants | relevant | sacrifice |
| backbone | sense of community | chaotic | |

## EXERCISE 1

### A. Work with a partner. Discuss the questions.

1. In her introduction, Professor Galvez lists three important medieval values and states that they remain important in society today. Do you agree that they are still important? Why?

2. What other values are important in your culture today? Why do you think so?

3. How do the values of your culture compare with those of North America? Explain.

### Glossary

Proximity: nearness in distance or time

Kinship: a family relationship

Forge: (v) to develop something new, especially a strong relationship

🔊 **B. Listen to a panel discussion on medieval culture and the value systems of the times. Match each panelist with the idea that person presents.**

............ 1. First Panelist: Zachary Hubbins

............ 2. Second Panelist: Madlyn Trotting

............ 3. Third Panelist: Anna Savings

a. Community was the priority.

b. It was most important to work for the kingdom.

c. Family, specifically extended family, was the priority.

🔊 **C. Listen again. Choose the characteristics of each panelist's presentation.**

|  | Panelist One | Panelist Two | Panelist Three |
|---|---|---|---|
| Spoke casually; less formal |  |  |  |
| Spoke formally; more direct |  |  |  |
| Spoke dramatically |  |  |  |
| Used persuasive language |  |  |  |
| Used emotional language |  |  |  |
| Used evidence to support his/her point |  |  |  |

**D. Work with a partner. Answer the questions below.**

1. In your opinion, which speaker makes a better argument? Why?

2. How do the arguments differ?

3. How does each speaker use his or her voice?

4. What impact do you think voice has on a persuasive appeal?

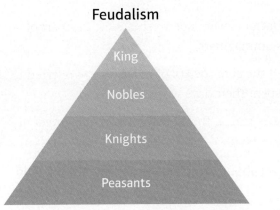

Feudalism

King

Nobles

Knights

Peasants

**CULTURE NOTE**

During medieval times, there was a feudal system of government. In a feudal system, there were higher social orders (kings, nobles, knights), and those that worked for them (peasants). In return for peasants working their social better's land, those of higher orders gave the resident peasants protection, and use of some of land for farming.

**E. Now listen to a conversation between two students who have just attended the panel discussion. Take notes on their comments.**

|  | Student One | Student Two |
|---|---|---|
| Style of each speaker |  |  |
| Key terms |  |  |

## VOCABULARY CHECK

A. Review the vocabulary items in the Vocabulary Preview. Write the definitions and add examples. Use a dictionary if necessary.

B. Complete the sentences with the correct vocabulary items.

1. During medieval times, family was an important part of daily life. However, people also had a deep ........................ , helping neighbors who needed it.

2. If you were a performer, performing for ........................ kings and knights was a great achievement.

3. While many believe that royals were the most important people in medieval society, the farmers were really the ........................ of the community; providing food for all.

4. Do you really believe that farmers were not a ........................ part of medieval society? It seems unimaginable.

5. Those who were not part of the elite society of royalty, were referred to as ........................ . They spent their days working the land.

6. Many knights would ........................ their life to protect the kingdom.

○ Go to MyEnglishLab to complete a vocabulary and skill practice and to join in collaborative activities.

# SUPPORTING SKILL 1
## IDENTIFYING AND DISTINGUISHING TYPES OF APPEALS

**WHY IT'S USEFUL** By recognizing and distinguishing different types of appeals, you are better able to understand speakers' motivations and identify their key argument.

Persuasion is part of our daily life. We listen to advertisers tell us why we should buy a product, and talk our friends into or out of doing things. The goal of persuasive speaking is to get listeners to change their attitudes, beliefs, or values. Speakers do this by making an **appeal** to their listeners. In an academic situation, a good appeal must be well-supported and use rhetorical devices. The rhetorical devices we use are determined by the type of appeal we are making. When listening to a persuasive speaker, you need to have a good understanding of different styles of appeal to determine the speaker's motive and to fully understand the argument.

There are three methods commonly used to make an effective appeal. These methods are known by their Greek names of *ethos*, *logos*, and *pathos*. *Ethos* is an appeal to one's ethics, or beliefs. In order to make an effective appeal using ethos, speakers need to establish their credibility as a speaker, by demonstrating that they are objective and have the right moral character to make that appeal. They use unbiased language and attempt to sound balanced and fair.

**CULTURE NOTE**

The methods for making an appeal were developed by the Ancient Greek philosopher Aristotle in 350 BCE and are still used today. In his book *The Rhetoric*, Aristotle divided persuasive appeals into *ethos* (*character*), *logos* (*word* or *reason*), and *pathos* (*suffering* or *experience*). These methods were designed so that his students could use the best available means of persuasion for any situation.

*Logos* is an appeal to logic. In other words, it is a persuasive technique that uses reason and good judgment to argue a point. Speakers who make an appeal with logos use a lot of statistics, facts, and other types of evidence to persuade listeners that they are knowledgeable and rational and their argument is sensible.

Finally, an appeal using *pathos* is an emotional one in which speakers attempt to produce strong feelings in their listeners. Speakers using pathos often use emotionally charged language, poetic effects, and dramatic vocal changes in pitch, intonation, speaking rate, and volume to communicate their feelings. The emphasis is on expressiveness rather than on balanced-judgment or reliable evidence.

**TIP**

One effective way to use your voice in an emotional appeal is by employing strong focal stress on key words or ideas. Focal stress is when the speaker makes stronger a certain word or syllable by saying it at a higher pitch, slightly longer, and the vowel is pronounced more clearly.

|  | Ethos | Logos | Pathos |
| --- | --- | --- | --- |
| Content | Establishes self as an authority, gives background or qualifications<br><br>Models success through stories | Presents facts, data, statistics, research, quotations | Tells emotional stories about effects on people, includes loaded and figurative (symbolic) language |
| Delivery | Eye contact<br><br>Clear intonation and focal stress | Repeats key words and phrases<br><br>Clear thought groups | Strong focal stress<br><br>Impressive changes in pitch, speaking rate, volume |

Many speakers use a combination of all appeals to present an argument. Using a combination of all three appeal styles makes the strongest appeal, and are often the most successful in persuasion.

## VOCABULARY PREVIEW

Read the vocabulary items. Circle the ones you know. Put a question mark next to the ones you don't know.

| destined | struggle | dusk | standards | condemned | plows (n.) |

## EXERCISE 2

### A. Work with a partner. Use the question to complete the Venn Diagram.

What are some differences between life during medieval times and today? Consider life/work balance, limitations on time and travel, and access to information.

Medieval Times                                    Today

**B. Listen to two students make claims about life during medieval times. Mark the ideas *1* (Speaker One) or *2* (Speaker Two).**

.............. People remained at home.

.............. People were forced to work the land.

.............. People suffered because of the lack of technology available to them.

.............. People suffered because of their inability to travel.

**C. Listen again. As you listen, take notes. Then check the appeal methods used by each speaker. Give examples.**

|  | Student One | Student Two |
|---|---|---|
| Establishes self as an authority, gives qualifications |  |  |
| Presents facts, data, statistics, research, or quotations |  |  |
| Tells stories that include emotional language |  |  |
| Has clear intonation and focal stress |  |  |
| Distinct thought groups |  |  |
| Repeats key words, phrases |  |  |
| Type of appeal |  |  |

## D. Work with a partner. Answer the questions.

1. Which style of appeal do you think worked better for the argument? Why?

2. How could you make the same argument, incorporating elements from each appeal style?

### VOCABULARY CHECK

A. Review the vocabulary items in the Vocabulary Preview. Write the definitions and add examples. Use a dictionary if necessary.

B. Write a synonym for each vocabulary item. Use a thesaurus to help you.

1. condemned ........................................................................................................................

2. destined ..............................................................................................................................

3. dusk ......................................................................................................................................

4. standard ..............................................................................................................................

5. struggle ...............................................................................................................................

○ Go to MyEnglishLab to complete vocabulary and skill practices and to join in collaborative activities.

## SUPPORTING SKILL 2

### IDENTIFYING THE RHETORIC OF APPEALS

**WHY IT'S USEFUL** By identifying the rhetoric, or language, used to make an appeal, you can better understand a speaker's argument, and successfully formulate your own arguments.

Throughout your college career, you will listen to a wide variety of speakers. Many of these speakers will be making an appeal. As you learned, appeals come in many formats. Distinguishing the type of appeal is the first step in understanding and interpreting the speaker's message. The next step involves identifying persuasive techniques and language. This helps you recognize a speaker's tone and intention. To successfully determine the speaker's motive, you need to identify the rhetoric, or language, for making appeals.

*Rhetoric* refers to language that has a persuasive effect on listeners. There are several techniques a speaker may use to persuade or appeal for change. We call these techniques *rhetorical devices*.

One of the most common rhetorical devices is alliteration. *Alliteration* is the repetition of an initial consonant sound. This repetition creates a rhythm that is attractive to listen to, and can easily draw listeners in. Famous people have utilized this technique to make an appeal, as well as storytellers and poets.

"<u>D</u>eep into that <u>d</u>arkness peering, long I stood there wondering, fearing,

<u>D</u>oubting, <u>d</u>reaming <u>d</u>reams no mortal ever <u>d</u>ared to <u>d</u>ream before."

From Edgar Allan Poe's poem, "The Raven"

"He found them <u>s</u>prawled in <u>s</u>leep, <u>s</u>uspecting nothing, their dreams undisturbed."

From the old English epic poem, "Beowulf"

Another common device is allusion. An *allusion* is a figure of speech that makes reference to a person or event. The reference can be real or fictional, come from folklore, literature, or history. Allusions use the background knowledge of the listeners to make a connection to the message. Look at the examples:

He's a real **Robin Hood**!

It's a **Titanic** problem!

The first example might be used to describe someone who is doing something illegal to benefit the poor, just as in the legend of Robin Hood. The second example, could be describing something huge or enormous by making a historical reference to the giant ocean liner that sank in the Atlantic in 1912.

A third valuable device for appeals is using a rhetorical question. *Rhetorical questions* are questions asked by speakers without expecting an answer. The question may not have an answer, or the answer may be obvious. Generally, speakers ask these questions to make a point, or to get the audience's attention. Look at this example:

Do young people of today have the same beliefs as the young people during medieval times?

## VOCABULARY PREVIEW
**Read the vocabulary items. Circle the ones you know. Put a question mark next to the ones you don't know.**

| | | | | | |
|---|---|---|---|---|---|
| extension | reflections | comprehensive | flawed | sincere | biased |

## EXERCISE 3

### A. Work with a partner. Answer the questions below.

1. Think about songwriting. What are some common themes or topics in today's music?

2. Do you think songwriters are influenced more by society or their own personal lives? Why?

3. How did the influences differ in medieval times? What do you think some common themes of song might have been during this time period?

---

### Glossary

Clergy: religious leaders

Minstrels: traveling singers or musicians

Caedmon: the earliest known English poet

Taliesin: a famous Welsh poet from the 6th century

Parodies: imitating the style of an artist or genre for humorous effect

---

### B. Listen to two panelists present their positions on the key factors that influenced songs and poetry during the medieval times. Choose the ideas each speaker presents.

| Panelist One | Panelist Two |
| --- | --- |
| .............. Songs and poems reflected life at that time. | .............. Songs and poems reflected life at that time. |
| .............. Contained the experiences of peasants, clergy, and noblemen. | .............. Contained the experiences of peasants, clergy, and noblemen. |
| .............. The change of seasons is an example of how daily life influenced songwriters. | .............. The change of seasons is an example of how daily life influenced songwriters. |
| .............. The individual songwriter or poet wrote for personal reasons. | .............. The individual songwriter or poet wrote for personal reasons. |
| .............. Poets like Taliesin wrote on personal tastes. | .............. Poets like Taliesin wrote on personal tastes. |
| .............. Believing songwriters and poets only wrote about society is biased. | .............. Believing songwriters and poets only wrote about society is biased. |

**C. Listen again. Choose the rhetorical devices that each panelist uses.**

**Panelist One**

............... Alliteration

............... Allusion

............... Rhetorical question

**Panelist Two**

............... Alliteration

............... Allusion

............... Rhetorical question

**D. Work with a partner. Read the sentences from the discussion. Underline any alliterations, circle any allusions, and double underline any rhetorical questions.**

1. The tales told in times past were truly reflections of what people took an interest in. Songs and poems were a mirror of the society around them.

2. Laborer songs like "Sumer is icumen in" suggest the wonder of seasonal change, an event tied to the farmers and peasants who worked the earth. Can you imagine the beautiful artistry of these peasants?

3. Weren't poetry and songs a reflection on the author that composed them? Dr. Becks is taking the individual out of the equation. Society had an influence, certainly, but the need to express personal views and demonstrate ability was more important. Don't we all write today for our own reasons?

**E. Work with a partner. Take turns persuading one another.**

Think of a favorite song or poem. Persuade your partner why it is great. Use at least one rhetorical device.

## VOCABULARY CHECK

A. Review the vocabulary items in the Vocabulary Preview. Write the definitions and add examples. Use a dictionary if necessary.

B. Replace the underlined words with vocabulary items from the box.

| biased | comprehensive | extension | flawed | reflect on | sincere |
|--------|---------------|-----------|--------|------------|---------|

1. Our professor gave our class a <u>full and complete</u> .................................... review of the chapters we previously studied.

2. I really think her argument is <u>imperfect</u> ..................................; there are many holes in her thinking.

3. I am not sure he was really being <u>real and genuine</u> .................................... when he offered his help.

4. It's important to <u>consider</u> .................................... your goals before you make a quick decision about dropping that class.

5. Do you think Professor Winters is <u>showing a preference</u> .................................... ? I think he is.

6. I feel like the knights were an <u>important part</u> .................................... of a king's power.

⬆ Go to MyEnglishLab to complete vocabulary and skill practices and to join in collaborative activities.

## INTEGRATED SKILLS

### RECOGNIZING DESCRIPTIVE IMAGERY

**WHY IT'S USEFUL** By recognizing descriptive imagery in written and spoken discourse, you can visualize presenters' meanings, and better understand their appeal. Additionally, you can make your own appeals more realistic and vivid.

Rhetorical devices create pictures in our minds. We use **descriptive imagery** to form those pictures. *Descriptive imagery* is when the speaker or writer uses language to paint a vivid picture for the listeners or readers that elicits certain emotions. Imagery is essential for deepening understanding, and engaging our audience. Descriptive imagery involves an appeal to our senses.

An appeal to our senses involves using sight, sound, touch, taste, and smell to describe someone or something. We use our senses in descriptions to make them more realistic, vivid, and comprehensible. Look at these two examples:

It was a rainy day. Rain fell from the sky.

The day was gloomy; soft cool rain fell from the gray sky.

Which sentence paints a better picture? The second sentence appeals to our sense of sight, as well as our as sense of touch. The words *gloomy*, *soft,* and *cool* all help to create an image. Word choice is essential in descriptive imagery; it involves choosing concrete words that cause a certain feeling. Review the chart below. It includes concrete words that elicit certain feelings.

| Sight | Sound | Touch | Taste | Smell |
|---|---|---|---|---|
| brilliant | faint | dusty | bitter | fragrant |
| dingy | growling | fluffy | creamy | moldy |
| faded | howling | icy | luscious | musty |
| gleaming | piercing | prickly | rotten | odorless |
| misty | roaring | rough | spicy | pungent |
| silvery | rustling | toasty | bland | perfumed |
| twinkling | sizzling | velvety | zesty | sweet |

## EXERCISE 4

**A. Work with a partner. Look at the list of descriptive words in the chart above. Which words are familiar? Which words are new? Circle the unknown words.**

**B. Read each sentence. Change the underlined word to a more descriptive word.**

1. The <u>soft</u> .......................... blanket covered the infant.

2. The old castle had a <u>bad</u> .......................... smell.

3. The fireworks made a <u>loud</u> .......................... noise.

4. Did you taste the dish she prepared? It was quite <u>good</u> .......................... .

5. The full moon is really <u>nice</u> .......................... tonight.

6. Can you smell those roses? They are so <u>lovely</u> ..........................

## C. Read the passage on court culture during medieval times. Complete the tasks.

Thanks to the popularity of the television series, *Game of Thrones*, and the series of books it is based on, interest in medieval history, and medieval court life in particular, has grown enormously. Aside from imaginary elements, such as dragons, sorcerers, and white walkers, these fantasy-based courts had much more in common with the real thing than might be imagined. However, there are a few important differences.

Like their fantasy counterparts, medieval courts of Europe were built on a unique and rigid series of hierarchies and focused on the behavior of nobles. Medieval courts were busy colorful places and included not just the immediate royal family, but dozens of attendants ranging from knights and ladies-in-waiting to minstrels and jesters. The sons of other nobles, dressed in brilliant colors, would wait on the court members. These young men served as pages, and later, as squires. Squires were apprentice knights; they learned about a knight's tasks by serving one. Their duties included carrying and polishing the knight's armor until it gleamed, and tending horses dusty from hunting and the battlefield. This practice of apprenticing young nobles helped keep the various noble families closely connected to one another.

Surprisingly, another similarity between the television series and medieval court life is where it took place. Many assume that court was always held in a brilliant castle, but this was not the case. Most spaces were quite dingy, musty, and cramped. Some courts took place entirely in a single room—a great hall where attendants worked, lived, and even slept! Frequent baths were not common, so you can imagine the pungent odors of these spaces. Eventually, the royalty would have their own bed chambers, but for everyone else a life at court meant a life *in* the court—waking, eating, and sleeping.

Unlike most people in the medieval era, kings and other nobles were free to travel a great deal and often visited elegant estates belonging to the king or other noble families throughout the country. Generally, the king traveled to see to the other nobles and make certain that the country was running smoothly. He always had to be alert for any possible schemes to remove him from the throne.

When the king traveled, he took his attendants, royal officials, and his favorite possessions with him—sometimes even his bed! On icy mornings, the king would awake, prepare himself, and then take meetings—all from the toasty comfort of the fluffy royal bed! This demonstrates an important point: the court was wherever the king happened to be at the time.

It was at court that the code of conduct we call chivalry developed. The word chivalry comes from the French word for knight: *chevalier*. This code, and the associated ideals of courtly love and its admiration for women, offers a stark contrast between the medieval world and the brutal world of Game of Thrones and the cruelty shown women in that show. According to the chivalric code, an ideal knight was brave, loyal to his king, and always courteous—especially to women. In the courtly love tradition knights promised their love and devotion to a woman, usually a noblewoman married to another, that the knight may have seen only a few times or perhaps had never even met. The woman's reputation for beauty, gentleness, and virtue made the knight adore her.

The ideals of chivalry and courtly love would go on to inspire the great poems and songs of the era, emphasizing intense bravery, undying love, and unquestioning loyalty to the king and church. It's worth remembering, that though knights aspired to these ideals, they could not always live up to them. Human behavior was and is a messy, hard-to-predict thing that does not always align with expectations—even in a royal court. Perhaps our ideas about knights and courtly love are as much of a fantasy as the Game of Thrones saga.

1. Circle all the words that appeal to our senses.

2. Read the passage without the circled words. How does it change?

3. Add two additional sense adjectives.

**D. Work with a partner. Tell your partner about a scary or exciting experience you have had. Add descriptive adjectives to your story to create a vivid image for your partner.**

⬆ Go to MyEnglishLab to complete skill practices.

# LANGUAGE SKILL

## USING SIMILES AND METAPHORS

**WHY IT'S USEFUL** By identifying and utilizing similes and metaphors, you can persuade your listeners with descriptive, engaging, concrete language.

⊙ Go to MyEnglishLab for Language Skill presentation and practice.

# VOCABULARY STRATEGY

## RECOGNIZE IDIOMS BASED ON MEDIEVAL CULTURE

**WHY IT'S USEFUL** By identifying idiomatic expressions related to medieval times and literature, you can build your vocabulary and better comprehend lectures, stories, and folktales from this time.

Idioms are common in speech, and are especially effective when making an appeal. Like other rhetorical devices, idioms can create vivid images for the listeners. To understand an idiom, you have to learn the idiomatic phrase; it is quite difficult to fully comprehend the meaning by just seeing them. However, understanding the context in which the idiom has been said can help you break it down and better comprehend its usage.

Many idioms have historical origins. Quite a few have originated from a story during a specific time in history, while others represent the culture of that time. Look at the idiomatic expressions in the chart. You will notice that they are related to court culture, fighting, punishment, and death. Many of these occur in literature and stories related to the medieval times because they capture life during that time.

| Idiomatic Expression | Meaning | Example |
|---|---|---|
| damsel in distress | a young woman in trouble who needs help | Today's role models are women warriors rather than **damsels in distress**. |
| heart of stone | to be cruel or unkind | The King has a **heart of stone**. He has made many suffer. |
| knight in shining armor | a male who comes to the rescue of someone or something | The **knight in shining armor** saved the small village from destruction. |
| make the ultimate sacrifice/pay the ultimate price | to die fighting for something | Many soldiers **make the ultimate sacrifice** for their country. |

| Idiomatic Expression | Meaning | Example |
|---|---|---|
| one's hour has come | going to die soon | The evil leader has been caught. **His hour has come**. |
| play devil's advocate | to take the opposing side just for argument | She didn't disagree with him, but decided to **play devil's advocate** anyway. |
| throw down the gauntlet | to challenge someone to a fight | Angered by his rudeness, the knight **threw down the gauntlet**, and challenged him to a swordfight. |

## EXERCISE 5

### A. Read the excerpted presentation. Underline all the idiomatic phrases

What you see on TV or in movies doesn't tell the whole story of knights during medieval times. While knights were the highest rank of those who fought, they weren't always knights in shining armor saving damsels in distress. In reality, many of the knights put their life on the line every day not for women, but for the noblemen they protected. And many more had hearts of stone, killing innocent people who challenged them. They were taught to fight fire with fire, and if you were caught in their sights, you may have been in danger. They were clearly rank and file members, responding the commands of their leaders. They were taught to hold their ground, and soldier on during the toughest times. They often stole from those they fought, and became quite rich. It was not the glorious life that is often painted in the movies.

### B. Match the idioms from Part A with their meanings.

1. damsel in distress
2. fight fire with fire
3. hold your ground
4. put your life on the line
5. rank and file
6. soldier on

a. risk own well being
b. ordinary members; non-leaders
c. keep fighting
d. a woman in danger needing help
e. use same methods as your opponents
f. not to stop fighting or lose your advantage

### C. Work with a partner. Retell a story you have heard. Use three of the idioms above.

🔊 Go to MyEnglishLab to complete a skill practice.

# APPLY YOUR SKILLS

**WHY IT'S USEFUL** By applying the skills you have learned in this unit, you will be able to identify the style of a persuasive appeal. You will also be able to recognize rhetorical devices used in different appeals, and actively participate in a college-level lecture or discussion.

### ASSIGNMENT

Prepare a persuasive presentation on the meaning behind a song, poem, or short story. Interpret how society, culture, or an individual has influenced its words.

## BEFORE YOU LISTEN

### A. Before you listen, discuss the questions with one or more students.

1. Who has the greatest influence on a society: leaders or everyday people? Why?

2. In addition to a government, what other organizations have great influence on a culture?

3. How do you think these influences might have differed during medieval times? Why?

### B. You will hear a panel discussion on the three social orders that existed during medieval times. As you listen to the lecture, think about these questions.

1. Each panelist argues that a different order of medieval society had the greatest influence. What are the three orders?

2. According to one panelist, who were the real thinkers, or brainpower, of the time?

3. What support does the panelist offer for laborers helping society to be fully functional?

4. According to one panelist, influence can only come from nobility. Why?

C. Review the Unit Skills Summary. As you listen to the lecture and prepare for your group presentation, apply the skills you learned in this unit.

## UNIT SKILLS SUMMARY

### DETERMINE STYLE AND GENRE USING THESE SKILLS:

**Identify an appeal**

- Recognize persuasive techniques.
- Distinguish between ethos, pathos, and logos appeal styles.
- Utilize content and delivery to differentiate appeal styles.

**Recognize rhetorical devices**

- Identify alliterations, allusions, and rhetorical questions.
- Utilize rhetorical devices to formulate a concrete appeal.

**Recognize and utilize descriptive imagery**

- Recognize words and phrases that appeal to our senses.
- Clarify meaning, create concrete images.

**Identify similes and metaphors**

- Identify grammatical patterns of similes and metaphors.
- Construct your own similes and metaphors.

**Recognize idioms related to medieval culture**

- Identify idioms related to historical events and times.
- Determine meaning of idiomatic phrases through context.

## LISTEN

A. Listen to a panel discussion on the three orders that existed during medieval times. Take notes.

B. Compare your notes with a partner. Do you both have the same key ideas? What skills from this unit can help you identify key ideas?

C. Review the questions from Before You Listen, Part B. Listen to the lecture again. Work with a partner and use your notes on the lecture to answer the questions.

Go to MyEnglishLab to listen more closely and answer the critical thinking questions.

## THINKING CRITICALLY

**Discuss the questions with another student.**

1. How does each panelist make his or her argument? What are some characteristics of each appeal?

2. Each panelist supports his or her idea. How does each panelist support his or her idea?

3. Based on the overall panel, how would you describe this academic discussion?

## THINKING VISUALLY

**A. Look at the graphic. What social system does it describe?**

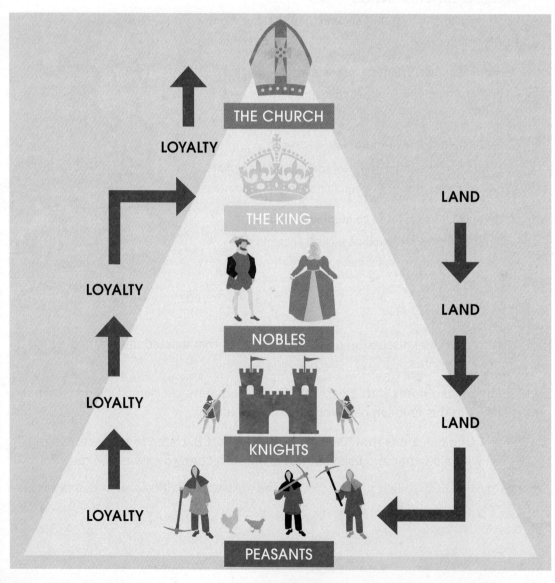

**B. Discuss the questions with a partner using the diagram on page 220 to help you.**

1. Which social order had the greatest number of people? How do you know?

2. How can you describe the relationship between the nobility (kings and knights) with the peasants? What did each gain from the relationship?

3. How can you describe the relationship between the church and the other two orders? What do you think noblemen and peasants gained from the church?

**C. Go online and investigate the other landholding system of medieval Europe, manorialism. How does it differ from feudalism? Create a visual like the one above. Share your visual with your classmates. Discuss the similarities and differences between the two systems.**

Go to MyEnglishLab to record your results.

## THINKING ABOUT LANGUAGE

Circle the two things being compared, and mark the statement *S* (simile) or *M* (metaphor).

............ 1. She was a kite, floating in the air.

............ 2. Watching the news is like getting teeth pulled.

............ 3. Love is a battlefield.

............ 4. The sea was a raging monster.

............ 5. The sun covered me like a warm blanket.

............ 6. The night was as black as coal.

## INDIVIDUAL PRESENTATION

A. Think about the lecture and the other information presented in the unit. Songs and stories played a vital role in medieval culture. The values and events of the time strongly influenced the songs and stories of the period. The same is true of cultural arts today. Use the chart to brainstorm a list of important themes popular in modern songs and films and provide examples.

| Themes of Medieval Songs and Poetry | Themes in Modern Songs and Films | Examples |
|---|---|---|
| Heroic deeds | | |
| Ideal women | | |
| Ideal knights | | |
| Forbidden love | | |
| Loyalty to king (head of state) | | |

She was as playful as a kitten.

B. You will prepare a persuasive presentation on how an important song or film is representative of today's society and cultural values. As you prepare, think about what style of appeal (logos, ethos, or pathos), rhetorical devices, and descriptive imagery you will use to convince your classmates. Use these questions to prepare. Listen carefully and take notes on each presentation.

1. Which song or film will you choose?

2. What parts of society or social order does it show?

3. What values does it illustrate?

4. What images does it use or evoke in order to make its point?

5. Why is it popular or important?

C. **Listen to each presentation.**

Listen carefully and take notes on each presentation. As you listen, identify the type of appeal, rhetorical devices, and images used in each presentation.

◐ Go to MyEnglishLab to watch Professor Galvez's concluding video and to complete a self-assessment.

# MATERIALS ENGINEERING

# Presentations

## UNIT PROFILE

In this unit, you will learn about the development of polymers and their role in materials engineering. You will also investigate why polymers are chosen for many everyday products, products used in space travel, and other potential future applications.

**You will give a formal presentation examining how synthetic polymers are aiding product development in a field of your interest.**

## OUTCOMES

• Determine presentation purpose and structure

• Select and integrate resources

• Synthesize information from various resources

• Connect resources with transitional words and phrases

• Acquire and retain new vocabulary by categorizing

For more about **MATERIALS ENGINEERING**, see ❶ ❸.

See also R and W **MATERIALS ENGINEERING** ❶ ❷ ❸.

# GETTING STARTED

⬤ Go to MyEnglishLab to watch Professor Heilshorn's introductory video and to complete a self-assessment.

**Discuss these questions with a partner or group.**

1. There is a lot of talk today regarding a lack of natural resources, including resources needed to make and create everyday products. What do you think companies and scientists are doing to resolve this problem?

2. Some materials are organic, like iron, while others are inorganic, like silicone. What are the advantages and disadvantages of using organic and inorganic materials to produce everyday products?

3. In Professor Heilshorn's introduction, she states that this section is about polymers. What fact does she state about polymers?

# CRITICAL THINKING SKILL
## PREPARING FORMAL PRESENTATIONS

**WHY IT'S USEFUL** By understanding how to effectively prepare a formal presentation, you can express your ideas clearly, cohesively, and confidently. This will also help your listeners' understanding of the material.

Speaking to a group is a regular activity in many college classrooms. These speaking opportunities may be formal or informal. Informal speaking opportunities often include answering questions, or working with a group or partner, while formal speaking opportunities often refer to giving a prepared presentation. **Presenting** a formal speech to a class or small group can be stressful. The best way to reduce the stress associated with presenting is to be well-prepared.

Preparing a presentation is much like preparing a written assignment, like an essay or research paper. Follow these steps:

1. Read the assignment carefully, and identify the key words or phrases that will help you determine a topic.

2. Use the key words to brainstorm a topic.

3. Examine your topic to be sure it meets the assignment.

4. Determine if it is a topic you know enough about that you can speak about it for the given time.

5. Write down everything you know about the topic.

6. Plan your presentation by outlining your ideas.

7. Identify resources to help you support your ideas.

8. Develop an introduction that has a clear focus and outlines your overall organization.

9. Add a conclusion that restates the important ideas.

10. Practice and time your presentation. Consider practicing with a friend or classmate, or record yourself.

11. Make any necessary changes.

When planning your presentation, you will need to determine the **organizational pattern** of your presentation. Formal presentations have three sections: a clear beginning (the introduction), body, and ending (conclusion). Understanding each of these parts, and their purposes, can help you better plan your presentation.

As you prepare each part of your presentation, you will need to support your ideas with evidence. Consider the **type of resources** you could use to support your ideas. These may include quotes, paraphrases, or summaries of articles, visuals, statistics, and surveys. The type of resources you use will depend on the assignment given, and the ideas you are supporting.

## VOCABULARY PREVIEW
Read the vocabulary items in the box. Circle the ones you know. Put a question mark next to the ones you don't know.

| satellite | on a large scale | linear | synthetic | bond | distinction |
| --- | --- | --- | --- | --- | --- |

## EXERCISE 1

### A. Work with a partner. Discuss the questions.

1. What are some great inventions from the 20th century?

2. Which of those inventions are made from plastic or contain plastic parts?

3. Why do you think plastic is widely used in manufacturing?

## Glossary

Polymer: a chemical compound that has a simple structure of large molecules

Macromolecule: a molecule containing a large number of atoms

Monomer: a molecule that can be bonded with another molecule to form a polymer

Cellulose: the material that cell walls of plants are made from

Acrylics: of or relating to acrylic acid or the products made from it

B. Listen to a lecture that introduces polymers. As you listen, number the images 1–4 in the order they are mentioned.

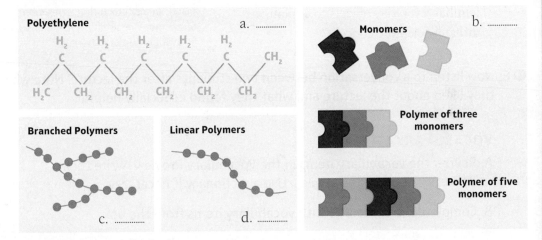

C. Listen again. Which section does each item come from? Mark each one *I* (introduction), *B* (body), or *C* (conclusion).

............... 1. They are all part of the last century's most exciting scientific developments. They all share something else, as well.

............... 2. To understand polymers we have to have a clear understanding of a macromolecule. Macromolecules are giant molecules.

............... 3. Now that we know what a polymer is, let's look at what makes it special.

............... 4. Dishwashers, microwaves, frozen foods, plastics, and satellites. What do these all share?

............... 5. Just imagine—what if you didn't have those plastic containers to bring in your leftovers, or the microwave to heat it up?

............... 6. Think about those long, molecular chains next time you take out the garbage or drink your coffee from an insulated cup!

**D. Discuss the questions with another student.**

1. How does the speaker introduce and conclude the topic?

2. Why do you think the speaker uses familiar, everyday objects to explain a difficult scientific concept?

**CULTURE NOTE**

Synthetic polymers include a large group of plastics, which have displaced many traditional materials like wood, stone, metal, and glass in manufacturing. Using plastic in manufacturing saves money, offers more versatility, and it can be used in a wide range of materials.

🎧 **E. Now listen to a conversation between two students after the lecture. Note what they liked about the lecture and what they found especially helpful.**

**VOCABULARY CHECK**

**A. Review the vocabulary items in the Vocabulary Preview. Write their definitions and add examples. Use a dictionary if necessary.**

**B. Complete the sentences with vocabulary items from the box.**

| bond | distinction | linear | on a large scale | satellite | synthetic |
|------|------------|--------|------------------|-----------|-----------|

1. Materials engineering involves developing ........................ materials that are not naturally occurring.

2. It is important to make a ........................ between ionic and chemical bonds.

3. Scientists try to observe how atoms ........................ or attach, to one another.

4. Scientists develop materials that can be used ........................ rather than those that have limited usage.

5. Because a ........................ has to be able to experience a wide range of environments, it must be constructed of durable and flexible material.

6. In a ........................ configuration, atoms attach in a line.

⬆ Go to MyEnglishLab to complete a vocabulary and skill practice and to join in collaborative activities.

# SUPPORTING SKILL 1
## DETERMINING PRESENTATION PURPOSE AND STRUCTURE

**WHY IT'S USEFUL** By determining the purpose and organizational structure of your presentations, you can be better prepared to effectively communicate your ideas in a logical manner. You can also deliver speeches with greater comfort and confidence.

In many of your classes, you will be asked to give a formal presentation. While standing up in front of a class may be an intimidating and nerve-wracking experience, with the right preparation, it can also be an effective way to demonstrate your learning and understanding of course content. Preparation is key. To prepare for a presentation, first **identify the type** of presentation you are being asked to give. Most presentations fall under two main categories: **informative** or **persuasive**.

*Informative presentations* use definitions, demonstrations, descriptions, and specific details to fully explain an idea, concept, person, or place. The goal of an informative presentation is to provide information for the audience. As such, an informative presentation can take a complex topic, like polymers, and break the topic down in a way that makes it easy for the audience to understand.

Likewise, *persuasive presentations* also use definitions, demonstrations, descriptions, and specific details. However, the goal of a persuasive presentation is to persuade, or convince, the audience to accept the presenter's point of view. A persuasive presentation is more emotional because it attempts to appeal to the emotions of the listeners. These presentations often include facts, like statistics, that listeners might react to in an emotional way. Look at the example:

90 percent of all trash floating in today's oceans is plastic.

While this is a fact, it is a fact that many will find shocking or alarming.

After determining the type of presentation, you need to develop its **organizational structure**. Like a well-written essay, a successful presentation has a clear introduction, body, and conclusion. Look at the chart on page 230 for elements of each section.

| Introduction | Body | Conclusion |
|---|---|---|
| • Gets attention<br><br>• Makes a connection to the audience<br><br>• Builds background knowledge on topic<br><br>• Defines key terms<br><br>• Build to topic or focus | • Broken into three or four key sections. Each section is identified by signal words, "First, Second,…"<br><br>• Moves from general to specific<br><br>• Includes resources (evidence, visuals)<br><br>• Specific examples given and highlighted by signal words, "To illustrate, for example, for instance" | • Returns back to context in introduction<br><br>• Leaves listeners with a final thought or desired action |

## VOCABULARY PREVIEW

Read the vocabulary items in the box. Circle the ones you know. Put a question mark next to the ones you don't know.

| | | | | | |
|---|---|---|---|---|---|
| revolutionize | react | reputation | preserve | durable | discarded |

## EXERCISE 2

A. Work with a partner. Look at the ideas for a presentation on synthetic polymers. Number the ideas 1–4 in the order you think they should be presented.

............... a. How synthetic polymers are used

............... b. Benefits of synthetic polymers

............... c. What is a synthetic polymer?

............... d. Environmental concerns of synthetic polymers

B. Listen to a lecture on synthetic polymers. Complete the tasks.

1. Is this an informative or persuasive presentation? How do you know?

2. Choose all that apply:

☐ The introduction gets the audience's attention.

☐ The introduction makes a connection to the audience.

☐ The introduction provides background knowledge to the audience.

☐ The introduction defines key terms.

☐ The introduction states the focus of the presentation.

3. Number the ideas 1–3 in the order that they were presented.

.............. a. Polymers used for food storage purposes.

.............. b. The environmental concerns associated with synthetic polymers.

.............. c. The reasons synthetic polymers make excellent food containers.

> **TIP**
>
> When preparing a presentation, it is best to outline your ideas. Using an outline format can help you build your presentation and visually see the connection between ideas. This allows you to easily choose the best signal words or transitional words to move from one idea to the next.

🔊 **C. Listen again and complete the outline of the presentation.**

I. Introduction

    Focus: ................................................................................

II. Body

    A. Why synthetic polymers are great food containers

        1. ................................................................................

        2. durable

        3. ................................................................................

    B. Polymers commonly used for food storage purposes

        1. ................................................................................

            a. example: milk

        2. PVC: polyvinyl chloride

            a. example: .........................................................

    C. ................................................................................

        1. Improper disposal negative impact

        2. ................................................................................

            a. being designed to be easily recyclable

III. Conclusion: ................................................................................

D. Work with a partner. Review the two slides. Take turns giving one-minute informative presentations on each topic.

## Plastics and children's toys

- **Introduction**
  - Benefits of using synthetic polymers in children's toys
- **Body**
  - Benefit One—Bends easily without breaking
  - Benefit Two—Is easily molded into variety of shapes
  - Benefit Three—Has low manufacturing costs
- **Properties**
  - Best material for children's toys

## Plastics and athletic clothing

- **Introduction**
  - Benefits of using synthetic polymers in athletic clothing

- **Body**
  - Benefit One—Is lightweight
  - Benefit Two—Does not restrict movement
  - Benefit Three—Wicks away moisture; keeps athletes dry
- **Conclusion**
  - Best material for athletic clothing

## VOCABULARY CHECK

A. Review the vocabulary items in the Vocabulary Preview. Write their definitions and add examples. Use a dictionary if necessary.

B. Choose the sentence that correctly paraphrases the meaning of each underlined vocabulary item.

1. a. Some materials are quite strong, or <u>durable</u>, while others are not.

   b. Some materials are quite flexible, or <u>durable</u>, while others are not.

2. a. Marta <u>discarded</u>, or threw away, the supplies she did not need.

   b. Marta <u>discarded</u>, or organized, the supplies she did not need.

3. a. There are some materials, like plastic, which have <u>revolutionized</u>, or supported, product development.

   b. There are some materials, like plastic, which have <u>revolutionized</u>, or completely changed, product development.

4. a. Many people agree that we need to <u>preserve</u>, or adjust, the rate at which we are developing new materials.

   b. Many people agree that we need to <u>preserve</u>, or continue, the rate at which we are developing new materials.

5. a. Plastic may have a bad <u>reputation</u>, or status, with environmentalists, but it has drastically changed our lives.

   b. Plastic may have a bad <u>reputation</u>, or characteristic, with environmentalists, but it has drastically changed our lives.

6. a. The properties of a material describe how it will <u>react</u>, or respond, to physical forces.

   b. The properties of a material describe how it will <u>react</u>, or replace, to physical forces.

🔵 Go to MyEnglishLab to complete vocabulary and skill practices and to join in collaborative activities.

# SUPPORTING SKILL 2

## SELECTING AND INTEGRATING RESOURCES

**WHY IT'S USEFUL** By selecting and integrating resources into your presentations, you can support your ideas with evidence and also demonstrate a deeper understanding of the topic. Using resources also aids your listeners in comprehending complex topics.

Presentations are a regular part of the college classroom. They not only effectively demonstrate your understanding of a topic, but also illustrate your ability to synthesize multiple resources in a clear, and logical manner. **Selecting** the right **resources and integrating** those **resources** into your presentations is a vital part of a successful presentation.

In order to select the best resources, you must first consider the parameters of the assignment. To be certain that you understand the assignment, look carefully at the key words used to describe the assignment.

| Key Word | Purpose |
| --- | --- |
| compare | State what is the same or similar. |
| contrast | State what is different. |
| define | State the meaning of something. |
| describe | Tell how something works, looks, or has happened. Consider answering WH-questions. |
| discuss | Consider all of the important characteristics. |
| enumerate | List or discuss each point separately. |
| evaluate | React to the topic by focusing on strengths and weaknesses. |
| explain | Give facts and details to make something clear. |
| illustrate | Explain something through the use of examples. |
| summarize | Cover all of the major points. |
| trace | Describe the development or progress of a thing or event. |

For more information about using WH-questions to organize information, refer to EARTH SCIENCE, Part 1

Once you have a clear idea of what to present on, look for resources that can improve your presentation. Using resources can add clarity and accuracy, and maintain audience interest. There are several types of resources you could use.

## Definitions

To help the listeners understand the overall topic, define key terms. Definitions can be quotations from a textbook, article, or your professor.

> According to our textbook, polycarbonates are polymers that contain carbon and are widely used in the manufacturing of many everyday products.

## Statistics, Graphs, and Illustrations

Using statistics, graphs, and illustrations (drawings and photos) can help support your ideas while visually showing a concept. They allow the listeners to either hear or see the significance of the information.

> "90 percent of all trash floating in the ocean today is plastic."

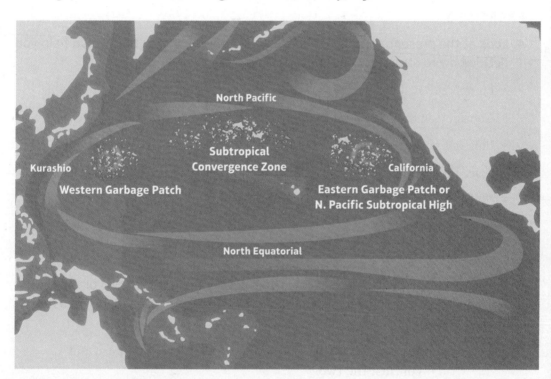

## Testimonials and Quotes

Testimonials are when speakers give their own opinions, beliefs, experience with, or ideas about a topic. They are most effective when they come from an expert and are often the result of an interview. This can take place face-to-face or virtually, via email. Quotes are the exact words someone has said, and these often come from textbooks, journal articles, or a lecture.

> "The use of polymers reduces manufacturing costs. According to the CEO of WorkIt Clothing, they have saved nearly 1.5 million dollars in productions costs by utilizing polymers in the development of their materials."

Integrating a combination of these resources demonstrates your ability to synthesize materials and maintains your listeners' interest.

## VOCABULARY PREVIEW

Read the vocabulary items in the box. Circle the ones you know. Put a question mark next to the ones you don't know.

| | | | |
|---|---|---|---|
| technical jargon | ingest | landfill | paint a picture |
| accumulation | jump in | incorporate | man-made |

## EXERCISE 3

A. Look at the presentation topics below. Circle the key words that would help you decide how to structure your presentation.

- Enumerate the ways in which synthetic polymers have improved human life.

- Consider synthetic and organic polymers. Compare and contrast the two.

- Illustrate the ways in which humans can reduce their use of plastic.

- Trace the development of synthetic polymers in athletic clothing.

- Evaluate the strengths and weaknesses of using synthetic polymers in the manufacturing of children's toys.

- Describe the environmental concerns of using synthetic polymers.

B. Work with a partner. Look at each of the supporting ideas for two of the topics above. Circle the resource you think would best support each idea. Discuss why that resource is best.

1. **Topic One: Consider synthetic and organic polymers. Compare and contrast the two.**

   Supporting Idea One: Cost of the two

   *Definition        Statistics, graph, or illustration        Testimonials or quotes*

   Supporting Idea Two: Environmental friendliness

   *Definition        Statistics, graph, or illustration        Testimonials or quotes*

   Supporting Idea Three: Durability

   *Definition        Statistics, graph, or illustration        Testimonials or quotes*

2. **Topic Two: Describe the environmental concerns of using synthetic polymers.**

Supporting Idea 1: Animals mistake for food

    *Definition*       *Statistics, graph, or illustration*       *Testimonials or quotes*

Supporting Idea 2: Increase in landfills

    *Definition*       *Statistics, graph, or illustration*       *Testimonials or quotes*

Supporting Idea 3: Manufacturing waste

    *Definition*       *Statistics, graph, or illustration*       *Testimonials or quotes*

C. Listen to the two students prepare for their presentation. Complete their presentation plan.

Topic: ........................................................................................................

Introduction:   Resource: ...........................................................................

               Definition of synthetic polymer

               Focus: ...................................................................................

Supporting Idea #1: ............................................................................................

               Resource: Quote from government website

               Example: ...............................................................................

Supporting Idea #2: Production pollution

               Resource: ...............................................................................

Supporting Idea #3: ............................................................................................

               Resource: ...............................................................................

Conclusion: Resource: ........................................................................................

D. Work with a partner. Select one of the topics from Part A. Create a presentation plan similar to the one in Part C.

## VOCABULARY CHECK

**A.** Review the vocabulary items in the Vocabulary Preview. Write their definitions and add examples. Use a dictionary if necessary.

**B.** Complete the sentences with vocabulary items from the box.

| | | | |
|---|---|---|---|
| accumulation | incorporate | ingest | landfill |
| jump in | man-made | paint a picture | technical jargon |

1. I understand our professor pretty well, except when he uses a lot of
   ........................................... .

2. It's amazing how many materials are ........................................... . I'm sure this helps with sustainability.

3. Dante is giving a presentation on ionic bonds, and he really hopes to ........................................... a visual that shows the process.

4. We really need to recycle more materials, and not throw everything away. Did you see how large that ........................................... was?

5. Be sure to ........................................... whenever you have an idea. I'd love to hear what you are thinking.

6. There is a large ........................................... of old tires in that junkyard. I hope they will be recycled.

7. I really appreciate how our professor uses a lot of visuals; it helps to ........................................... for me.

8. Careful—don't ........................................... that chemical; it is toxic.

⬆ Go to MyEnglishLab to complete vocabulary and skill practices and to join in collaborative activities.

# INTEGRATED SKILLS
## SYNTHESIZING RESOURCES

**WHY IT'S USEFUL** By using multiple resources and synthesizing the information, you can better comprehend a topic and differentiate between a variety of different opinions and beliefs.

Throughout your college career you will be asked to present information either in writing or speaking on a wide range of topics to demonstrate your understanding of a concept, event, or theory. To fully comprehend a topic, you will need to research it using a variety of resources. Once you have investigated a topic thoroughly, you will need to synthesize the information in these resources.

**Synthesizing resources** refers to the comparing and contrasting of information. It involves thinking about what you already know about the topic, what you are learning about the topic through different resources, and combining that information in a clear, logical manner. It is a lot like putting a puzzle together. You have a few pieces, you look for a few pieces, and you determine how they best fit together. Using a graphic organizer can help you organize information. There are several graphic organizers that are useful when researching.

### Key Concept Synthesis

In this chart, you list the key concepts you learn from each source, put the idea in your own words, and then explain why it is important and how it relates to other concepts.

| Key Concepts | My Words | Why Important |
|---|---|---|
| Low cost in manufacturing (from Wills article) | Creating products from synthetic polymers saves money | Benefit of using polymers |
| Durability of material (from Wills article) | Synthetic polymers are the material of choice in many areas because they are strong, and not easily broken | Benefit of using polymers |

## Venn Diagram Synthesis

In a Venn diagram, you record information that is the same in sources, and information that is new or different between sources. This can help you see the major ideas or concepts of a topic, and the supporting ideas, details, and examples. Venn diagrams work best with two to three sources.

Lecture                                                     Textbook article

*Environmental concerns:*
*Landfills expanding*
*Pollution*
*Damage to ecosystems*

*Uses of synthetic polymers— widespread*

*Benefits: lower cost in manufacturing, durability, wide variety of uses*

## EXERCISE 4

A. Imagine you need to give a presentation on organic and synthetic polymers. What do you know about the topic? Use the T-chart to brainstorm your ideas.

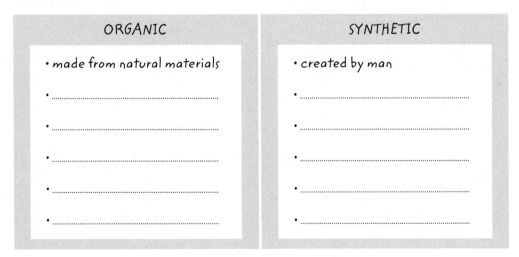

| ORGANIC | SYNTHETIC |
| --- | --- |
| • made from natural materials | • created by man |

B. Now read the textbook excerpt on page 241 and complete the key concept table.

# Natural and Organic Polymers

In all forms of materials science, both natural and synthetic polymers have been the focus of much research and development. Polymers range from natural materials like cellulose and protein to synthetics like polyesters and polyurethane. These helpful molecules have been at the forefront of human innovation ever since our ancestors chose to clothe themselves in animal skins and weave simple baskets of leafy cellulose. Studying the polymers that make up the human body led to discoveries like DNA, while the study of synthetic polymers brought us not only more efficient clothes and storage containers, but also exciting advances like artificial hearts and corrosion-resistant plumbing.

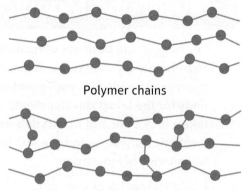

Polymer chains

Cross-linked Polymer chains

Polymers are large molecules or *macromolecules*. They are formed by chaining together smaller, repeating sets of molecules. These smaller links are called *monomers*. Polymers can have a great range of chemical properties depending on their size, shape, and chemical composition. The specific monomer, including how many there are and what the molecules consist of, is especially important.

Some characteristics worth considering when choosing a synthetic polymer for a manufacturing project are polymer crosslinking and the related thermal properties of the polymer. Through various chemical processes, many synthetic polymers can be *cross-linked*: polymers will covalently bond with *other* polymers, turning the entire mass into an enormous molecular web. This creates a material that is *thermoset*: strongly bonded and highly resistant to heat. Thermoset polymers are well suited to applications that require long term durability.

Conversely, other synthetic polymer materials that have not undergone this procedure remain *thermoplastic*. These materials are not as resistant to heat, but because they can be melted, they are especially easy to recycle and reuse for other purposes. Thermoplastic polymers are rapidly becoming a preferred choice in disposable food storage containers since the material can later be melted down and recycled, saving money and minimizing their environmental impact.

| Key Concepts | My Words | Importance |
|---|---|---|
|  |  |  |
|  |  |  |

C. Read a trade magazine article on the same topic. Complete a key concept table.

# Music and Manufacturing

I've been in the business of manufacturing musical instruments for over three decades and am continually impressed by the innovative and creative uses our industry finds for the latest developments in manufacturing. Let's take a look at one of our trade's core resources—the synthetic polymer—and see just how far we have pushed the boundaries of innovation.

Musicians may have been using organic polymers since the beginning of human history; after all, the long molecules formed by the repeated linking of monomers help form the bones, skin, and plant material that ancient drums and flutes are made of. The problem is that natural polymers are vulnerable to the elements; many a hopeful amateur has pulled grandpa's accordion or aunt Edna's guitar out of the attic only to find that moisture, heat, and fungi have turned a potential heirloom into a tragic, unplayable mess.

Synthetic polymers, however, can be made resistant to many of the things that harm instruments made from organic materials. By crosslinking polymers, and covalently bonding the various polymer molecules in a given product, manufacturers were able to make clarinets for beginners that would stay in tune longer and be resistant to the drops and dings likely to occur in the hands of a novice.

Speaking of beginner instruments, light and easily manufactured plastic instruments have been helping to bring the joy of music to interested youngsters for years. As early as the 1950s, instrument makers answered a nationwide ukulele craze with cheap plastic ukuleles—often branded with a particular celebrity or cartoon character. While many of these were little more than toys, modern manufacturing has led to surprisingly rich-sounding brass instruments being created from thermoplastics such as ABS. Plus, that plastic is recyclable, letting us turn tubas into trumpets into trombones and back! Not only is this great for the environment, it means that one manufacturer can create a wide variety of products from the same raw materials.

| Key Concepts | My Words | Importance |
|---|---|---|
|  |  |  |
|  |  |  |
|  |  |  |

**D. Work with a partner. Using your key concepts charts, complete the Venn diagram.**

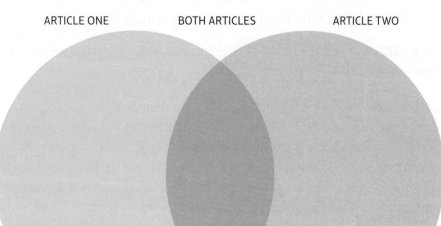

ARTICLE ONE          BOTH ARTICLES          ARTICLE TWO

◑ Go to MyEnglishLab to complete a skill practice.

## LANGUAGE SKILL

### LANGUAGE FOR LINKING IDEAS

**WHY IT'S USEFUL** By identifying and utilizing language for linking ideas, you can help your listeners understand the relationship between key points, which will allow them to better follow complex topics.

◑ Go to MyEnglishLab for the Language Skill presentation and practice.

# VOCABULARY STRATEGY

## LEARNING VOCABULARY THROUGH CATEGORIZATION

**WHY IT'S USEFUL** By using categories to group new technical terms, you can identify and learn new vocabulary and better understand its usage.

Subjects like science can be challenging because of their complex vocabulary. Memorizing these terms, and how to use them often presents a whole other challenge. One effective way to learn new technical terms is by categorizing, or classifying. **Categorizing** refers to grouping terms by a common theme, or function. For example, you may group all the characteristics of synthetic polymers together. By classifying terms, you can better understand their relationship to other terms. Grouping not only helps you learn difficult vocabulary words, but it can also provide you with an effective study aid.

Notice the organization and pattern of these categories.

| Characteristics of Synthetic Polymers | Cross-linked Polymers |
|---|---|
| inorganic | chained |
| durable | covalent |
| heat resistant | ionic |

## EXERCISE 5

A. Look at the words in the box. Using what you have learned in this unit, determine which words and phrases go under each category in the chart.

| | | | | |
|---|---|---|---|---|
| DNA | nylon | naturally-occurring | silk | Teflon™ |
| moldable | durable | made by scientists | nonresistant | |

| Synthetic Polymers | Organic Polymers |
|---|---|
| | |
| | |
| | |
| | |

**B. Look at each set of terms. What do they have in common? Categorize each set.**

1. metallic, ionic, chemical .........................................................

2. green, biodegradable, recyclable .........................................................

3. durable, malleable, strong .........................................................

4. macromolecule, monomer .........................................................

5. linear, branched, cross-linked .........................................................

**C. Work with a partner. Read the excerpt. Categorize the underlined words.**

One of the greatest innovations of modern science has been the development of a class of materials known as polymers. Many refer to polymers as plastics. They are known for their extensive <u>versatility</u> and <u>formability</u>. During production, they can be easily produced into a wide variety of shapes. These synthetic materials share many traits with metals. They have the mechanical property of <u>ductility</u>, and they are <u>not brittle</u>. Additionally, they are <u>lightweight</u>, and provide a <u>cost-effective</u> alternative to metals in the production of many every day products.

## APPLY YOUR SKILLS

**WHY IT'S USEFUL** By applying the skills you have learned in this unit, you will understand and successfully give well-organized formal presentations in academic settings.

### ASSIGNMENT
Prepare a formal, academic presentation on how synthetic polymers are aiding the development of a product in a field of your interest. You will use a wide variety of synthesized resources to support your ideas, and connect ideas using cohesive devices.

### BEFORE YOU LISTEN
**A. Before you listen, discuss the questions with one or more students.**

1. We live in a time of technological advancement. Ideas and concepts that appeared in the movies 20 or 30 years ago are now real. We can carry our phones with us and see and chat with anyone, anywhere in the world. What role has materials engineering played in the development of these products?

2. The fields of medicine and aerospace are both developing more products with synthetic polymers. The medical field plans to develop organs for transplants from synthetic polymers. What do you see as the advantages of this? Are there any disadvantages?

3. How do you think the aerospace industry might be using synthetic polymers? How could synthetic polymers assist our pursuit to find life on other planets?

B. You will listen to a lecture on the future use of polymers, specifically in the fields of medicine and aerospace. As you listen, think about these questions:

1. How could synthetic polymers be used in medicine?

2. Do you think it is likely that human organs (hearts, livers, etc.) created from synthetic polymers can be successfully transplanted in humans? Why?

3. What do the human body and outer space have in common?

4. How can synthetic polymers be used in the development of materials for space? What advantages do they provide?

C. Review the Unit Skills Summary. As you listen to the lecture and prepare for your presentation, apply the skills you learned in this unit.

## UNIT SKILLS SUMMARY

### PREPARE FORMAL PRESENTATIONS USING THESE SKILLS:

**Determine the purpose and structure of presentations**
- Identify the purpose of the presentation by recognizing key words.
- Organize presentations by using an introduction, a body, and a conclusion.

**Select and identify resources to support your presentations**
- Determine the type of presentation.
- Identify the type of resources needed.
- Incorporate definitions, statistics, graphs, illustrations, testimonials, and quotes into your presentation.

**Synthesize resources**
- Utilize the key concept chart to extract key ideas from a resource.
- Identify similarities and differences between resources by using a Venn diagram.

**Utilize language to make connections between ideas**
- Distinguish the relationship between ideas.
- Select the most appropriate cohesive device to signify the relationship.

**Identify new terms by category**
- Categorize new words to learn meaning and usage.

## LISTEN

A. Listen to the lecture on the potential future uses of synthetic polymers. Take notes.

B. Compare your notes with a partner. Do you both have the same key ideas? What skills from this unit can help you identify key ideas?

C. Review the questions from Before You Listen, Part B. Listen to the lecture again. Work with a partner and use your notes on the lecture to answer the questions.

Go to MyEnglishLab to listen more closely, and answer the critical thinking questions.

## THINKING CRITICALLY

### Discuss the questions with another student.

1. Based on the lecture, what products include synthetic polymers?

2. What can you infer by the amount of research put into using synthetic polymers in artificial organ development?

3. Why do you think the professor does not mention any environmental concerns regarding the manufacturing of products from synthetic polymers?

## THINKING VISUALLY

### A. Look at the graph. Discuss the questions with a partner.

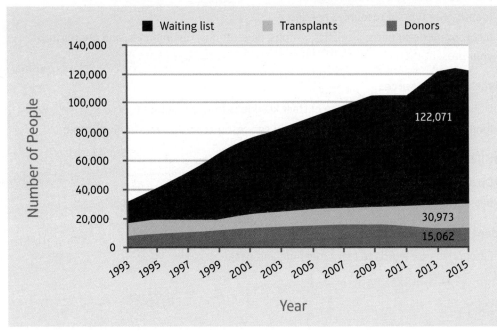

1. Using the information in the graph, why do you think they are researching this area?

2. How could the development of artificial organs change the graph?

3. In your opinion, if artificial organs are not developed, what will the graph look like in 2020? 2025?

For language to describe trends using graphs, see LINGUISTICS, Part 1

### B. Go online and investigate the need for heart valve transplants. Create a visual like the one in Part A. Share it with your classmates by summarizing the information.

◉ Go to MyEnglishLab to record your results.

# THINKING ABOUT LANGUAGE

## Complete each sentence with a cohesive device.

1. Scientists are looking into developing artificial organs from synthetic polymers. ........................ , they are also looking into their applications in space travel.

2. The human body often rejects non-organic matters. ........................ , doctors must carefully watch patients who receive non-organic implants.

3. The demand for donor hearts by patients with heart disease now exceeds the available supply. ........................ , more and more types of artificial hearts are being developed.

4. There have been many great achievements in the research of synthetic polymers. ........................ , the development of synthetic heart valves has greatly helped surgeons and patients.

5. A new group of synthetic polymers is under development that will change our world. ........................ , "bioplastic," a substance made from organic materials rather than petroleum products, would be biodegradable and environmentally-friendly.

6. Scientists are developing self-repairing polymers. ........................ , these polymers have great applications in satellite and space station repairs.

---

**TIP**

Cohesive devices make the connections between ideas clear for your listeners. Cohesive devices have several functions, such as adding information, emphasizing points, giving examples, listing exceptions, and showing cause and effect. For specific examples, refer to the Language Skill presentation in MyEnglishLab.

---

**CULTURE NOTE**

According to the US Department of Health & Human Services, there are about 3,100 people on waiting lists for donor heart transplants every year. However, only about 2,300 donor hearts a year are available. The shortage of hearts means not only that people have to wait longer for transplants, but also that they risk dying while they wait. To help meet the need for donor hearts, artificial hearts have been implanted in some people. Typically, these hearts help patients survive the wait until a suitable human heart is available for transplant. One of the most commonly used artificial heart costs about $125,000 for the initial implant and an additional $18,000 a year to maintain. The first artificial heart to be implanted in a human was in 1969, however the patient later died following the implantation of the donor heart. The first successful artificial heart implant in a human was the Jarvik-7 in 1982, designed by a team including Willem Johan Kolff and Robert Jarvik.

## INDIVIDUAL PRESENTATION

A. Think about the lecture, and other information presented in the unit. There are definite benefits to utilizing synthetic polymers in the production of certain products. Brainstorm the characteristics of synthetic polymers that make them a material of choice.

B. You will prepare a presentation on how a field of your interest (for example, medicine, construction, transportation, electronics, agriculture, or sports) is currently using synthetic polymers in the manufacturing of goods. Use the questions to help you prepare.

1. Which field will you examine?

2. What is the product used or produced for that field?

2. How are synthetic polymers used in the production of that product?

3. Why is it a material of choice? What are the benefits?

4. Are there any drawbacks to using synthetic polymers? Are there any environmental concerns?

C. Listen to each presentation.

Listen carefully and take notes on each presentation. As you listen, note the organizational pattern and resources used. Were the presentations clear and easy to follow? Were the resources appropriate and effective? Discuss the benefits of synthetic polymers. Do the benefits outweigh the drawbacks?

◑ Go to MyEnglishLab to watch Professor Heilshorn's concluding video and to complete a self-assessment.

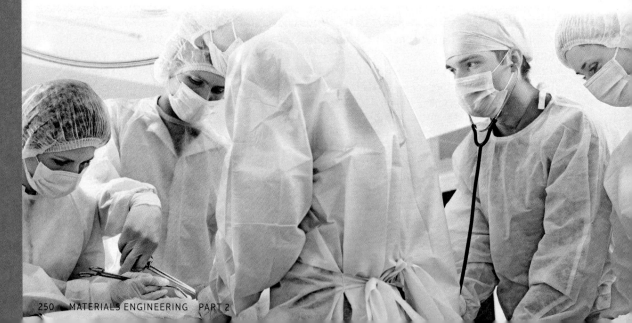

# Extended
# Lectures

*Part 3 presents authentic content written and delivered by university professors. Academically rigorous application and assessment activities allow for a synthesis of the skills developed in Parts 1 and 2.*

*Language communicates who we are*

# LINGUISTICS

# What Accents Tell Us

## UNIT PROFILE

In this unit, you will watch a lecture on how our accents tell those around us where we came from and who we are. Additionally, you will learn what segmental and prosodic features are and how they help us recognize where someone's accent originated.

You will research and prepare a presentation about the regional and educational background of a well-known American and use that information to analyze that person's accent.

For more about **LINGUISTICS**, see ❶❷. See also Ⓡ and Ⓦ **LINGUISTICS** ❶❷❸.

# EXTENDED LECTURE

## BEFORE YOU VIEW

Think about these questions before you view the lecture "What Does My Accent Say About Me?" Discuss them with another student.

1. What can you tell about people by their accent?

2. What are the features of speech that help you decide where someone is from? How about if they are male or female?

3. Do you think you can identify if someone is happy or sad by his or her speech? Why or why not?

4. How does accent affect how other people perceive you?

## LECTURE

Go to MyEnglishLab to view Professor Podesva's lecture. Take notes while you listen. Then answer the questions in Check What You've Learned.

---

### Glossary

Convey: to communicate something without using words

Consciousness: awareness of your thoughts

Phonology: the study of the sounds or the system of the sounds in a language

Segmental features: individual sounds, such consonants and vowels

Prosodic features: intonation, rhythm, pitch, and volume of speech

Ideology: a set of beliefs which influences how one behaves

Affect: (n) emotional response

Isogloss: a line on a map differentiating one regional linguistic feature from another

Nerd: a slang term for someone who is very studious and interested in science, computers, etc.

Jock: a slang term for someone who is very athletic and plays a lot of sports

Burnout: (n) a slang term for someone who habitually abuses drugs

---

**TIP**

When taking notes, it is important to distinguish between facts and opinions. Speakers highlight facts and opinions with signal words and phrases. To learn more or to review these methods, refer to LINGUISTICS, Part 2.

## CHECK WHAT YOU'VE LEARNED

**A. Think about the lecture you have just viewed, and refer to your notes. Answer each question.**

1. Professor Podesva states that our accents say a lot about us. Name four things an accent says about a person.

2. He states that our accents are resources. What three things are they resources for?

3. Professor Podesva begins by defining an accent. How does he define it? Why does he define it? How is the definition important for the lecture?

4. The professor notes that he will only be referring to accents in one's native language. What is he implying by mentioning this?

5. He states that our accents say much more about us than the geographical area we have come from. How does he support this idea?

## B. View the lecture again and answer the questions.

**TIP**

When listening to a lecture, you can identify the speaker's opinion through verbal and non-verbal signposts. For more on identifying opinions and on distinguishing opinions from facts, refer to LINGUISTICS, Part 2.

1. How does Professor Podesva distinguish between an accent and a dialect?

   .................................................................................................

   .................................................................................................

2. What is his opinion about people having an accent?

   .................................................................................................

   .................................................................................................

3. According to the lecture, what is the relationship between phrase lengthening and gender in California?

   .................................................................................................

   .................................................................................................

4. Based on research studies, what is the relationship between social class and "creaky voice" among central California's residents who earn a living off the land?

   .................................................................................................

   .................................................................................................

5. What is the main relationship that Professor Podesva hopes to emphasize?

   .................................................................................................

   .................................................................................................

## THINKING CRITICALLY

**Think about the situation considering what you heard in the lecture. By yourself or with a partner, use what you know about accents and identity to respond.**

**Situation:** In the lecture, Professor Podesva describes several accent features that reveal information about a person's background (family, education, and experiences) and identity. One example is the pronunciation of two words: *cot* and *caught*. According to the lecture, how these words are pronounced can inform us where someone grew up. A second example is phrase-final lengthening, which helps to determine the age and gender of a speaker. The next feature, creaky voice, helps to determine social class. Additionally, Dr. Podesva illustrated how a dark or light "L" can be used to determine ethnic background. Choose a famous person and apply these rules to his or her speech. What can you determine about this person based on his or her accent and the information presented in the lecture?

▶ Go to MyEnglishLab to complete a critical thinking activity.

## THINKING VISUALLY

Read the lecture excerpt and underline the phrases that identify how to label the graph. Add labels for gender and age to the graph showing differences in phrase-final lengthening.

### Excerpt

It's worth considering whether accents that typify geographic areas tell us about other dimensions of identity. ... I'm going to focus on accent features used in California. Even though these might be considered regional features, they also differentiate speakers along other social dimensions. The first social dimension is gender and age. The relevant accent feature is known as phrase-final lengthening. Because speakers typically slow down at the ends of phrases, sounds at the ends of phrases tend to be longer. But how much people lengthen sounds at the ends of phrases varies. ... In a project on 50 Californians that I investigated with my colleagues, we found that phrase-final lengthening varies between men and women and also varies with age. We see that female speakers across the whole age range, as represented by the blue line, have a greater degree of lengthening than male speakers, who are represented by the lower red line. We also see that younger speakers, toward the left of the graph, regardless of gender, lengthen more than older speakers. So, phrase-final lengthening is more prevalent in the speech of women, especially young women. And as it turns out, young women lead in the use of most innovative accent features.

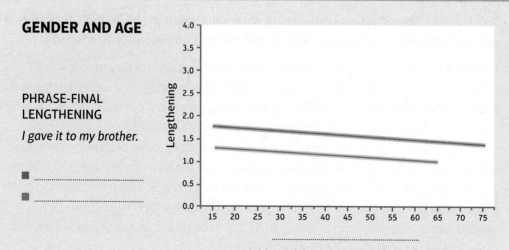

**GENDER AND AGE**

PHRASE-FINAL
LENGTHENING

*I gave it to my brother.*

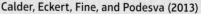

Calder, Eckert, Fine, and Podesva (2013)

**B. Work with a partner. Partner A describes the trends between ages. Partner B describes the trends between genders.**

## THINKING ABOUT LANGUAGE

### IDENTIFYING AND UTILIZING INTERJECTIONS

**Read the sentences from the lecture. Add an interjection from the box to indicate how you feel about the information.**

1. A: An accent might indicate that you come from a particular region of the country, or it might say something about how old you are, your gender, or even your social class.

   B: .............................................................................................

2. A: I want to stress the fact that everyone has an accent.

   B: .............................................................................................

3. A: Surfers are stereotypically male, they're young, and they can generally afford to spend time at the beach instead of working.

   B: .............................................................................................

4. A: Young women lead in the use of most innovative accent features.

   B: .............................................................................................

5. A: Political persuasion is another dimension of identity that can be conveyed by your accent.

   B: .............................................................................................

6. A: It looks like accent features don't just offer clues to where you grew up. Instead they serve as resources for constructing identities.

   B: .............................................................................................

# RECOGNIZING CHANGE OF TOPIC SIGNALS

Read the excerpt below. Circle the signal used when the speaker changes topics.

The way you speak tells people where you came from geographically. There is a clear distinction between regions in North American speech, often referred to as the *cot/caught merger*. In some places these vowels are pronounced the same while in others there is a distinct difference between them. By the way, this applies only to native speakers. With regards to accents and identity, we can also be informed on age. Younger people tend to phrase-final lengthen. In other words, the end of their phrases is often longer. On the subject of phrase-final lengthening, this is also a feature more marked in females. Anyway, it looks like it's time to summarize today's key points.

## INDIVIDUAL PRESENTATION

Dr. Podevsa highlighted many characteristics of speech that can help us determine more about a person. Think about a famous person who is a native English speaker. Consider someone you are familiar with from TV or movies. In this presentation, you will use the features Dr. Podesva explored to research a person's background and analyze his or her accent.

   Topic: A Famous American and Features of His or Her Accent

## RESEARCH

A. Investigate a famous person in the United States. Research that person's background, including birthplace, where he or she grew up, his or her educational experiences, and where that person lives now.

   *Person:* ..............................................................................................

B. Research the regional and educational accent features of the areas where he or she has lived and gone to school. Be sure to select appropriate evidence that adds authority and interest to the topic.

C. Prepare your presentation. Be sure to present your main ideas clearly and to support your ideas with examples.

D. Practice presenting to a partner.

E. While listening to your partner, be sure to distinguish between factual and opinion-based information.

**TIP**

It's important to clarify your ideas by providing clear examples for your listeners. Speakers use a variety of different types of examples. For more on different types of examples, refer to LINGUISTICS, Part 1.

## PRESENT

A. Listen to each class member's presentation. As you listen, complete the chart below.

| Person | Location | Features of accent |
| --- | --- | --- |
|  |  |  |
|  |  |  |
|  |  |  |
|  |  |  |
|  |  |  |
|  |  |  |

B. After the presentations, have a class discussion about each person. Discuss their similarities and differences. Be sure to actively engage in the discussion by signaling interest and using appropriate idioms in your discussion.

🜂 Go to MyEnglishLab to complete a collaborative activity.

## BUSINESS ETHICS

# Moral Inquiry Through Literature

### UNIT PROFILE

In this unit, you will watch a lecture on how great works of literature can help business leaders develop a sense of moral or ethical behavior by understanding and analyzing fictional characters in novels and plays.

**You will research and prepare a presentation on how the behavior of prominent business leaders can reflect on their companies' brands and reputations.**

For more about **BUSINESS ETHICS**, see ❶❷.

See also Ⓡ and Ⓦ **BUSINESS ETHICS** ❶❷❸.

# EXTENDED LECTURE

## BEFORE YOU VIEW

Think about these questions before you view the lecture "Developing Character—Moral Inquiry Through Literature." Discuss them with another student.

1. How does a person learn to behave ethically?

2. What role can literature, movies, and TV play in modeling ethical behavior?

3. How are business leaders often portrayed in books, stories, and movies?

4. Are you familiar with any works of literature that focuses on a business leader and his or her behavior? Describe the character to your partner.

## LECTURE

⬆ Go to MyEnglishLab to view Dr. McLennan's lecture. Take notes while you listen. Then answer the questions in Check What You've Learned.

| TIP |
| --- |
| When listening to a lecture, it is important to listen for cues that signal a main idea and a supporting detail. These signal words can help you better understand the overall organization of the lecture. For more on these signal words, refer to BUSINESS ETHICS, Part 1. |

### Glossary

Vices: immoral behavior or habits

Integrity: being honest and fair-minded

Pragmatic: finding practical solutions to problems

Protagonist: the main character of a novel, play, or movie

Tycoon: an extremely powerful business leader

Across the board: affecting everyone or everything

Workaholic: a person who has a deep need to work all the time

Full of hot air: an idiom for someone who says a lot of foolish or untrue things

Adultery: a married person having sex with someone other than his or her spouse

Diligence: showing careful, constant work or effort; not giving up

Temperance: self-control

Aren't cut out for (something): not well-suited for something

## CHECK WHAT YOU'VE LEARNED

**A. Think about the lecture you have just viewed, and refer to your notes. Answer each question.**

1. According to Dr. McLennan, what can talented playwrights and authors do more successfully than historians or biographers?

   .............................................................................................................................................

2. Why do you think Dr. McLennan uses fictional characters rather than real-life examples to illustrate moral virtues and failings in business?

   .............................................................................................................................................

   .............................................................................................................................................

3. Dr. McLennan uses three stories to illustrate the moral successes and failures of three businessmen. Why do you think these specific stories were chosen?

   .............................................................................................................................................

   .............................................................................................................................................

   .............................................................................................................................................

4. What kind of background information does Dr. McLennan provide for each story? Why?

   .....................................................................

   .....................................................................

> **TIP**
>
> Understanding your audience helps you determine what kind of background information to provide for your listeners. For more on the kind of background information needed for different audiences, refer to BUSINESS ETHICS, Part 2.

5. What can you infer from Dr. McLennan's statements, "Siddhartha has his own share of moral failings along the way. But he seems to learn from them. And he ultimately finds his way to an understanding of what he calls 'the unity of all things.'?"

   .............................................................................................................................................

   .............................................................................................................................................

## B. View the lecture again and answer the questions.

1. What connection does Dr. McLennan make between work and life outside of work?

......................................................................................................................................

......................................................................................................................................

2. How does Dr. McLennan characterize Monroe Stahr's behavior in the workplace? Does he feel he is a moral person? Why or why not?

......................................................................................................................................

......................................................................................................................................

3. How does Willy Loman compare to Monroe Stahr? How are they similar? How are they different?

......................................................................................................................................

......................................................................................................................................

......................................................................................................................................

4. What can be learned from Siddhartha? How does the lecture characterize him?

......................................................................................................................................

......................................................................................................................................

5. What message do you think Dr. McLennan is trying to make clear to listeners?

......................................................................................................................................

......................................................................................................................................

## THINKING CRITICALLY

Think about the situation considering what you heard in the lecture. By yourself or with a partner, use what you know about business and personal ethics to respond.

Situation: In the lecture, Dr. McLennan outlines how literature is an effective way to "see deeply into the minds and emotions and spiritual centers of individuals" both inside and outside the workplace. Do you think movies and TV provide similar insight into the human mind, heart, and spiritual center? Consider a TV show or movie you have recently seen showing someone's life "in the bedroom and the boardroom." Choose a character to analyze as Dr. McLennan did. What moral victories and failings does this character have, and how do they impact his or her business and personal life?

Go to MyEnglishLab to complete a critical thinking activity.

A. Review three excerpts from the lecture. Each excerpt gives a description of one of the characters. Use words and phrases from the excerpt to complete the Venn diagram below.

### Excerpt One

Its hero, Monroe Stahr, has been enormously successful by the age of 34 when we meet him. "He was a marker in industry like Edison. He felt a great purposefulness. He'd been a money man among money men." And he cared about making a quality picture even though it would lose money, knowing that it would also bring in new customers through goodwill for the studio. There's a wonderful section of the novel, near the beginning, which is described as a producer's day. The reader sees Monroe's star as he sympathetically reinstates a cameraman who'd been wrongly terminated. He reinvigorates a talented person who has writer's block. He counsels an actor having problems in his private life. He replaces a director who isn't working well with his actors. And he reviews and cuts film scenes and much more. Across the board in his business, he shows sensitivity, knowledge, insight, decisiveness, and wisdom. Virtues of character that come through are passion for his craft, hard work, genuine caring for people, integrity about the quality of his products, composure, and a capacity for self-reflection. His great failing, however, literally his fatal flaw, is that he's a workaholic, without any sense of proportion about his own life. The good part of this is his inability to form close friendships and find a life companion. In short, to give and receive love. He has, he has heart problems, which his doctor says will actually kill him within a year if he doesn't slow down and develop a capacity to rest and relax.

### Excerpt Two

Willy Loman has exactly what Stahr lacks. He's married with two children, and as we're told in the stage instructions at the beginning, Linda, his wife, more than loves him: She admires him. His sons have admired and idolized, almost lionized him, as they grew up. And his message to them has always been, be liked and you will never want. He has a close friend, Charlie, who lives next door, but Willy goes too far with loving relationships. And he has an affair on the road as a salesman. His older son finds out about it during high school and is never the same again…. Willy is a hardworking salesman surrounded by a loving wife and children as well as a loyal friend, Charlie. Exactly the relationships that Monroe Stahr doesn't have. But his life becomes a lie when he betrays his wife in a relationship with another woman, when he finds himself in the wrong line of work and doesn't get out. And his final and most terrible failing is when he tries to convince his adoring children to follow in his footsteps at work rather than find their own careers for which they have a genuine passion and ability.

### Excerpt Three

Siddhartha's moral character was shaped by the traditional virtues of diligence, patience, temperance, kindness, charity, and humility. But then we're told slowly the soul sickness of the rich crept over him. As the narrator explains, "the world had caught him, pleasure, covetousness, idleness, and finally that vice he'd always despised and scorned as the most foolish: acquisitiveness. Property possessions and riches had also finally trapped him. They were no longer a game and a toy. They'd become a chain and a burden." So, he turns to gambling and alcohol and profligate sex. At the same time, he lost his patience with slow-paying debtors, and he was no longer kind-hearted to beggars. He became more hard and mean in business and sometimes dreamt of money at night. And eventually he comes close to committing suicide, saved by an old friend. Luckily for him, Siddhartha had developed some close relationships during his life, starting with loving and giving parents. He had a long liaison with a woman who bore him a son, for whom he had the deepest of love. He also had a lifelong friend who was always loyal to him. And in his later years he began working with an experienced ferryman, taking travelers and cargo back and forth across a river. And this was the business in which it finally all came together for Siddhartha. Together these two provide an important service. Siddhartha and the ferryman were always respectful of their customers, some of whom turn to them for comfort and advice as well as for transportation. It is through practicing the classic virtues of diligence, patience, temperance, kindness, charity, and humility that Siddhartha finds true success.

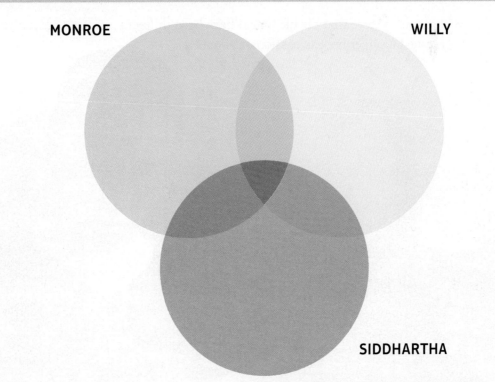

MONROE

WILLY

SIDDHARTHA

B. Work with a partner. Compare your Venn diagrams. How are they similar? How are they different?

> **TIP**
>
> Venn diagrams help you to organize information visually so you can see the relationships between two or three sets of items. These diagrams can then identify similarities and differences. For more on Venn diagrams, refer to LINGUISTICS, Part 2.

## THINKING ABOUT LANGUAGE
## DESCRIBING RELATIONSHIPS WITH ADVERBIAL CLAUSES

Add an adverb to complete each sentence.

> **TIP**
>
> Adverbial clauses describe relationships. They tell us when, where, how, and to what extent something happens. For more on adverbial clauses, refer to BUSINESS ETHICS, Part 1.

1. ............................ Willy was not passionate about his job, he still worked hard.

2. Monroe was happy ............................ he was working.

3. Siddhartha found happiness ............................ he experienced a personal low.

4. ............................ to better understand the human mind and spirit, we will look at famous characters in literature.

5. ............................ Monroe hesitates about proposing to his love, he loses her.

6. Willy's sons believe that his life would have been different ............................ he pursued a career he was passionate about.

## CLARIFYING WITH NOUN CLAUSES

### Circle the noun clause in each statement.

1. Willy believed that he could be happy working a job he was not cut out for.

2. His objective was to see how much money he could make.

3. Why it is so hard for some to find happiness is a mystery.

4. It is critical that you have balance in your life.

5. The story suggests that being ethical involves both work and life balance.

6. Siddhartha knew that he needed self-fulfillment and friends.

> **TIP**
>
> Speakers often use a noun clause to describe something or someone with more precision. For more on utilizing noun clauses to clarify meaning, see BUSINESS ETHICS, Part 2.

## PAIR PRESENTATION

Dr. McLennan analyzed three famous works of literature and illustrated how readers can gain insight into moral behavior in business by evaluating the main characters in each work. He implied that people must not only behave ethically in their work lives but in all aspects of their lives. Consumers often evaluate a company by their leader. If they feel a leader is ethical, they are more likely to purchase that company's products or use their services. This is known as the "halo effect." Conversely, if a corporate leader is regarded as dishonest, unfair, or unethical, consumers will react in the opposite way. This is known as the "reverse-halo" or the "devil effect."

In this presentation, you will use the virtues outlined in the lecture (sensitivity, compassion, insight, diligence, patience, temperance, integrity, and fairness) to evaluate a business leader and determine how moral or ethically that person behaves and how that behavior has affected the company's reputation.

Topic: The behavior of today's tycoons and its impact on their companies

## RESEARCH

**A. Work with a partner. Discuss the questions.**

1. What are some specific examples of ethical and unethical behavior?

2. Which prominent businesspeople are viewed by the public as being highly ethical? Which are viewed as being unethical?

3. What effect do these leaders' reputations have on their companies? Give examples.

........................................................................................................................................

........................................................................................................................................

**B. Research a famous business leader – living or dead. Work with your partner. Investigate the leader's characteristics and the impact of the halo or devil effect on the company and its brand. Be sure to select appropriate examples and evidence that clarify your topic and add authority and interest.**

> **TIP**
>
> It's important to use a variety of evidence to support your ideas. Certain types of evidence can clarify or explain your ideas while other types of evidence might add authority or interest to your topic. For more on how to select appropriate evidence, refer to BUSINESS ETHICS, Part 2.

**C. Prepare your presentation. Decide which sections each of you will present. Be sure to present your main ideas clearly and to support your ideas with examples.**

**D. Practice presenting to another pair.**

**E. While listening to the other pair present, suggest places where words with strong connotative meanings can be used to make the ideas more compelling.**

# PRESENT

A. Listen to each pair's presentation. As you listen, complete the chart below.

| Business Leaders | Ethical characteristics | Unethical characteristics |
| --- | --- | --- |
|  |  |  |
|  |  |  |
|  |  |  |
|  |  |  |
|  |  |  |
|  |  |  |
|  |  |  |

B. After the presentations, have a class discussion on the different leaders presented. Discuss their similarities and differences. Who has demonstrated the most ethical behavior? Who has demonstrated the least ethical behavior? Be sure to actively engage in the discussion.

⬤ Go to MyEnglishLab to complete a collaborative activity.

*Decisions we make today will shape our future*

# EARTH SCIENCE

# What Is the Anthropocene?

## UNIT PROFILE

In this unit, you will watch a lecture on the importance of the geological timetable. Additionally, you will learn how geological forces shape the rules on the planet. Last, you will be introduced to a potential new geologic framework, the Anthropocene, which asserts that humanity itself is an agent of geologic change.

**You will research and debate whether human damage to the environment could potentially lead to catastrophic consequences.**

For more about **EARTH SCIENCE**, see ①②. See also ⟨R⟩ and ⟨W⟩ **EARTH SCIENCE** ①②③.

# EXTENDED LECTURE

## BEFORE YOU VIEW

Think about these questions before you view the lecture "What Is the Anthropocene, and Why Is It Important?" Discuss them with another student.

1. What changes have occurred on our planet? What has been the cause of these changes?

2. What caused the dinosaurs to go extinct?

3. In what ways has the climate affected the planet?

4. How have humans affected the planet?

## LECTURE

Go to MyEnglishLab to view Dr. Osborne's lecture. Take notes while you listen. Then answer the questions in Check What You've Learned.

### Glossary

Hard to get your head around:  difficult to understand

Fossils:  animals or plants that lived in the distant past and are preserved in rock

Plate tectonics:  the movement of the large sheets that form the Earth's surface

Fluctuate:  rising or falling irregularly in number or amount

Carbon cycle:  The cycle where carbon dioxide is incorporated into living tissue via photosynthesis and released back to the atmosphere via respiration, decay, or the burning of fossil fuels.

Mass extinction:  when an extremely large number of species stop existing

Paleo-climatologist:  someone who studies the climate of the distant past

Sacrosanct:  something considered too important to interfere with

### TIP

When taking notes on geological time, it is important to distinguish between time frames. Speakers use signal words to indicate when something happened. For more information on these signal words, refer to EARTH SCIENCE, Part 1.

## CHECK WHAT YOU'VE LEARNED

**A. Think about the lecture you have just viewed, and refer to your notes. Answer each question.**

1. Dr. Osborne presents a case that the concept of the Anthropocene is critical for humans today. Why does he want us to be aware of the Anthropocene, and what does Dr. Osborne hope we will do with this information?

   ................................................................................................................................................

   ................................................................................................................................................

   ................................................................................................................................................

   ................................................................................................................................................

2. Why does Dr. Osborne assert that climate change and global warming provide critical evidence of the Anthropocene?

   ................................................................................................................................................

   ................................................................................................................................................

   ................................................................................................................................................

3. What major effect of climate change did he use to demonstrate the power of past climate changes?

   ................................................................................................................................................

   ................................................................................................................................................

4. Why does Dr. Osborne talk about the future? What does he want his listeners to understand?

   ................................................................................................................................................

   ................................................................................................................................................

5. What might the fossil record look like in a million years from now?

   ................................................................................................................................................

   ................................................................................................................................................

### CULTURE NOTE

Dr. Osborne refers to a time machine, a flux capacitor and a DeLorean car when describing how we might travel into the future. These terms refer to a famous American movie, *Back to the Future*. In the movie, a scientist creates a time machine using a flux capacitor, and a DeLorean automobile. However, the scientist mistakenly went back in time rather than forward and then needed to return to the current time.

## B. View the lecture again and answer the questions.

1. According to Dr. Osborne, what do geologists do?

    ....................................................................................................................

    ....................................................................................................................

**TIP**

When listening to a lecture, speakers often define new key terms. The speaker may use a defining verb, or an example to explain each term. For more on listening for definitions, refer to EARTH SCIENCE, Part 2.

2. What does Dr. Osborne mean when he states that plate tectonics is often referred to as "the unifying theory of geology?"

    ....................................................................................................................

    ....................................................................................................................

3. During the 1950s, what human-created event took place that changed the chemistry of the atmosphere?

    ....................................................................................................................

    ....................................................................................................................

4. What does Dr. Osborne imply when he states that scientists from a variety of scientific fields will need to collaborate?

    ....................................................................................................................

    ....................................................................................................................

5. Dr. Osborne is very passionate about the Anthropocene, and stresses the importance of this potential new epoch. Why does he state the Anthropocene concept is so important today?

    ....................................................................................

    ....................................................................................

    ....................................................................................

**TIP**

When listening to a lecture, it's important to determine a speaker's intensity. Identifying boosting language can help you measure a speaker's level of assertiveness or passion about a topic. For more on boosting words, refer to EARTH SCIENCE, Part 2.

## THINKING CRITICALLY

Think about the situation considering what you heard in the lecture. By yourself or with a partner, use what you know about geological forces and the Anthropocene to respond.

**Situation:** In the lecture, Dr. Osborne explains the importance of the geological timetable, its role in describing Earth's history, and how the past of the planet can help us predict its future. He discusses geological forces, including the climate system, and how they impact the planet. He also introduces the concept of the Anthropocene and makes a case for humans as another agent of geologic change. With this in mind, choose a human behavior or human-caused event that has negatively impacted our planet, and discuss its potential effect on our climate.

⊙ Go to MyEnglishLab to complete a critical thinking activity.

## THINKING VISUALLY

A. Review the timeline indicating when five mass extinctions occurred. Dr. Osborne uses one extinction event as an example. At what period boundary did it occur?

## Geologic Time Scale

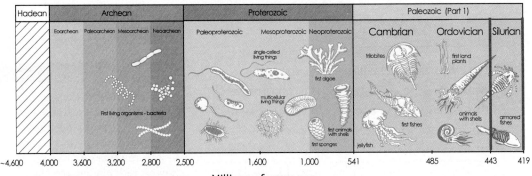

Millions of years ago

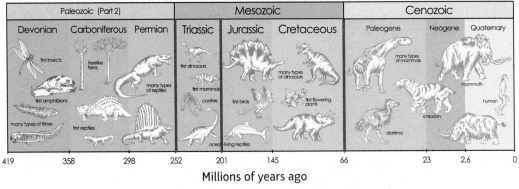

Millions of years ago

### Five **Mass Extinctions** in Earth History

B. Work with a partner. Using the timeline from Part A, and the excerpt below, summarize the five extinctions.

> About 66 million years ago, a giant meteor struck the Earth and led to a cascade of events that eventually killed the dinosaurs. More than 65 percent of species were wiped out in this event. But this is actually just one of five examples from Earth's history. There have been five mass extinction—five periods where large numbers of species were wiped out, never to return again.

**TIP**

Summarizing involves stating the event actions or events. In order to organize information to be included in a summary, consider using a graphic organizer. For more on graphic organizers for summarizing, refer to EARTH SCIENCE, Part 1.

## THINKING ABOUT LANGUAGE
## USING MODALS FOR POSSIBILITIES AND PROBABILITIES

A. Read the sentences from the lecture. Based on the modals used, determine if Dr. Osborne feels the information is *PR* (probable or very certain) or *PO* (possible but less certain).

............. 1. This is being taken seriously in the Earth Science and the Earth System Science community. And you can make arguments for a lot of different places.

**TIP**

Speakers use modals to indicate their certainty and the reliability of what is being said. There are different strengths of modals of possibility and probability, and listeners can interpret how certain speakers are by which modals they use. For more on modals expressing possibility and probability, refer to EARTH SCIENCE, Part 1.

............. 2. Chemistry tells about conditions on the planet millions of years ago and fossils tell us which organisms have come and gone. All of this information tells us about the immense powers that must have operated on this planet.

............. 3. You probably live in a city. And if you do, then you would think that the sediments of the future may be pavement, may be skyscrapers, may be sewer systems, or subway systems.

B. Rewrite each statement with a different modal to change the level of certainty.

## NOTICING BOOSTING LANGUAGE

**Read each sentence from the lecture and circle the boosting language. If there is none, add boosting language where appropriate.**

1. So one of the things that our future geologist is almost definitely going to see is a layer of plastics.

**TIP**

Speakers often add boosting words to show enthusiasm and interest about what is being said. Adverbs, definitive phrases, and *it + is+* adjective constructions all help boost, or intensify what is being said. For more on boosting language, see EARTH SCIENCE, Part 2.

2. We've also changed the chemistry of the atmosphere, and in particular in the 1950s there were a lot of nuclear tests by the United States and the former Soviet Union, and this actually changed the isotopic composition of many elements that exist in our air.

3. And then of course there's climate change, which I'm sure you've heard of.

4. We have now transformed over half of Earth's surface in the name of food production to feed the world.

5. There are all kinds of exponential changes underway on the Earth's surface today.

## CLASS DEBATE

Dr. Osborne made a case that human beings are responsible for recent changes in the Earth's atmosphere, climate, oceans, and land surface. He contends that these changes put life on Earth at risk for possible extinction. Although many scientists agree with Dr. Osborne, others argue that the current climate change is just a part of a recurring cycle, like many others throughout history. These people feel that the danger has been greatly exaggerated. What do you think? Do you believe that disregard for the environment could result in another mass extinction event? Or, do you believe the current global temperature extremes are just a cyclical event, without consequences for the planet in the long run?

You will participate in a debate in which the class is divided into two teams. Team A will argue in favor of the proposition. Team B will argue against the proposition.

Proposition: Human damage to the environment could lead to another mass extinction event.

## RESEARCH

A. Investigate the history of global climate changes, and determine if current changes in climate are similar to or different from previous ones. Find evidence that supports or refutes humanity's role in the current climate change. Discuss your team's position and write a claim. Brainstorm a list of points that support your claim.

Claim: ..................................................................................................................................

B. Choose team members (individuals or pairs) to give the opening and closing statements. Then divide the supporting arguments among the other team members.

C. Research alone, or with a teammate, the best arguments to support your position.

D. Prepare your statements. Be sure to use signal words and break down complex steps with details. Present your main ideas clearly and support your ideas with examples. If applicable, prepare visual aids.

E. Practice presenting your argument with your team members. While listening to your team members, be sure to ask for specifics when you want more information.

## DEBATE

A. Establish the rules and time limits of the debate before beginning. Begin the debate and follow these steps:

1. Team A delivers its opening statement.

2. Team B delivers its opening statement.

3. Team A and B alternate presenting specific arguments and responses.

4. Team A delivers its closing statement.

5. Team B delivers its closing statement.

B. After the debate, have a class discussion. Discuss your experience with the points raised. Which team's arguments were the strongest? Why? Are there any issues you would like to know more about?

◆ Go to MyEnglishLab to complete a collaborative activity.

# MEDIEVAL CULTURE

# Lyrics and Poetry

## UNIT PROFILE

In this unit, you will watch a lecture on how songbooks and medieval lyrics have shaped poetry. You will also learn about the influence lyrics, song, and poetry continue to have on our lives today.

**You will research and prepare a panel discussion on the cultural influences still felt today from a historical time period.**

For more about **MEDIEVAL CULTURE**, see ❶ ❷.
See also ⟦R⟧ and ⟦W⟧ **MEDIEVAL CULTURE** ❶ ❷ ❸.

# EXTENDED LECTURE

## BEFORE YOU VIEW

Think about these questions before you view the lecture "How Lyrics Became Poetry: Troubadours and Songbooks." Discuss them with another student.

1. What are some characteristics that occur both in song and poetry?

2. What role do you think rhyming has in song? How about poetry?

3. What are some common themes in song and poems today?

4. Which of those themes do you think occurred in songs and poems during the Middle Ages (1100–1300 CE)?

## LECTURE

▶ Go to MyEnglishLab to view Professor Galvez's lecture. Take notes while you listen. Then answer the questions in Check What You've Learned.

---

**TIP**

When listening to a lecture on a new or unfamiliar topic, it is important to take clear notes. One effective note-taking method is spider mapping. Spider mapping allows you to visually see, and connect main and supporting ideas. For more on spider mapping, refer to MEDIEVAL CULTURE, Part 1.

---

### Glossary

Troubadour: a singer, composer, and poet who performed for aristocrats in southern France

Vernacular: a form of language that ordinary people use, especially one that is not the official language

Secular: not connected to religion or controlled by the church

Feudal: relating to the system in which people received land and protection from a lord in exchange for working and fighting for him

Social agenda: a set of issues or policies people want done for a society

Elite social milieu: the social environment of the highest, best-educated social class

Skeleton: the basic structure or framework of a poem of song

Chansonnier: a Medieval songbook popular in Northern Italy

Resonate: to appeal to someone in a personal way

## CHECK WHAT YOU'VE LEARNED

**A. Think about the lecture you have just viewed, and refer to your notes. Answer each question.**

**TIP**

Speakers use a variety of styles and rhetorical devices to make an appeal. Sometimes they combine styles to be more effective. Three common styles include: ethos, pathos, and logos. For more about the characteristics of these appeals, refer to MEDIEVAL CULTURE, Part 2.

1. What main ideas did Professor Galvez present in her lecture? Choose the three main ideas.

   ☐ a. How the lyrics of troubadours were made into songbooks

   ☐ b. Who the medieval poets were, and how they influenced Western literary tradition

   ☐ c. Why songbooks developed from poetry

   ☐ d. How poetry was inspired by religious events

   ☐ e. The two ways in which someone can read the troubadours' lyrics through songbooks to see how music, image, and text combined

2. What were two common themes in songs of the troubadours?

   ......................................................................................................................................

   ......................................................................................................................................

3. According to Professor Galvez, what was a dominating element of poetry in medieval culture?

   ......................................................................................................................................

4. Which of these styles did Professor Galvez use to make her appeal?

   ☐ a. *Ethos*: Establishes authority, gives background or qualifications, uses success stories, makes eye contact

   ☐ b. *Logos*: Presents facts, data, statistics, research, quotations, repeats key words and phrases

   ☐ c. *Pathos*: Tells stories, includes emotional and figurative (symbolic) language

   ☐ d. Both *logos* and *pathos*

   ☐ e. All three: *ethos*, *pathos*, and *logos*.

5. What can you infer about the talents of troubadours from Professor Galvez?

   ......................................................................................................................................

   ......................................................................................................................................

## B. View the lecture again and answer the questions.

1. What dates are given in the lecture for the beginning and end of the "Troubadour Period?"

.................................................................................................................................

2. When Professor Galvez recites a piece of poetry in the Occitan language, what does she ask you to notice?

.................................................................................................................................

.................................................................................................................................

3. Professor Galvez uses a simile to describe how the ending of a song could be addressed to a specific person. She says within the song there is something "kind of like a wink." What does she mean?

> **TIP**
>
> *Similes* are a type of figurative language. They compare two things using very descriptive language. For more about similes and other types of figurative language, refer to MEDIEVAL CULTURE, Part 2.

.................................................................................................................................

.................................................................................................................................

4. Professor Galvez points out that few texts were written down due to the costs and labor of producing materials, such as parchment and vellum (prepared animal skins) to write on. Why do you think she points this out?

.................................................................................................................................

.................................................................................................................................

5. How does Professor Galvez illustrate how songbooks combined word, image, and music?

.................................................................................................................................

## THINKING CRITICALLY

**Think about the situation, considering what you heard in the lecture. By yourself or with a partner, use what you know about Medieval history and the troubadour tradition to respond.**

**Situation:** In the lecture, Professor Galvez states that the troubadours came from many different social classes and could be knights, clerics, or bakers. As entertainers of kings, troubadours had some measure of celebrity, and access to the rich and powerful at the courts where they performed. Dr. Galvez cites examples of songs on themes of love, social agendas, and moral instruction. Considering such things as social class, access to power, and themes, compare today's celebrities and entertainers to the troubadours.

🔾 Go to MyEnglishLab to complete a critical thinking activity.

## SCRIPT ANALYSIS

**A. Review the excerpt from the lecture. Find and circle the five collocations. The first one has been done for you.**

The troubadours by this time and in this place had enough (cultural status) to be placed in such books. These songbooks organize this poetry in a certain way so that audiences who were not there at the original performance could make sense of the troubabours. Songs were grouped by author and genre. Categories included love songs, moral or satirical songs, or dialogue songs between two poets. Sometimes poets might be ranked by their social status. The majority of troubadour chansonniers transmit no musical notation. Just lyrics. This tells us much about what this audience valued and how they viewed poetry as separate from music. Their view of poetry is similar to the poetry that we read in books today which is different than the lyrics of songs we hear on the radio. Other ways the chansonniers archived the lyrics and instruct readers in how to understand them is through the pictures that accompanied the lyrics of one troubadour and prose biographies, or *vitas*, that gave a snapshot of a troubadour's life—where he is from, his status in life, was he a knight, was he a cleric, was he a baker's son, the patron he served, or the court in which he was active, and finally what motivated him or her to compose poetry. Most of these biographies were drawn from the lyric themselves.

> **TIP**
>
> *Collocations* are two or more words that often appear together. Understanding collocations is important because language meaning is often determined by groups of words rather than individual words. For more on collocations refer to MEDIEVAL CULTURE, Part 1.

**B. Review the alliteration in the example excerpt from the lecture. Find and circle ten examples of alliteration in the second excerpt below.**

> **TIP**
>
> *Alliteration* is the repetition of an initial consonant sound. This repetition creates a rhythm that makes it appealing to listen to. For more on rhetorical devices, such as alliteration, refer to MEDIEVAL CULTURE, Part 2.

My heart draws me toward love, and I'm better made for his command. Heart, body, knowledge, (se)nse, (s)trength, and energy, I (s)et all on love. The rain draws me (s)traight toward love and I cannot (t)urn (t)owards anything else.

**Excerpt**

The image represents one version of the ideal lover celebrated by the troubadours. The lover is powerless, passive, pensive, and in adoration of the high-born lady. Once he finally reaches the object of his desire, he dies in her arms. In his lyrics, Jaufre sings about how he is unable to touch or talk to his lady, and soon he converts this sadness to a celebration of her separation, a desire of desire.

**C. Work with a partner. Take turns reading each excerpt. Be sure to use what you learned about rhythm, melody, speaking rate, and volume.**

## THINKING ABOUT LANGUAGE
### RECOGNIZING TIME FRAME AND ASPECT IN NARRATIVES

Read a story about a troubadour named Roland. Underline all the verb forms, then use the verb forms to determine the time frame and aspects used.

> **TIP**
>
> Verbs have two parts: time frame and aspect. The time frame tells us when, and the aspect tells us how. A storyteller's choice of time frame and aspect can convey an additional meaning. For more on time frames and aspects in narratives, refer to MEDIEVAL CULTURE, Part 1.

Long, long ago, a boy was born into a royal family. His name was Roland, and he was the nephew of Charlemagne, king of the Holy Roman Empire. Roland loved music, lyrics, and stories. He wanted to become a troubadour. As he grew, so did his passion for music. He played a musical horn, and entertained people throughout the land.

Then his country went to war. Roland served as a knight and was sent to fight. It was a terrible battle, and Roland found himself and a few other knights and soldiers surrounded by the opposing army. He knew they needed help, so Roland pulled out his horn. He began playing to alert others to come and help. However, help arrived too late. Roland and his band were all dead. King Charlemagne, Roland's uncle, was heartbroken. The King insisted that all troubadours carry a horn with them, as a reminder of the sacrifices made by Roland.

The Knight Roland

Time frame ........................................................................................................................

Aspects ...............................................................................................................................

## USING SIMILES AND METAPHORS

Circle the two nouns or noun phrases being compared.

1. Troubadours are like stage actors today.

2. The King was as cold as ice.

3. The poem flowed like a river.

4. Women were treasured like diamonds.

5. Love was as powerful as war.

6. The professor recites the poem like a troubadour.

**TIP**

The use of figurative language, like similes and metaphors, can create a more vivid picture for listeners. Similes and metaphors compare two nouns or noun phrases. For more on forming similes and metaphors, refer to MEDIEVAL CULTURE, Part 2.

## PANEL DISCUSSION

In the lecture, Professor Galvez spoke of how the great influence of lyrics, songs, and poetry of the Middle Ages helped to shape much of the literary, musical, and artistic traditions of the Western world. She pointed out how themes that arose in medieval times, such as unanswered love and social issues, are still popular in contemporary story and song. The arts of the medieval times continue to impact our lives today. Can you think of other historical periods that have caused new themes to appear in our arts—music, poetry, drama, painting, sculpture, or movies? How did the events of that time impact the arts?

You will prepare a panel discussion on the influence that another historical period continues to have on contemporary life. How have these periods influenced our lives today? What has continued to be part of our lives from those periods in history?

Topic: The Most Important Historical Influence on Contemporary Life.

## RESEARCH

A. Investigate an influential historical period. Consider such periods as the renaissance, the enlightenment, the romantic period, the industrial revolution, the atomic age, the information age, or your own idea. Working with your group, choose a time period to focus on, and decide which appeal style(s) you will use to convince your listeners.

B. Research your time period alone. Be sure to select appropriate evidence that adds authority and interest to the topic. As you research, consider these questions:

1. What was invented, discovered, or introduced into society at that time?

2. What effects did these new objects have on people's lives?

3. How were these effects reflected in the themes of literature, art, or songs of the period?

4. How and where can these cultural themes still be seen in contemporary life?

C. Prepare your discussion. Decide which sections each of you will talk about. Be sure to state your main ideas clearly and to support your appeal with appropriate examples.

D. Practice your discussion with another small group. While listening to the other group, suggest how they can utilize prosodic features more effectively.

> **TIP**
>
> Prosodic features in speech, rhythm, and melody, can keep the attention of your listeners, and communicate how you feel about the topic. Rising in pitch, elongating key syllables, utilizing non-verbal cues, and using facial expressions and gestures can all help you better engage your audience. For more on prosodic speech features, and use of gestures and expressions, refer to MEDIEVAL CULTURE, Part 1.

## DISCUSS

A. Listen to each group's panel discussion. As you listen, complete the chart below.

| Period in history | Cultural themes | How influences our lives today |
|---|---|---|
|  |  |  |
|  |  |  |
|  |  |  |
|  |  |  |

B. After the presentations, have a class discussion on the different time periods presented. Which time periods do you feel have had the greatest influence on our lives today? Why? Be sure to actively engage in the discussion.

⬆ Go to MyEnglishLab to complete a collaborative activity.

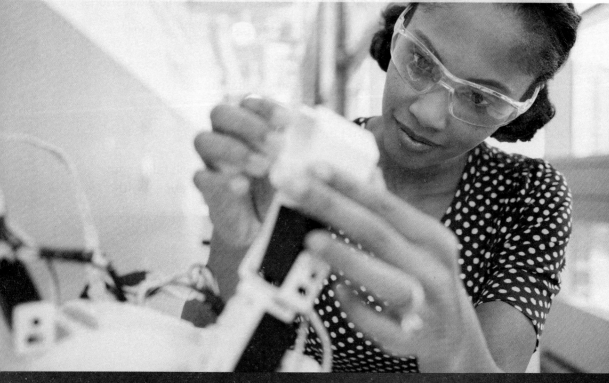

*How the study of molecules relates to the real world*

## MATERIALS ENGINEERING

# Engineering Biomedical Materials

### UNIT PROFILE

In this unit, you will watch a lecture on materials science and engineering. You will learn what materials science and engineering is, some applications of this field, and how new devices are being developed to improve human health and well-being. Finally, you will see the critical role materials engineering plays in our everyday lives.

**You will research and prepare a presentation on why a product material was replaced by another material and how that new material is an improvement over the previous one.**

For more about **MATERIALS ENGINEERING**, see ①②.

See also ⓡ and ⓦ **MATERIALS ENGINEERING** ①②③.

# EXTENDED LECTURE

## BEFORE YOU VIEW

Think about these questions before you view the lecture "An Introduction to Materials Science and Engineering and Their Application to Biomedical Materials." Discuss them with another student.

1. Look around and consider some of the objects near you. What materials are they made of?

2. What determines which material is used in the production of an object?

3. How many objects near you appear to be made from plastic?

4. What are some everyday objects made from plastic? How about objects used in the healthcare industry?

## LECTURE

Go to MyEnglishLab to view Professor Heilshorn's lecture. Take notes while you listen. Then answer the questions in Check What You've Learned.

> **TIP**
>
> When listening to a dense lecture, it is important to listen for cues that signal the organizational pattern of the lecture. Signal words can help you better follow and take notes on dense lectures. To learn more on signal words, refer to MATERIALS ENGINEERING, Part 1.

### Glossary

Microstructure: the arrangement of molecules that can be seen under a microscope

Real-world properties: obvious, practical characteristics rather than theoretical ones

Metallic bonds: chemical bonds that hold metal together through the attraction of fixed and mobile, positive, electrons

Ductile: able to be deformed or distorted; not brittle (easily broken)

Conductors: materials that allow heat and electricity to move freely

Ionic bonds: chemical bonds in which an atom loans one or more electrons to another atom

Insulator: a material that allows little or no heat to go into or out of something

Polymers: long molecules made up of repeating units

Covalent bonds: a chemical bond which is formed by a shared electron

Elasticity: the ability to return to an original shape

Crystalline: a three-dimensional arrangement of atoms

## CHECK WHAT YOU'VE LEARNED

**A. Think about the lecture you have just viewed, and refer to your notes. Answer each question.**

1. Which of these points from the lecture is <u>not</u> a key idea?

   ☐ Materials science is the study of how molecules are connected together.

   ☐ Chemical bonds hold molecules together.

   ☐ Glass is fragile and prone to mechanical failure.

   ☐ Materials science and engineering has applications in the biomedical field.

2. What three categories are materials generally separated into?

   ..........................................................................................................................................

   ..........................................................................................................................................

   ..........................................................................................................................................

3. Professor Heilshorn walks listeners through the properties that are associated with each type of material. What is the connection between their properties and their use?

   ..........................................................................................................................................

   ..........................................................................................................................................

4. According to Professor Heilshorn, what is the underlying cause of the real-world properties of a material?

   ..........................................................................................................................................

5. Why does she describe the unique properties that polymers have?

   ..........................................................................................................................................

   ..........................................................................................................................................

**B. View the lecture again and answer the questions.**

1. Professor Heilshorn begins by defining exactly what material science and engineering is. What can be implied by her explaining what the field is, and the fundamental disciplines it represents?

   ..........................................................................................................................................

   ..........................................................................................................................................

   ..........................................................................................................................................

2. According to the lecture, in what two ways are the properties of metals different from the properties of ceramics?

.............................................................................................

.............................................................................................

3. What are the similarities between polymers and metals, and polymers and ceramics?

.............................................................................................

.............................................................................................

4. Professor Heilshorn mentions that polymers are used in contact lenses because they have several excellent mechanical properties. What are some of those properties?

.............................................................................................

.............................................................................................

5. What are three examples from the lecture showing how these materials are being used in our bodies today?

.............................................................................................

.............................................................................................

## THINKING CRITICALLY

**Think about the situation considering what you heard in the lecture. By yourself or with a partner, use what you know about material science and engineering to respond.**

**Situation:** In the lecture, Professor Heilshorn outlines why certain materials are more suitable for manufacturing a product than others. She carefully describes the properties that help determine why one material is better than another. Choose any everyday object. Based on the information in the lecture, and what you have learned in the units, explain why the properties of the material used for that object are suited to its function.

⚓ Go to MyEnglishLab to complete a critical thinking activity.

## THINKING VISUALLY

A. Review the slide and the excerpt from the lecture. Underline key words and phrases in the excerpt that describe similarities between the toys and polymer chains.

## Why do polymers have unique properties?

● **They have a unique structure: Flexible, dynamic chains**

○ Flexible, dynamic chains can be thought of as molecular springs

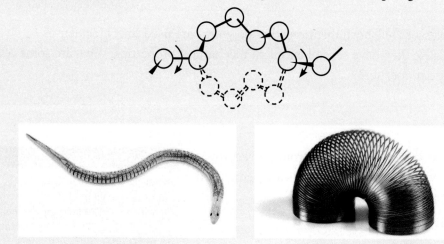

### Excerpt

So why do polymers have these unique properties? It's all because of their underlying unique molecular structure. It's because they're these great big, long, worm-like molecules. And although we often draw them as straight lines, we need to remember that these are flexible molecules that are dynamically moving around. They're always wiggling. And so, I like to think of them as molecular springs. They're like a, a combination of two children's toys. So, you might have played with pretend snakes, where if you wiggle one part of it, it makes the whole part move. So, if you wiggle the tail, that movement wiggles all the way down to the head. Now I'd like you to imagine each of those little segments within your toy snake are held together by a spring. And that's what a polymer is like. If you stretch the polymer out of its original position, it has a restoring energy that wants to pull those parts back together. And the movement can propagate down the chain. Now we don't just have one molecule of these things. We actually have a whole bunch of them all mixed together.

B. Work with a partner. What other everyday objects or toys have the same characteristics as those found in Part A?

## THINKING ABOUT LANGUAGE

## LANGUAGE FOR COMPARISON AND CONTRAST

Read the sentences from the lecture. Add a word or phrase to indicate if the items are being compared or contrasted.

> **TIP**
>
> When comparing and contrasting two items, speakers generally use signal words and phrases that indicate if two things are being compared or contrasted. For more on language for comparison and contrast, refer to MATERIALS ENGINEERING, Part 1.

1. ............................... metals and ceramics, the microstructure of the polymer material is the underlying cause of the real-world properties of that material.

2. Polymer chains are ............................... a bowl of noodles where each individual noodle is a different polymer chain. Now these chains could be semi-rigid or flexible, just like your noodles could be more rigid before you cook them or could be very floppy after you cook them.

3. ............................... glass, polymers are less expensive, and not as heavy.

4. Metals are good at conducting heat; ............................... , ceramics are not. They are insulators.

5. So ............................... the types of elements that are used to make up metals and ceramics, polymers have much lower molecular weights and that means overall they have a very low density, typically 1 to 2 grams per milliliter.

6. ............................... amorphous structures where molecules occur randomly, crystalline structures are well ordered.

## LANGUAGE FOR LINKING IDEAS

Read the sentences from the lecture. Circle the signal words used to make connections between ideas.

> **TIP**
>
> Speakers often use cues to link ideas, and help listeners see connections between ideas. For more on language for linking ideas, refer to MATERIALS ENGINEERING, Part 2.

1. And, in addition, the ultra-high-density polyethylene that we talked about in the knee implant, we also use a variety of polyesters and other polymers for implantable devices inside the body.

2. When we think about materials, we generally separate them into three main categories: metals, ceramics, or polymers, which we also call plastics.

3. Then we'll evaluate whether that material does a good job in that application. In particular, we're going to apply this to the field of biomaterials.

4. Although we often draw them (polymers) as straight lines, we need to remember that these are flexible molecules that are dynamically moving around.

5. We learned today that the same polymer can have different types of material properties depending on how its molecules are arranged into different microstructures, for example, the linear polyethylene versus the branch polyethylene. Finally, we talked about how different materials from all three categories of materials—metals, ceramics, and polymers—can all be used for medical applications inside the body even though they're not living materials, they can still perform important mechanical functions in patients.

## INDIVIDUAL PRESENTATION

Dr. Heilshorn highlighted the reasons why certain materials are better suited than others for particular applications. Understanding the mechanical properties of materials can help determine if they can be effectively used in the manufacture of a product.

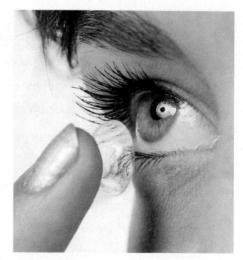

Materials used to make many everyday products have been changed dramatically by materials science: for example, soccer balls were once made from the lining of a pig's bladder, footballs were once made from pig's skin and false teeth were once made from wood.

In this presentation, you will describe the reasons for changing the production material of a product and compare and contrast that material's properties with the material currently being used.

Topic: Why ............................................ is no longer used to make ............................................

## RESEARCH

A. Investigate a product that is no longer produced with the same material it was made from originally. Consider such issues as durability, availability, cost, effectiveness, and weight.

Product: ...............................................................................................................................................................

B. Research the product you've chosen by seeking out primary sources. Use more than one source, and synthesize your sources by using a Key Concept Chart.

C. Prepare your presentation. Be sure to present your main ideas clearly and to support your ideas with examples.

D. Practice presenting to a partner.

**TIP**

It's important to use more than one source when giving an academic presentation. When using more than one source, you need to organize the information from each source in a cohesive manner that makes it easy to reference. Using a Key Concept Chart to synthesize information can help you stay organized, and clearly see the similarities and differences between the sources. For more on Key Concept Charts, refer to MATERIALS ENGINEERING, Part 2.

## PRESENT

A. Listen to each class member's presentation. As you listen, complete the chart below.

| Product | Original Material | Current Material |
|---|---|---|
| | | |
| | | |
| | | |
| | | |
| | | |
| | | |
| | | |

B. After the presentations, have a class discussion about each product presented. Discuss their similarities and differences. Be sure to organize your ideas and present them clearly and cohesively.

◯ Go to MyEnglishLab to complete a collaborative activity.

Page numbers followed by f and t indicate figures and tables, respectively. Page numbers followed by ● refer to terms found in Student Book audio referenced on those pages. Page numbers followed by ● and ●(LS) refer to terms found in MyEnglishLab audio and Language Skill presentations referenced on those pages.

# Credits

Cover image: Alamy F8NFBD = Oleksandr Prykhodko / Alamy Stock Photo; Page viii (top): Welcomia/123RF; viii (middle, right): Pearson; ix (bottom, left): 501room/Shutterstock; x (middle, left): Rawpixel.com/Shutterstock; viii (middle, right): Pearson; Page 1: (multiple uses): Budai Romeo Gabor/Fotolia (gold coins); Nik_Merkulov/Fotolia (green leaf with drops of water); Scisetti Alfio/Fotolia (old letter); Vichly4thai/Fotolia (red molecule/DNA cell); Tobkatrina/123RF (hands holding Earth); orelphoto/Fotolia (honeycomb background); 2: Digital Storm/Shutterstock; 4: Martinova4/Shutterstock; 8: Asafeliason/123RF; 11: Rafael Ramirez Lee/Shutterstock; 16: Everett Collection/Shutterstock; 18: Monkey Business Images/Shutterstock; 22: Monkey Business Images/Shutterstock; 25: Jacob Lund/Shutterstock; 26: Rawpixel.com/Shutterstock; 31: Bearsky23/123RF; 34: Vitaliy Vodolazskyy/123RF; 43: Weerapat Kiatdumrong/123RF; 45: Pressmaster/Shutterstock; 50: Uncle Leo/Shutterstock; 54: Welcomia/123RF; 56: Alinabel/Shutterstock; 58: Rainer Albiez/Shutterstock; 68: Ssuaphotos/Shutterstock; 70: 501room/Shutterstock; 76: James Steidl/123RF; 78: Aalphaspirit/123RF; 82: Truhelen/Shutterstock; 86: Ion Chiosea/123RF; 87: Fernando Gregory Milan/123RF; 91 (left): Pearson Education Ltd; 91 (right): ArtMari/Shutterstock; 99: TwilightArtPictures/Shutterstock; 102: Ion Chiosea/123RF; 104: Alicephoto/123RF; 107 (left): Honglouwawa/Shutterstock; 107 (right): Vasilyev/Shutterstock; 111: Bogdan Vasilesuc/Shutterstock; 119 (bottom, background): Solarseven/Shutterstock; 119 (top): Pearson Education Ltd; 120 (top): Snapgalleria/Shutterstock; 120 (bottom): Oxford Designers & Illustrators Ltd/Pearson Education Ltd; 128: Markus Mainka/123RF; 130: Vitchanan Photography/Shutterstock; 133: Stylephotographs/123RF; 134: Mama_mia/Shutterstock; 138: Lculig/123RF; 142: Ammentorp/123RF; 149: IQoncept/123RF; 150: Fernando Blanco Calzada/Shutterstock; 152: Minerva Studio/Shutterstock; 155: Krisckam/123RF; 165: Creativa Images/Shutterstock; 167: Richard Foote/Shutterstock; 169 (top): Piotr Wawrzyniuk/Shutterstock; 169 (bottom): Forest Badger/Shutterstock; 171: Danil Roudenko/123RF; 173: Rabia Elif Aksoy/123RF; 176: Krisckam/123RF; 178: Kittikorn Phongok/123RF; 181: Robin2/Shutterstock; 182–183: Andreanita/123RF; 185: William Roberts/123RF; 188: Sergey Borisenko/123RF; 191: Mikeledray/Shutterstock; 195: Esbobeldijk/Shutterstock; 199: Grynold/Shutterstock; 200: Freeartist/123RF; 207: Dmitriy Cherevko/123RF; 211: View Apart/Shutterstock; 214: Christopher Elwell/Shutterstock; 215: Hein Nouwens/Shutterstock; 222: Nadinelle/Shutterstock; 224: Sergio Schnitzler/Shutterstock; 231: Sozaijiten; 232 (top): Silverpin Design Company Ltd/Pearson Education Ltd; 232 (bottom): Phadventure/Shutterstock; 238: Huguette Roe/Shutterstock; 242: Irabel8/123RF; 243: Onizu3d/123RF; 246: Matej Kastelic/Shutterstock; 250: Poznyakov/Shutterstock; 252: Rawpixel.com/Shutterstock; 260: ER_09/Shutterstock; 266: ARENA Creative/Shutterstock; 267: iQoncept/Shutterstock; 268: Pistolseven/Shutterstock; 270: Auttapon Moonsawad/123RF; 274: Alinabel/Shutterstock; 278: JeniFoto/Shutterstock; 283: Antony McAulay/Shutterstock; 286: Hero Images Inc/Alamy Stock Photo; 290 (left): KVaSS/Fotolia; 290 (right): Paul Lampard/123RF; 292: Lukas Gojda/123RF.